Mastering Contract Law

Carolina Academic Press Mastering Series
Russell L. Weaver, Series Editor

Mastering Administrative Law
William R. Andersen

Mastering Appellate Advocacy and Process
Donna C. Looper, George W. Kuney

Mastering Bankruptcy
George W. Kuney

Mastering Civil Procedure
David Charles Hricik

Mastering Constitutional Law
John C. Knechtle, Christopher J. Roederer

Mastering Contract Law
Irma S. Russell, Barbara K. Bucholtz

Mastering Corporate Tax
Reginald Mombrun, Gail Levin Richmond, Felicia Branch

Mastering Corporations and Other Business Entities
Lee Harris

Mastering Criminal Law
Ellen S. Podgor, Peter J. Henning, Neil P. Cohen

Mastering Criminal Procedure, Volume 1: The Investigative Stage
Peter J. Henning, Andrew Taslitz, Margaret L. Paris,
Cynthia E. Jones, Ellen S. Podgor

Mastering Elder Law
Ralph C. Brashier

Mastering Employment Discrimination Law
Paul M. Secunda, Jeffrey M. Hirsch

Mastering Contract Law

Irma S. Russell
DEAN AND PROFESSOR
UNIVERSITY OF MONTANA SCHOOL OF LAW

Barbara K. Bucholtz
PROFESSOR
UNIVERSITY OF TULSA COLLEGE OF LAW

CAROLINA ACADEMIC PRESS
Durham, North Carolina

Library of Congress Cataloging in Publication Data
Russell, Irma S.
  Mastering contract law / Irma S. Russell, Barbara K. Bucholtz.
    p. cm.
  Includes index.
  ISBN 978-1-59460-287-0 (alk. paper)
  1. Contracts--United States. 2. Contracts. I. Bucholtz, Barbara Kay, 1939-
II. Title.
  KF801.R87 2010
  346.7302--dc22

                                2010032402

Carolina Academic Press
700 Kent Street
Durham, NC 27701
Telephone (919) 489-7486
Fax (919) 493-5668
www.cap-press.com

Printed in the United States of America

Contents

Table of Authorities

Table of Cases

Series Editor's Foreword

The Carolina Academic Press Mastering Series is designed to provide you with a tool that will enable you to easily and efficiently "master" the substance and content of law school courses. Throughout the series, the focus is on quality writing that makes legal concepts understandable. As a result, the series is designed to be easy to read and is not unduly cluttered with footnotes or cites to secondary sources.

In order to facilitate student mastery of topics, the Mastering Series includes a number of pedagogical features designed to improve learning and retention. At the beginning of each chapter, you will find a "Roadmap" that tells you about the chapter and provides you with a sense of the material that you will cover. A "Checkpoint" at the end of each chapter encourages you to stop and review the key concepts, reiterating what you have learned. Throughout the book, key terms are explained and emphasized. Finally, a "Master Checklist" at the end of each book reinforces what you have learned and helps you identify any areas that need review or further study.

We hope that you will enjoy studying with, and learning from, the Mastering Series.

Russell L. Weaver
Professor of Law & Distinguished University Scholar
University of Louisville, Louis D. Brandeis School of Law

Preface

The authors dedicate this book to their families and colleagues and to their students, past, present, and future. They appreciate the ideas and suggestions on earlier versions of this work from many colleagues and friends, especially Professors Frank Snyder, Martin Frey and Robert Spoo. The authors thank their research assistants, Brittany Littleton Woodard, Anthony Craiker, Jared Nelson, Todd Musick, Avon "Chauncy" Whitworth, Bradford Dickson, and Julie Rostad for their dedicated research on the project and Cyndee Jones and Rebecca Krantz for their work on the manuscript. We also express gratitude to Professor Russell Weaver for inviting us to be authors in the *Mastering Series* and for his tireless work in legal education.

Introduction

This book covers the major points included in first year courses in contracts. It is intended to give students an overview of contract doctrine and analysis rather than exhaustive coverage of the myriad details of this vast field of law. The book explores basic principles and purposes of contract law including discussions of background principles and traditions of private ordering. It explains contract formation, interpretation, the requirement of written evidence for enforcement of certain types of promises. It examines the themes and doctrines of reliance, restitution and the importance of public policy in contract law. The text includes the bargained-for exchange, unenforceable contracts, performance and breach, obstacles to performance, modification, precontractual obligation, remedies and damages, and stakeholders other than contracting parties, which is to say the third party beneficiary doctrine, delegation, and assignment.

While no introductory book covers every point of law relating to its subject, we hope that this text prepares you to master both the framework of contract doctrine and the themes that inform contract law. The book is designed to be a comprehensive but accessible introduction to the law of contracts. In addition to explaining the major concepts traditionally covered in Contracts classes, the authors present common sense examples linking intuitions about fairness and competition to the law of contracting.

Casebooks and courses in Contracts are organized in a variety of ways. Some courses begin with the principles of contract formation. Some begin with the doctrine of consideration. Some begin with contract remedies. It does not matter where you start; you will need to learn it all, and it is all part of the whole. This book is organized according to the typical approach used in many contracts classes. It takes up the issues of contract law and contracting in the sequence in which courts consider a dispute or claim based on contract law.

Despite the organization built on the elements of proving a contract claim, the book also explores in depth the transactional aspects of contract law. It discusses practice pointers and aspects of contract law from the viewpoint of lawyers putting together contracts and deals as well as from the perspective of lawyers litigating contract disputes.

Chapter 1

Preliminary Matters

Roadmap

- Sequential Analysis of Contract Law
- The Seriousness of Promising
- Interest Protected
- Implied-in-law Contracts and Implied-in-facts Contracts
- Sources of Contract Law
- Common Law
- Statutory and Regulatory Law
- Reading the UCC and Statutes Generally
- The Movement toward Uniform Law
- International Law
- Tensions among Different Sources of Law

Sequential Analysis of Contract Law

The basic course in contract law can be organized and understood by thinking about five sequential questions. These questions frame the legal analysis of contract issues and the thought processes of lawyers and judges. They are sequential because they map the order in which courts analyze a contracts case. For example, a judge doesn't ask whether a party's nonperformance of his promise amounts to a breach (Chapter 10) unless the judge is first satisfied that the promise was part of an agreement that was, indeed, a valid enforceable contract (Chapters 3–6). The sequential questions of contract law are:

1. Was there an agreement between the parties that the law would consider to be a contract?
   If the answer is yes, then ask:

2. Are any of the terms of the contract enforceable?
   If the answer is yes, then ask:

3. Was there a nonperformance (or a defective performance of a promise) that amounts to a breach?
   If the answer to the question is yes, then ask:

4. What remedies are available to compensate the non-breaching party?
   And finally, ask:

5. Are there any enforceable third party interests under the contract?

Some concepts we deal with can be addressed in more than one of these questions. For example, a court may treat the issue of capacity as a question of formation, and, thus, within the first sequential question ("Was there an agreement between the parties that the law would consider to be a contract?") Another court may deal with the issue as one of enforceability. (For example: "If the contract itself was valid, can it be enforced against a minor?") As a student and as a lawyer, you can use alternative sequential questions to craft your arguments. Principles of interpretation assist you in developing those arguments. Learning these five sequential questions and applying them as a template will help you, as they help judges, lawyers, order and give direction to the myriad legal questions and rules of contract law.

The Seriousness of Promising

The serious business of contracting prevails even when an individual is not serious. For example, the classic case of *Lucy v. Zehmer*, a case we will discuss in Chapter 4 on formation, the court enforced a promise based on the reasonable expectations of a buyer who believed the transaction was serious, even accepting as a matter of law the seller's assertion that he intended a joke. Thus, it is not necessary that both parties regard a promise as serious—only that the one seeking enforcement reasonably expected the promise to be weighty. The weightiness of promises comes from the law's regard for the promises.

Interest Protected

A general understanding of the interests that courts protect under the general heading of contract law will help you understand the functioning of courts in this broad area of law. The three important fundamental interests are: (1)

expectation, (2) reliance, and (3) restitutionary interests. The majority of cases in today's world of contract law fall into the first area of expectation. We cover this area under the concept of bargained-for-exchange. The protection of the expectation interest is a fairly new phenomenon in the law, not arising until around the time of the industrial revolution. Before that time courts rejected the idea of enforcing an interest based on a "mere expectation." Comparing these three interests shows the progression of protection for economic activity.

The person with the restitutionary claim has the strongest argument for protection. Plaintiff is saying that he has lost something that is rightfully his, and, further, defendant has that something. This is clearest in the case of a loan. If money was given by Plaintiff to Defendant and was never intended to be a gift, Plaintiff has lost a unit of property (X) and Defendant has gained a unit of property (X). Plaintiff's claim is that it is unjust for Defendant to retain X. In restitutionary cases courts determine whether Defendant received a benefit and whether it is unjust for Defendant to retain the benefit. The debate is all about the movement of one unit of economic interest (X) from one party to another.

In the case of reliance, Plaintiff is claiming loss of a unit of value (X). That unit of value is not in the hands of Defendant. Thus, it is different than the restitutionary claim—and not as pronounced from this view of shifting units of value. Plaintiff has changed his position. This has cost him some unit of economic value. Defendant has not been enriched by the loss, however. Something more is necessary as a basis for recovery in such a case. That something more is found when there is a promise on which Plaintiff relied. Not every promise is sufficient to support a claim in reliance. The requirements for the promise that show the promise is of sufficient significance to justify enforcement are covered under *Restatement § 90*.

Finally, the expectation interest from this comparison of economic units is the weakest from the perspective of economic analysis. Plaintiff has lost something, but it is something he never had, as a matter of property law. What he has lost is the expectation of gain based on the transaction. This interest of expectation was called a "mere expectation" by courts before courts began to recognize this interest as sufficiently important to be protected by the law.

These three interests are also seen as measures for damages. The expectation measure seeks to put the Plaintiff in a position he would have been in if that promise had been performed. The reliance measure seeks to return to Plaintiff the economic unit he lost by relying on Plaintiff's promise. The restitution measure returns to Plaintiff what he lost. There is some flexibility in the reliance area. As *Restatement § 90* notes courts have the discretion to measure Plaintiff's recovery either by an expectation measure (based on what was promised) or a reliance measure (based on what was lost). In the restitution area, some flexibility is also seen. The traditional measure of returning the benefit to the plaintiff has been expanded in a few courts to allow a recovery on a promise in the expectation measure. This only occurs when a promise is made. This situation is explored in our treatment of enforcement of promises for a benefit received.

Implied-in-law Contracts and Implied-in-facts Contracts

You will see references in your casebook and in the cases to two different contracts created by implication. These are the implied-in-law contract and implied-in-fact contract. Implied-in-law contract is not really a contract but an enforcement of an obligation basis of restitution. This basis of enforcement does not involve assent by the parties. It is an obligation created by the court. The implied-in-fact contract, on the other hand, is recognition by a court that the parties created an obligation, even if they did not do so in a clear-cut manner. *Wood v. Lucy Lady Duff-Gordon* is the additional vehicle for seeing this situation. In the *Wood* case, the Plaintiff entered an agreement with Defendant, Lucy Duff-Gordon, who Mr. Wood served as an agent to place the lady's endorsement on various fashionable products. The contract the parties entered was written and quite detailed. It did not, however, specify in "so many words" that Mr. Wood had an obligation to place the products. The contract made no sense if that promise was not seen as a part of it. Accordingly, the court recognized an implied-in-fact promise. This is a promise that is not stated precisely but is the promise parties intended according to a judgment by the court.

Lucy, Lady Duff-Gordon was an interesting celebrity in her day. You might want to Google her and get a sense of how important she was in her day. She lost her fame and celebrity because of public perception that she had dishonorably escaped from the Titanic when it sank. You can read the testimony transcript at: http://www.titanicinquiry.org/BOTInq/BOTInq11LDuff-Gordon01.html.

The *Sullivan v. O'Connor* case is often used in casebooks and contracts courses to show the difference between different interests protected in contract law. This case involved a bad result in cosmetic surgery. It was a failed "nose job." Plaintiff claimed that defendant doctor promised to make her a beautiful nose. She was an actress and would obviously have benefited by having a beautiful nose. The evidence indicated that the end result of two surgeries was far from beautiful. Plaintiff's tort claim failed. The jury was not convinced that the doctor was negligent. The plaintiff recovered, however, on the contract claim. You can see the three interests involved in this claim. Expectation, the value of the nose promised minus the value of the nose delivered. Reliance, the value of the original nose minus the value of the nose delivered. Restitution would be what was lost by plaintiff and gained by defendant. Restitutionary interest in the case is simply what plaintiff paid the doctor. The reliance interest would also include money paid to the hospital. The reliance interest measures what plaintiff lost, not what defendant gained.

Sources of Contract Law

Like most areas of law in the United States, contract law is a mixture of common law and statutory law. It also includes regulatory law in some areas. The basic principles of contract law in the United States are based on common law, meaning that judicial decisions are the source of the law. Nevertheless, the common law has been modified by statutes, sometimes in significant ways. Consumer statutes are an example of the modification of the common law by statutes. Some statutes that govern contract law, like the Magnuson Moss Warranty Act, are federal. Others are state law. The move to change the common law relating to consumers has been the response by legislatures that see the common law as inadequate or unfair in some way. For example, some consumer protection statutes allow for an award of attorneys' fees, which would not be recoverable at common law. Some consumer protection statutes prohibit particular deceptive trade practices. Others attempt to level the playing field by requiring disclosure of information in loans or sales of real estate or other types of transactions. Insurance commissions and other regulatory bodies control business in certain areas. Licensing commissions control to some extent the right to enter certain contracts. If you are not licensed to practice law, for example, you may be violating statutory and regulatory laws prohibiting the unauthorized practice of law. Regulatory agencies now play a role in many areas of modern life. Some of the cases in Contracts class present a combination of statutory law and common law, but the focus of your class is likely to be common law.

Common Law

The common law is a body of law created by courts and enunciated in judicial decisions. The common law recognizes and relies on basic principles that apply to relations between parties. This type of law is sometimes referred to as "decisional law," or "judge-made law." Although statutes are of increasing importance in contract law, the basic principles of contract law come to us from the judge-made common law. Thus, contracts courses depend in large part on studying judicial decisions in contract cases. The common law varies from state to state. This is true in all common law subjects, such as property, contracts, and torts. It is also true of statutory law. The statutes of states vary in their interpretation of contract common law principles. These variations can sometimes create problems. Modern law recognizes that our country engages in nationwide commerce. Thus, while some areas of the law, such as the sale of land, retain local context that may vary greatly from state to state, conflicts in rules among states may impede the flow of relationships such as contracts. With the growth of the national economy, the variations among the states imposed the costs of learning the law of different states and the uncertainties of complying with the law of different states in commercial transactions. This is particularly true of the sale of goods because the sale of goods is a national market in many respects. If a company is selling grain all around the country, it would bear the cost of knowing the law of each state in order to comply with that law. Thus, the move to harmonize the law can be seen as a necessary response to the movement toward nationwide or region wide commerce. The most obvious or pressing need for a single set of rules arose in the sale of goods area. Thus, a uniform law was seen as essential for the economy.

Statutory Law and Regulatory Law

Statutory law is law created by legislatures. It is of increasing importance in the modern world. In the area of contracts, state and federal statutes deal with specific areas of contracting, such as sale of consumer goods, employment law, insurance law, and many other areas. Federal law can also change the common law of contracting. For example the Magnuson-Moss Act creates warranty law relating to the sale of goods. Statutory law may either change the common law or codify the common law.

When a federal statute applies, it will preempt state law—both statutory and common law. Additionally, statutory law can preempt or change the common law. However, a statute will not always make clear whether it is changing the common law or simply attempting to clarify or codify the common law. This creates an issue of interpretation. While state or federal legislation can change or displace the common law, courts often need to decide the extent to which the law changes the common law.

Because of the growing importance of statutory law, lawyers are increasingly called upon to interpret statutes both to give advice to their clients and to advocate for their clients in controversies. Statutes set forth law that is, at least on the surface, more defined than most common law doctrines. The coverage of the subject of Contracts includes an overview of the Uniform Commercial Code. In addition to setting forth a more determinate statement of the law than often occurs in common law, the Code offers the benefits of uniformity in an increasingly mobile society.

In reading statutes take each word seriously. Pay attention to function words such as "unless," "except," and "provided." Charting or outlining a statute is well worth your time. Read the statutory provision three or four times and outline the provision whenever you find that a statute applies.

Reading the UCC and Statutes Generally

The skill of reading and understanding statutes is every bit as important as the skill of reading cases. Because of the growing importance of statutory law, lawyers are increasingly called upon to interpret statutes both to give advice to their clients and to advocate for their clients in controversies. Statutes set forth law that is, at least on the surface, more defined than most common law doctrines. The coverage of the subject of Contracts includes an overview of the Uniform Commercial Code. In addition to setting forth a more determinate statement of the law than often occurs in common law, the Code offers the benefits of uniformity in an increasingly mobile society.

The Movement toward Uniform Law

The Uniform Commercial Code ("UCC") is a dramatic example of the move toward uniformity in state law. Most or all of the UCC has been adopted by all states. For the purposes of contract law and the study of contracts in the first year course, Article 2 is the most significant part of the UCC. Article 2 deals with the sales of goods. It is the law in every American state except Louisiana. Article 2A is closely related. It deals with the leasing of goods. It is not generally covered in any depth in the first year contracts course. In many of the explanations of contract doctrine in this book, we explain the UCC approach to the doctrine as well as the common law approach to the doctrine. The UCC often accepts or codifies the common law. In other instances, it changes the rules of contract law to make them clearer or more precise in the scope of the area involved (in this example, the sale of goods).

The movement toward uniformity of law is not limited to statutory law. The American Law Institute ("ALI"), an organization made up of leading lawyers, scholars, and judges, responded to the growing sense that a more uniform approach is desirable by drafting "restatements" of the common law. These restatements deal with all the major common law areas, including contracts. They summarize the law, meaning that they seek to state the majority rule for each doctrine of the common law. This is a daunting task, of course, but the necessity for the *Restatements* is clear: articulating the majority approach, when it can be discerned makes it easier for parties to do business, making the economy and the work of the courts more efficient. It is basically a compilation of state decisional law. It also includes choices of what the drafters regard as the better rule on points where state doctrine varies.

The *Restatements* provide commentary on the law but very important commentary since they actually influence the law by summarizing the various views of the law and making courts more aware of the law of other states on each doctrine.

Restatements are not "The Law." Although the presentation of the *Restatement* in sections of "black letter law" looks like a code, they are not law. Rather they are commentary on the state of the law across the country. They are, literally, *restating* the law. Thus, a *Restatement* is not a source of law, but, rather "persuasive authority" just as scholarship is persuasive authority—the kind of statement of law a court may consult and find persuasive. Courts sometimes even say that they "adopt" the *Restatement* view. Nevertheless, this is not an enactment. Only legislatures can enact laws. The highest court in the state can adopt the same approach endorsed by the *Restatement.* This is not an enactment but it does make the State's common law consistent with the *Restatement.* The decision of the highest court is binding on all courts in the jurisdiction and persuasive to courts in other jurisdictions. Statutory law is binding on all courts in the legislature's jurisdiction, including the highest court. The work of the ALI continues. The organization is now working on the third restatement of the law in some areas.

The first *Restatement of Contracts* was adopted by the ALI in 1932. We would not say it is "promulgated" since that term is generally used in the law to mean that a legislature created law. Actually the word "promulgate" can mean simply to proclaim something, but the confusion that sometimes results about the force of the *Restatements* being law makes us want to avoid the term in this context. The ALI adopted the *Restatement (Second) of Contracts* in 1972. Of course when you are practicing law you will need to find the rule on any particular doctrine in your state's law. The *Restatement* may have influenced courts in your jurisdiction, but it is the courts and the legislature of that jurisdiction that create the applicable law. The *Restatement* may help you find the law of your state. It can be a valuable research tool. As you can tell from this discussion, we want to make clear that while the *Restatements* may have had an influence on what the law is they are not the law itself. In this book, we use the title "the *Restatement*," to refer to the *Second Restatement*.

International Law

International law is an important source of law in the modern world. A significant source of contract law is the United Nations Convention on Contracts for the International Sales of Goods (CISG"). The CISG is an international treaty that has been ratified by the United States and many other countries. Because the treaty has been adopted by the U.S., it has the force of federal law. It trumps state law and is part of the law of every American jurisdiction. The CISG applies to international sales of goods that occur between parties in different countries, provided those countries are signatories of the treaties. Although many countries have signed this treaty, parties to a contract can opt out of the treaty, choosing the law that will apply to their contract. The treaty expressly states the power of parties to opt out of the CISG and choose applicable law. The CISG provides a backdrop of accepted norms for those engaging in international sales. The United Nations Commission on International Trade Law (UNCITRAL) drafted the CISG, and in 1980 the original parties signed the convention in Vienna, making it one of several treaties referred to as the "Vienna Convention." The CISG required ratification by eleven countries to come into force. This occurred in 1988.

The convention applies to the contract unless the parties expressly opt out of the law by terms of their contract when the parties' places of business are in different nations and those nations are parties to the CISG. Except in limited circumstances, the CISG supplants domestic law (such as the state versions of the UCC provision). Many of the terms of the CISG are consistent with the UCC. The CISG makes some notable departures from the UCC, however. For example, the CISG rejects the formation rule of most U.S. jurisdictions that a contract is formed when the offeree places his acceptance in the mail. It also rejects the UCC statute of frauds, which renders oral contracts unenforceable without a writing if the purchase price is $500.00 or more.

Tensions among Different Sources of Law

Modern law is the product of historical fact as much as from the force of analysis. Many default rules of contract law and other areas of law are not inevitable or incontestable. The law of other modern countries and sophisticated economies rest on significantly different policy choices in numerous areas. Likewise, different judges, practitioners, and scholars view doctrines and even the interaction of the common law and statutory law from radically different points of view. In the popular press today, many commentators criticize "activist judges." They assert that legislatures should create the law and judges should merely enforce the law. This assertion rests on an assumption that the law is basically statutory in nature and judges should be bound by what the legislators have promulgated. It also assumes that the words of the law are unambiguous and that the only role of judges is to apply the clear words of the law to the facts of a particular case.

Some scholars assert that the constitutional doctrine of separation of powers means that judges should limit their role to applying law created by legislators. The criticism that judges should merely enforce the law rather than creating law overlooks the fact that the basis of much of the doctrine in contract law and other law in the United States is common law, which is judge-made law. Historically, the common law consisted the essential universe of law. Thus, in the common law area, judges are not activists in the negative sense of the charge. They are the legitimate source of the common law. It is generally accepted that the legislature can change the common law within the bounds of the U.S. and state constitutions. Nevertheless, a rich body of common law provides the backdrop for statutory and regulatory law. Today, the common law is supplanted or modified in many contexts. However, it continues to provide a significant and still viable body of law that has not been altered by legislatures.

Significant tensions also exist among scholars and judges regarding basic principles of fairness in contracting. Consider the issue of fairness from the perspective of the current hot topic of high interest rates on outstanding credit card debt and other consumer transactions. Some commentators would say that fairness is not at issue because the market will set the rate at "what the market will bear." The other perspective on this issue is that if there is a limit on interest rates, lenders will lend to higher risk borrowers at the top rate. In order to maintain the volume of their business they will need to keep the interest rate at a reasonable level in the market generally. Society has traditionally recognized the need for a limit on interest rates. Until recently, all jurisdictions had effective limits on interest. Indeed usury laws predate the existence of currency. That seems like a remarkable statement. Indeed it seems impossible that usury could predate currency. Nevertheless, it is true.

Most contract terms are not inherently good or bad. In rare cases, it is clear that a term will not benefit one party in any circumstances. In such cases, however, the party absorbing the cost of that of term may have received a reduction in price because it accepted the term. For example, goods sold "as is" bear the risk of being flawed but a buyer may accept that risk in exchange for a below-market price for the goods.

Checkpoints

- The sources of contract law include the common law, which is decisional law of the jurisdiction.

- Statutory and regulatory laws play a significant and growing role in contract law.

- The movement toward greater uniformity in the law affects contract law as well as many other areas of law.

- The United Nations Convention on Contracts for the International Sales of Goods (CISG) has the force of federal law because the U.S. Congress has ratified the treaty.

- Because tensions and contradictions exist among different sources of contract law, determining which law is applicable is an important step in contract law.

- The sequential analysis of contract law provides a way of determining what issues are determinative in particular cases.

Chapter 2

Basic Concepts and Guiding Principles

Roadmap

- Defining a Contract
- Defining an Agreement
- Freedom of Contract
- Illegal Contracts

Defining a Contract

A contract is an obligation recognized by the law. Lawyers and judges use several different terms to refer to dealings between parties that result in transfers and legal obligations. These terms include "contract," "agreement," "deal," "bargain," and others. The *Restatement (Second) of Contracts* states that a contract is "a promise which the law regards as enforceable or which the law recognizes a duty to perform." While this definition may not seem very helpful, it captures the point that the court has the final word on whether it will enforce a promise. Be careful not to take this point to mean that no contractual obligations exist until a court finds them. This line of reasoning leads to the mistaken view that the court creates the obligations and that a party is not truly obligated by contract until a court declares the obligation real. This is not the case. The parties create the obligations of contract law and courts enforce those obligations once the plaintiff makes his case for the existence of the contract.

The word "contract" is used in contracts class to mean both the enforceable promise and also the recorded statement of the agreement — the contract. Courts and parties also use the terms "agreement" and "bargain" to refer to the deal between two parties, with or without asserting that the deal will be enforced by a court. The word "bargain" is often used as a synonym for contract and agreement. It includes completed exchanges, even those in which the parties

13

do not make a promise. The common law conceptualizes a contract as an agreement by which two parties voluntarily and knowingly intend to bind themselves to certain conduct ("I will sell you my house for $500,000"). Often courts and scholars use the terms "contract" and "agreement" as interchangeable synonyms. Sometimes the term "agreement" is used to refer to the larger scope of the parties' deal, which includes default terms and general principles as well as the specifically negotiated items found in the contract itself.

Defining an Agreement

Restatement Section 3 defines "agreement" as a "manifestation of mutual assent on the part of two or more persons." It defines "bargain" as a subset of "agreement," noting that a "bargain is an agreement to exchange promises or to exchange a promise for a performance or to exchange performances." The term "agreement" is generally treated as a broader category than the other terms. It does not include a judgment about the legal consequences of the arrangement. In other words, a contract is an agreement but agreement may not always be a contract, enforceable at law. Parties generally manifest their assent to be bound by words. Courts also find manifested assent by the actions of parties. In rare cases, even silence can provide the basis for finding assent.

We will discuss the idea of assumed concepts and default terms shortly in this discussion of basic concepts and guiding principles. Noteworthy guiding principles of contract law include the following:

- commercial reasonableness and fairness,
- mutual assent or consent to be bound by the promises,
- determining the intent of the parties from their manifestations,
- enforcing the reasonable expectations of the parties at the time of the contract, and
- effectuating public policy.

Every contract includes an obligation to act in good faith in performing the obligations of the deal. Likewise, every contract includes an obligation to act in good faith in enforcing a contract. Another foundational principle of contract law is that courts will seek to enforce the intent of the parties in enforcing the contract. Of course when parties are in a dispute they are likely to disagree about the intent they held at the time of contract formation.

While the basic concept of "mutual assent to be bound" provides the basis for enforcing agreements that parties have voluntarily entered, agreement alone is not enough. A party may have agreed to terms based on inaccurate or misleading information. Enforcing such a contract would undermine the fundamental requirement of mutual assent to be bound. In some cases, even assent by both parties fails to justify enforcement when the agreement conflicts with public policy. Obvious examples of such contracts include promises to break the law or to undermine public purposes such as policies against anticompetitive conduct.

Freedom of Contract

The concept of freedom of contract plays an important role in modern American law. The agreement in contract cases makes private ordering and the free market possible. It is an essential component of legal analysis and, therefore, is essential to the lawyer's role. The law of contracts reflects over 200 years of competing views of society and the public good. Modern contract law is influenced by tensions between competing values relating to freedom and obligation. Freedom of contract is an important aspect of the traditional American idea of liberty. Like all rights, it is tempered by considerations of the public interest and social order. Controls on contracting often flow from the idea that inequalities in bargaining power can undermine social order. Contract law seeks to ensure that people are free to organize their relations as they choose, while protecting parties in some circumstances and furthering other social goals.

Illegal Contracts

Freedom of contract is not limitless. The concept of a free market rejects government control of contracting except for clear violations of public policy such as antitrust violations, illegal contracts or unconscionable contracts, or areas where the legislature has spoken expressly. It makes sense that contracts that the legislature has deemed illegal to have no effect. It is clear, then, that freedom of contract is not an absolute. The federal or state legislature can prohibit contracts to do a certain thing or to purchase certain products. Drug laws are a good example of the prohibition against purchasing certain products. *Restatement Section 580* explains this area of contract law. It uses the term "bargain" rather than "contract," perhaps because the drafters do not want to give an illegal contract the name "contract." It states that a bargain is illegal if "either the formation or the performance thereof is prohibited by constitution or statute." It also gives guidance on the ways a court can determine legislative intent regarding whether the contract is prohibited. The range of ways a legislature can make a bargain illegal include express prohibition, making the formation of the bargain or the performance thereof a crime, or requiring a license for particular bargains.

A clear case of prohibited conduct is the Mafia "contract" to kill someone. Much less dramatic violations of law are also, prohibited, ranging from prohibitions against interference with property or contract rights of another to prohibitions against the unauthorized practice of law. A person who practices law without a license will not be able to enforce a contract for a fee for legal services. This is true of people who are not lawyers and also of lawyers who are practicing without authorization in the state where the person's services are rendered. In other words, the fact that you are a lawyer in one state does not authorize you to practice in all states. Arguments regarding whether particular conduct is prohibited by a statute can raise interesting interpretation questions.

The idea of freedom of contract has another important corollary in our system of law: freedom from contract. Thus, courts will not impose contracts on parties. (In a sense the law of restitution is an exception to this idea but the major principle is, nevertheless, of great importance.)

When parties enter into contracts, they do not discuss every possible question that could arise. To specify every point relating to the contract would require recounting essentially all of contract law. Parties do not need to explicitly address every point of their obligations because the cost of specifying everything would reduce the profitability of contracting. Rather than doing a deal for goods or services, the parties would be spending their time and money articulating contract law. Naturally parties enter contracts with a whole host of assumptions built into their deal. General rules of reasonableness and the expectations of the parties are implicit. Courts recognize and apply "background" rules and a rule of reasonableness when the parties have not expressly addressed issues. Such background rules are sometimes called "default" rules or "gap-fillers."

Many of the background rules of contract law operate like the default on a computer. The parties can change the rule commonly accepted in most cases. Thus, if parties do not specify in a sale of goods whether the delivery of the goods will be in multiple deliveries or a single delivery, the rule is that it will be a single delivery. The law applies the assumption that the parties intend a single delivery. Of course the parties can alter this assumption simply by indicating multiple deliveries. There are limits on the power of parties to alter the defaults of contract law. These limits generally come from concepts of fairness. Sometimes the reason the law limits the power of parties to alter a rule will not seem clear. For example, the default rules on the issue of multiple or single delivery of goods can clearly be altered, but once the parties have identified a contract as allowing multiple deliveries, it is deemed an installment contract and the rules for judging performance and breach are set by this fact. The parties cannot choose different rules for judging the performance by simply declaring the contract a series of single deliveries. This is a good example of the line between default rules and rules imposed by law because the rule imposed by law relates to judging the right of a party to reject performance. The court has chosen a different rule for the single delivery contracts — called the Perfect Tender Rule. This rule allows the buyer to reject goods if they are not "perfect" in all respects. Later in the book we will take up the contours and exceptions that relate to the Perfect Tender Rule. For this discussion, it is enough to note that when the issue relates to choosing the legal rule by which to judge performance and breach, the power of the parties to alter the "defaults" of the law has limits.

Checkpoints

- A contract is an agreement between two or more parties that the law will enforce or give effect in some way.
- The sources of contract law include:
  - Common law,
  - Statutory law, including a state's version of Article 2 of the UCC,
  - Federal law, including federal treaties like the CISG,
  - State and federal consumer protection laws,
  - Regulatory laws for specific industries or types of contract.

Chapter 3

Interpretation

Roadmap

- Purpose of Interpretation
- Interpretive Rules for Statutes
- Public Policy Considerations
- Contract Interpretive Rules
  - Canons (or Maxims) for (Contract) Construction
  - Extrinsic Evidence of Contract Construction
- UCC Rules for Construing Contracts
- Parol Evidence Rule

Purpose of Interpretation

In contract cases, courts interpret the agreement of the parties with the goal of effectuating the intent of the parties. Section 200 of the *Restatement* states: "Interpretation of a promise or agreement or a term thereof is the ascertainment of its meaning." Courts use their powers of interpretation to look at the evidence presented to determine both the meaning of a contract and the very fact of a fact, i.e., whether the parties consented to be bound in a contract. The consistent theme in interpretation in contract law is manifested intent. The intention of the parties is relevant to formation as well as to the meaning of the contract. In both realms (formation and interpretation) a party should not be held to a meaning unless he has reason to know that meaning.

This chapter deals with the issue of interpretation once the court has determined the terms of the contract. The process of interpretation plays a larger role than this particular aspect. This is because courts need to interpret the communications of the parties in nearly every aspect relating to contract doctrine. For example, the Parol Evidence Rule, which we cover in Chapter 9 on Special Issues of Enforceability, is not a rule of interpretation. Rather, the Parol

Evidence Rule deals with the issue of what terms are included in a contract. The question—after determining the terms—is the question of interpretation that we take up here. In a larger sense, courts engage in interpretation of the events and language of parties in every issue that comes to them. In the next chapter on Formation, for example, we will discuss the question of whether a communication is an offer to enter a contract or a preliminary negotiation. This question involves the court in interpretation. That is not the kind of interpretation we discuss here. This chapter on interpretation deals specifically with the more precise task of interpreting the language parties used in articulating their agreement.

Interpretation is the process of determining what the parties intended. Once the court has interpreted the words, conduct and circumstances, it may decide that the parties are not bound or that their mutual meaning is not the plain meaning of the words. Thus, determining intent can be seen as the overriding purpose of interpretation. With regard to a contracts case, courts must interpret two sets of rules. First, the public law of contracts rules; second, the private law of the contract provisions in a particular bargain. Both of these sets of rules are generally considered questions of law for the courts (rather than questions of fact for juries) to resolve.

The role of the court in interpreting words and documents is larger than contract law, however. It encompasses interpretation of other writing by individuals such as wills and leases and, additionally, the law itself in the form of statutes, rules, treaties, and case law. Thus, the points you learn here on interpretation will serve you well in many areas of law.

An important and sometimes overlooked point is the power of the court in interpreting the law. Benjamin Hoadley, Lord Bishop of Winchester is credited with saying that "whoever hath an absolute Authority to interpret any written, or spoken Laws; it is He, who is truly the Lawgiver, to all Intents and Purposes; and not the Person who first wrote, or spoke them." The overarching purpose of interpretation is to give effect to the intent of the drafters of the rules. In the case of Public Law, the drafters are: 1) the legislature, if the rule is statutory and 2) the highest court in the jurisdiction, in the case of a common law rule. In the case of private law, the drafters are the parties to the contract at issue. In both cases interpretive devices will be applied to resolve the question of what the drafters intended the public law or private contract to mean.

Interpretive Rules for Statutes

The rules for interpreting statutes are the most formalized and structured. For this reason, we begin with them to get a general understanding of interpretation. Some of the Rules of Statutory Construction are listed below:

- The Plain Meaning Rule and other Canons of Statutory Construction
- Definitional Statutes
- Legislative History
- Case Law (interpreting a statute)
- Case Law (establishing and interpreting the Common Law)

Public policy considerations and the rule of reasonableness play a role generally in interpretation. Remembering that the purpose of each of these rules is to illuminate the intent of the legislature, we will discuss the above rules and conventions in interpretation.

1. Plain Meaning and the Canons of Statutory Construction

The canons look exclusively at the language of the statute, while other rules of statutory construction consider extrinsic evidence. Courts sometimes use the terms "interpretation" and "construction" interchangeably. Professor Williston, a famous contracts professor from generations back, distinguished between interpretation and construction. He restricted "interpretation" to refer to the "process of applying the appropriate standards to words the parties have used in their agreement in order to determine the meaning of the words." He contrasted this meaning with the term "construction," which he used to refer to a "court's role in determining, as a matter of law, not the sense of the words or symbols, but the legal meaning of the entire contract."

The canons are common law rules developed by courts over time as a means of discovering both the legislative intent of a statute and the intent of parties to a contract. Most courts begin their interpretive analysis with *The Plain Meaning Rule*. It declares that, absent any other evidence of legislative intent, the words of a statute mean what they mean in ordinary usage. Although traditionally, courts have looked at the legislative history to help interpret the meaning of a statute, some judges and justices reject legislative history in favor of dictionary definitions and the judge's own interpretation of meaning. The same themes of restricting the court's view apply to interpreting contracts. The common law at one time refused to consider anything other than the language of an unambiguous contract. The "Four Corners" rule required a court to find a contract ambiguous before looking at other evidence to interpret the contract.

Nevertheless, one party may view the meaning of the words in a particular statute as clear while the other party sees them as fraught with ambiguities or clear but with a different meaning from that asserted by the first party.

> ▸ Suppose a city ordinance states that "vehicles are prohibited in city parks." That seems clear. Its meaning seems plain. Would it apply to Bernice riding a skateboard through the park? What if "Granny" drives a motorized wheel chair through the park? Is a skateboard a "vehicle"? Is a motorized wheelchair a "vehicle"? What if the wheelchair is not motorized, should that make a difference?

Applied to a particular situation, ordinarily plain words may not be clear. Context can render apparently plain words ambiguous. This inherent tension in the application of the Plain Meaning Rule occurs in statutes and contracts. Karl Llewellyn, the principal drafter and chief reporter of the Uniform Commercial Code, explained that the canons are more accurately described as grounds for argument or tools of persuasion than bright line rules amenable to a simple ministerial task of application. Llewellyn demonstrated that the canons provide persuasive arguments but, given the malleability of language itself and the difficult nature of the collective "intent" in the case of statutes, we should not see the canons as hard-edged rules. For example, one canon declares that remedial rules (changing the common law) should be construed broadly but another canon states that statutes in derogation of the common law (changing the common law) should be construed narrowly. If a particular statute is remedial it will be a change in derogation of the common law. These particular canons are in direct conflict. A court will decide which canon, in a particular case, is more persuasive.

2. Definitions

When interpreting a statute or a contract, always look to see if there is a definitional section. Applicable definitions are found in separate sections in the statute at issue or by more general statutory definitions in a definition section of a code applicable to the particular subject matter. For example, a statute may expressly state how a term is to be understood within its provisions or, more generally, a section in an entire code of the law may be devoted to defining terms for provisions within that code. An example is the definitional section of a criminal code for a particular state. The Uniform Commercial Code has a definitional section in Article 1, which applies to the entire code with its many pages and articles. Article 2 of the Uniform Commercial Code also has a definitional section, which applies only to the provisions of that article, dealing with the sale of goods. Significant contracts with multiple provisions and obligations also often contain a definitional section. It is often found near the beginning of the contract. Courts give these "bargained for" terms in the contract great deference. Accordingly, if the terms are given special definitions, these definitions are likely to control the meaning ascribed to the contract by the court, even when the meaning is not consistent with the plain meaning ordinarily given those terms.

3. Legislative History

If the legislature has an official reported legislative history, you can sometimes find persuasive arguments about what the legislature intended the statute to mean in a Committee Report, or other legislative record. The U.S. Congress has an official history. Most state legislatures do not. The argument against using legislative history to interpret a statute is that opponents and proponents of a statute sometimes seek to influence the interpretation of a statute by loading up the committee report with testimony and documents that support the interpretation they prefer. In the realm of contract interpretation, a party may wish to introduce notes or correspondence as a kind of private history memorializing the intent of the parties. The Parol Evidence Rule often creates a bar to the use of such private history.

4. Case Law

In both contract and statutory interpretation, case law is the most common interpretive tool other than the language of the document to be interpreted. Other cases may have defined the language in dispute. Like the canons, however, case law does not present an open and shut case. Opinions from different courts may have differing and conflicting results. Factual differences often justify differing results. Even when precedent exists courts must ask whether the earlier case is sufficiently similar to control the current case. Only binding precedent is conclusive, and determining whether precedent is binding is a matter of judgment. Courts are free to disregard persuasive precedent that defines a term. When a party cites binding precedent that appears to be favorably analogous to its theory of the case, the opposing party may seek to distinguish the precedent.

5. Common Law

While statutes can preempt the common law, a common law definition of a term will prevail unless the statute clearly displaces the common law. Conversely, if a statute fails to define an ambiguous term, then a common law definition can "fill the gap" in the statute. Courts may conclude that the gap indicates that the legislature intended the common law definition to be incorporated into the statute. The common law is judge-made law. The process of interpretation of the common law engages courts in interpreting the law created by other courts. *The Restatement of Contracts* also plays an important role in the interpretation of contracts. Although *Restatement* provisions are persuasive, rather than binding, courts are often influenced by the reasoning and formulation of the provisions.

Public Policy Considerations

Courts often view legislative intent through the perspective of public policy interests arising out of certain economic, political or sociological circumstances. Attempts by courts and parties to argue a certain interpretation of statutory language must be viewed through the lens of legislative intent: What did the legislature intend for this statute or the ambiguous words of this statute to mean? In contract law these interpretive rules apply to a state's version of the Uniform Commercial Code and to other state and federal statutes (like the Magnuson-Moss Act) related to contract law issues.

Contract Interpretive Rules

The points above on interpretative rules for statutes have application in contract law for at least two reasons: (1) often statutes affect contracts and the law applied to contracts, and (2) courts use the same interpretive rules when interpreting contractual commitments. In this context the overriding purpose of interpretation is give effect to the intent of the parties to the contract, subject to any constraints of law and public policy. All of the principles should be used with a sense of the "Rule of Reason," meaning that a nonsensical result should be rejected, even if one of the maxims seems to support it.

1. Canons (or Maxims) for (Contract) Construction

As was true with statutes, courts view the text of the agreement as the first source for determining the intent of the drafters (the parties to the contract). Thus, the interpretive process for contracts begins with the words of the contract itself. All of the maxims should be read in light of the purpose of the statute (or contract). The beginning point focuses on the words used. This point of beginning with the words the drafters chose is referred to as the Plain Meaning Rule. Some jurisdictions go further, limiting interpretation of contracts and statutes by the "Four Corners" Rule. Both maxims reject extrinsic evidence unless the contract or statute is ambiguous. Modern courts are less likely to require a showing of ambiguity as a precondition to allowing the introduction of extrinsic evidence to interpret a statute or contract.

The canons or maxims the common law courts developed for statutory construction also apply to contract interpretation. Here are a representative few:

a. *The Plain Meaning Rule*—Words are construed the way they would be in ordinary discourse, absent evidence that some other meaning was intended by the drafters.

> ► A demolition contract that calls for the removal of "all houses" within a geographical area will certainly include single family residential dwellings. It is likely to exclude commercial buildings. Whether the term includes residential apartment buildings or duplexes may be subject to dispute.

Modern courts often employ a softer approach to contract interpretation, allowing evidence of intent and meaning to be considered even when the words of the contract seem unambiguous when they are seen in isolation. When the words are "reasonably susceptible" the alternative interpretation should be considered. Chief Justice Traynor of the California Supreme Court explained this approach in *Pacific Gas & Elec. Co. v. G. W. Thomas Drayage & Rigging*, saying: "The test of admissibility of extrinsic evidence to explain the meaning of a written instrument is not whether it appears to the court to be plain and unambiguous on its face, but whether the offered evidence is relevant to prove a meaning to which the language of the instrument is reasonably susceptible." Rejecting the idea of "perfect verbal precision" in contracting, Justice Traynor asserted that a rational approach to interpreting contracts must include "preliminary consideration of all credible evidence offered to prove the intentions of the parties." Chief Justice Trayor's view clearly influenced the approach adopted by the *Restatement*, both in its statement of interpretive rules and its approach to the Parol Evidence Rule. We set forth the interpretive rules suggested by Section 202 of the *Restatement* at the end of this chapter.

b. *Contra Proferentem*—Where two or more meanings are possible, courts often construe the contract "against the drafter." This phrase means that the court is likely to reject the meaning that favors the drafter in preference for the meaning that favors the party who did not draft the language. This is not canon based on finding meaning so much as an incentive for the drafter to use clear language since unclear language creates a risk that a court may construe the words to favor the other party. You can see this canon as a way of leveling the playing field for the non-dominant party. For example, a landlord who drafts a lease to include a provision that "rent shall be paid monthly" runs the risk that the court will construe this language to permit the renter to pay on the last day of the month. The landlord may have intended the first day of the month. If so, as the party in charge of the language, he should make that meaning clear.

c. *Expressio Unius Est Exclusio Alterius*—The identification of certain things in a class implies the exclusion of all others in the same class.

> ▸ A term in a lease for a "furnished apartment" that lists "sofa, coffee table, 2 occasional chairs, book case, and queen-size bed" may be read to exclude other furnishings that might be included as furnishings for an apartment.

d. *Ejusdem Generis*—When general words describing a class are followed with specific words, courts interpret the general terms to embrace only similar items with the same character as the specific objects or items listed. Thus, the specific items in the class limit the applicability of the general terms to other like-kind specific items. This maxim limits the class to the types of things of the same general character as those specified.

> ▸ Bernice's grandpa sells his "working farm" along with "farm animals" which he identifies as "chickens, pigs and ducks." The court is likely to interpret the term "farm animals" to exclude his pet monkey and his herd of cattle which he intends to sell by separate auction.

The terms of construction work together. If Grandpa is the drafter of the contract, the Rule of *Contra Proferentem* puts this result at risk. The court may decide that the drafter (Grandpa) was ambiguous about which animals were included. Did he mean all the animals on the farm or only the animals typically found on a farm? The result would be clearer if the contract defined the term "farm animals" to exclude the monkey and the cattle.

e. *In Pari Materia*—Both statutes and contracts should be read as a whole, considering the primary purpose of the provisions, whether the provisions are created by parties or by legislators. A corollary of this point is that a term in a contract generally should be read consistently, to mean the same thing throughout the contract. A court could be convinced that different meanings were intended for its several uses. Use of a definition section helps to maintain consistency of usage.

> ▸ Each time the term "farm animals" appears in the contract Bernice's Grandpa prepared, it implicitly excludes his herd of cattle unless the context or other evidence establishes a different meaning.

f. *Specific Terms Control General Provisions* — A well-established maxim is that when there is a conflict between a specific provision and a more general provision, the specific controls. This is a common sense canon applied to interpret statutes and contracts. The more specific trumps more general provisions. This maxim, like the others, will not control when the court finds that the specific language is contrary to the purpose of the contract. For example, in a case interpreting a loan agreement the court rejected the argument of specific over general when it deemed the result reached under that approach conflicted with the overall purpose of the agreement by allowing an outside group a right to representation in a closely held family corporation.

The Rule clearly establishes that exceptions to general provisions trump the general provisions. To take a clear cut example from the UCC, the UCC Statute of Frauds declares that a contract for the sale of goods "for the price of $500 or more is not enforceable ... unless there is some record" that indicates that the parties entered a contract. This general bar to enforcement is defeated in the case of the specific exceptions set forth in the statute for specially manufactured goods when the seller made a substantial beginning in manufacturing the goods.

Consider the following example from a change in the grandpa's contract to sell the farm.

> ▸ The term "farm animals" appears in several parts of the contract that Grandpa prepared. In an addendum, Grandpa expressly identifies some particular cattle (all bulls "over two years of age") as being included as part of the sales transaction for the farm.

Although a court is likely to see the term "farm animals" as implicitly excluding his herd of cattle without the specific clause, the court may see the specific term on bulls "over two years of age" as trumping the general definition. Of course the Grandpa could seek to impeach or challenge the evidence. The Parol Evidence Rule would be a likely counter argument to Grandpa's challenge. The end of this chapter discusses the Parol Evidence Rule in detail.

g. *Additional Points*—The medium in which the provision is memorialized is important when terms within a contract appear to conflict: handwritten terms control over typewritten (or word processor) terms; and both control over printed terms. Similarly, courts hold negotiated terms prevail over inconsistent "form contract" terms.

> ▶ If Bernice's Grandpa writes by hand "including my herd of cattle" in the margin after the typed term "farm animals," his handwritten term will prevail over the meaning of the typed term "farm animals."

h. *Titles and Captions*—A title or caption will be preempted if it contradicts an operative term of the contract. The following provision in a residential lease includes a heading, which, without more, suggests a right to assign the lease. The text of the agreement clearly indicates that this right is subject to approval by the lessor.

> *Rights of Assignment and Subletting.* Lessee shall not assign this lease, nor sublet nor grant any concession or license to use the premises or any part thereof without the prior written consent of Lessor. Consent by Lessor to one assignment, subletting, concession, or license shall not be deemed to be consent to any subsequent assignment, subletting, concession, or license. An assignment, subletting, concession, or license without the prior written consent of Lessor, or an assignment or subletting by operation of law, shall be void and shall, at Lessor's option, terminate this lease.

i. *Legality, Reasonableness, and Public Policy or Public Interest*—Where more than one interpretation is possible, the interpretation that renders a legal and reasonable meaning to the contract along with one that is consistent with the public interest or public policy will be favored.

> ▶ A construction contract that calls for a building to be completed on a date certain will be interpreted to allow for an extension for government inspections required by law.

We end this part of the discussion on interpretation where we began: courts consider the evident purpose of the contract in interpreting the language. The canons are not conclusive, bright line rules. Rather they are grounds for legal argument or tools of persuasion. Thus, a particular term might suggest two or more conflicting canons. The court's view of the reasonable interpretation is likely to trump all of the canons. The purpose of the canons is to help courts discern the manifest intent of the parties and the logical and most likely construction of the language the parties used in their contract.

2. Extrinsic Evidence of Contract Construction

Despite the Plain Meaning Rule, modern courts often consider extrinsic evidence of the contract's meaning as long as the evidence is relevant and credible. While most issues of interpretation and construction are to be considered questions of law for the court's resolution, modern courts may turn to juries on questions of interpretive fact where reasonable but conflicting inferences can be drawn from the evidence. Section 202 of the *Restatement* summarizes rules in aid of interpretation. They are similar to the rules noted here, though they do not necessarily refer to the traditional maxims of interpretation courts use. Section 202 states:

(1) Words and other conduct are interpreted in the light of all the circumstances, and if the principal purpose of the parties is ascertainable it is given great weight.

(2) A writing is interpreted as a whole, and all writings that are part of the same transaction are interpreted together.

(3) Unless a different intention is manifested,(a) where language has a generally prevailing meaning, it is interpreted in accordance with that meaning; (b) technical terms and words of art are given their technical meaning when used in a transaction within their technical field.

(4) Where an agreement involves repeated occasions for performance by either party with knowledge of the nature of the performance and opportunity for objection to it by the other, any course of performance accepted or acquiesced in without objection is given great weight in the interpretation of the agreement.

(5) Wherever reasonable, the manifestations of intention of the parties to a promise or agreement are interpreted as consistent with each other and with any relevant course of performance, course of dealing, or usage of trade.

UCC Rules for Construing Contracts

The Uniform Commercial Code is essentially consistent with the common law approach to interpretation. It formalizes the canons and extrinsic evidence of a contract's meaning with four succinct rules and the Parol Evidence Rule of UCC 2-202. We will discuss the UCC Parol Evidence Rule separately as a bar to evidence. The Revised Article One of the UCC expresses the four rules in a hierarchy, a descending order of authority:

1. Express Terms — 1-303(e) — While all evidence of a contract's meaning (express terms and extrinsic evidence) should be construed as consistent with each other, if it is reasonable to do so, whenever express terms are irreconcilable with extrinsic evidence of meaning, express terms shall prevail over extrinsic evidence.

2. Course of Performance — 1-303(a) — is extrinsic evidence of conduct by the parties under the contract. Course of performance is only possible when the contract involves "repeated occasions of performance by a party. Courts allow such evidence only when the other party acquiesces or agrees with knowledge of the performance and has the opportunity to object to the conduct.

3. Course of Dealing — 1-303(b) — is extrinsic evidence of how the parties performed under other similar contracts with each other. And, 1-303(e) states that course of dealing prevails over conflicting extrinsic evidence of trade usage or industry practice.

4. Usages of the Trade — 1-303(c) — is extrinsic evidence of common practice "in a place, vocation or trade as to justify an expectation that it will be observed with respect to the transaction in question." The interpretation of a trade rule or code is a question of law. The existence of a trade practice is a question of fact, which is established by expert evidence. UCC 1-303(g) indicates that when a party seeks to offer evidence of trade usage, he must give the other party sufficient notice of the trade usage proffered.

Express terms prevail over course of performance. Evidence of course of performance prevails over other types of extrinsic evidence, and course of dealing prevails over usage of trade. This creates a hierarchy in which the evidence most closely associated with the contract is given superior weight. The terms are at the heart of the contract. Course of performance evidence relates to this particular contract and these particular parties; thus it is very central to the contract. Course of dealing is the same parties to the contract although this evidence is somewhat more remote because it relates to prior dealings between these parties. Usage of trade is evidence of parties to the trade to which the parties belong. Of course there are things to dispute as fact issues. One party may argue that the parties are not both members of the same trade or that the prior dealings of the parties did not establish the practice that the other is asserting.

UCC 1-303(f) states that evidence of course of performance under the contract is also "relevant to show a waiver or modification of any term inconsistent with it." This rule is subject to the requirements of UCC 2-209 on modification. We discuss modification in detail later.

Some explanation is necessary here to make the hierarchy of terms clear. The first attempt of the court is to read the terms as consistent with each other. Courts believe that parties are taking for granted their past dealings and their understandings from the trade in which they deal. If we read express terms literally, we might believe that any express term will exclude a usage of trade understanding of the term. For example, in a pre-UCC case, a dealer in horse meat entered an agreement with a purchaser (a dog food manufacturer), which specified a price per ton and also provided for an additional price of $5.00 for each ton delivered with over 50 percent protein. When the purchaser paid the flat rate rather than the premium rate, the seller put on evidence that the usage of trade for 50 percent protein involved rounding up from 49.5 percent. Thus, for every ton that measured 49.5 percent protein, the seller claimed the additional $5.00 per ton. The court agreed, noting that the express term of 50 percent did not destroy the usage of trade of rounding up because the parties had not clearly displaced the usage of trade in their agreement.

It may seem that the hierarchy of the UCC would require a different result. After all, the statute says that express terms control over usage of trade. Nevertheless, the same process of trying to read all of the terms together is required under the UCC. The result should be the same under the UCC as the common law decision discussed above. This is because the UCC respects the meaning of the usage of trade unless the parties carefully negate the usage. Courts believe that parties who are members of a trade negotiate contracts with reference to the usage of trade. In other words, the members of the trade take for granted the usage of trade. Only when they reject the usage by their express terms will the express terms displace the usage of trade. The comment to UCC 2-202 makes this point when it states that parties must "carefully negate" usage of trade if they wish to reject or displace a meaning established in a trade.

Additionally, Article 2 of the UCC makes it clear that evidence of course of performance, course of dealing, or usage of trade can be introduced in court without establishing first that the term at issue is ambiguous. This approach of allowing evidence to establish the meaning of a contract has been accepted by some courts in interpreting contracts outside the context of a sale of goods as well.

Parol Evidence Rule

The Parol Evidence Rule is a doctrine that Contracts books generally mention in connection with issues of interpretation. It is not truly a rule of interpretation, but it is related to interpretation. The Parol Evidence Rule presents an exception to the general practice of allowing admissible evidence to be presented to the trier of fact. It bars the evidence, even when it is relevant if the evidence offered contradicts the parties' final expression of the terms of the agreement. Rather than a rule of interpretation, the Parol Evidence Rule determines what the agreement should include. In a sense this is a threshold issue that should be dealt with prior to the issue of the meaning of the agreement. In other words, it does not decide the meaning of the contract but rather the *terms* of the contract. Clearly this rule interfaces with issues of contract interpretation. Because the Parol Evidence Rule creates a limitation on what evidence is admissible to determine the meaning of a contract, we include coverage of the Parol Evidence Rule in the chapter dealing with other limitations (i.e., Statutes of Limitations and the Statute of Frauds). For purposes of our coverage of interpretation of contracts, it is good to remember that the Parol Evidence Rule encourages parties to write down their agreements and may bar evidence relating to assertions of what the parties intended when those assertions are contrary to the written agreement.

The Rule of Reason is the ultimate interpretive tool. Courts often note that rules must yield to reason when interpreting contracts. As one court stated: "According to context and surrounding circumstances, a statutory "shall" is to be read as "may" and vice versa." *Comcoa, Inc. v. Coe*, 587 So. 2d 474 (Fla. Dist. Ct. App. 1991). Similarly, you can think of the Fifth Amendment of the U.S. Constitution, which states that private property is not to be taken "for public use" without reasonable compensation. No one suggests that the government has the right to take private property for private use without compensation, despite the rule of *exclusion unius*. This fact gives a memorable example of the Rule of Reason.

Checkpoints

- The purpose of interpreting contracts is to effectuate the intent of the parties.
- Principles of interpretation relate to interpretation of statutes as well as contracts.
- The canons of statutory construction look to the words of a statute to interpret its meaning.
- Definitional statutes may clarify the meaning of ambiguous terms.
- The common law provides gap fillers for missing terms in statutes.
- Courts interpret both legislative intent and the intent of parties with an eye toward public policy.
- Both statutory construction and interpretation of contracts depend on construing the meaning of the words of the contract.
- Both statutory construction and interpretation of contracts start from the plain meaning of the words of the document.
- Courts frequently reach an understanding of what the parties intended by considering the context and the circumstances of the contract.
- Courts consider extrinsic evidence of course of performance, course of dealing, and usage of the trade to interpret contracts.

Chapter 4

Formation: Mechanics of Mutual Assent

Roadmap

- Capacity
- Formation
- Unilateral and Bilateral Contracts

Capacity

Contract law recognizes the right of people to enter contracts as a general matter. Having legal capacity can be seen as a condition to the formation of a contract in some situations. In other situations, a party may have capacity to contract but may also have the power to void the contractual obligation. It may seem contradictory to say that someone may lack capacity and yet may enter a contract. This is the case, however, because contract law recognizes the right of some individuals to contract even though they could disaffirm (and thus undo) a contract. Capacity issues generally arise in the area of enforcement. This is the sequential question 2 in our organization. For this reason, we touch on the point here in the section on formation and we also deal with it more fully in the section on enforcement.

Restatement Section 12 deals with the requirement of capacity to contract. It states that no one can be bound by contract unless the person has legal capacity "to incur at least voidable contractual duties." The rules on capacity have the general purpose of protecting people the law deems not fully able to protect themselves. The rules can have negative effects on the people protected, however. We can see the negative effect of the rule if we consider history. In the past married women were denied the power to contract, for example. Some states had statutes that allowed for invalidation of contracts on a showing that a person was a habitual drunkard, a convict, or a spendthrift.

The law recognizes that some people lack full capacity, however, and has developed rules relating to people who are under the care of a guardian by virtue of an adjudication, minors, people who are mentally ill or defective, and people who entered a contract while intoxicated. Young people have the right to enter contracts but they can choose to disaffirm the contracts until they reach the age of majority. In fact, the right to disaffirm contracts extends some period of time past the age of majority. Most cases arise under the categories of people who are minors ("infants") and the mentally incompetent or mentally impaired. The way the law treats these categories of people will vary based on the type of incapacity and the circumstances. Another factor that plays a role in some situations is the knowledge of the person who entered the contract with the person who was partially or completely without capacity.

In some cases the capacity to contract may be partial. The nature of the transaction and circumstances can mean that the law treats everyone in a category as lacking capacity under some protective rules. Thus, some states have special rules, generally as a matter of statutory law, that provide special protection to designated groups of people, based on a legislative decision that the groups of people are vulnerable in some types of transactions. You can see this type of statute as imposing incapacity on all people in some transactions. Or you can see it as making the contract invalid despite the fact that the people protected actually have capacity. Incapacity sometimes relates only to particular types of transactions. It means that particular constraints are imposed on particular transactions.

This is a good example of how statutory law varies the common law. Examples of such statutes are limits allowing the borrower to disaffirm a contract to refinance a mortgage on a residential property, contracts resulting from a door-to-door sales transaction, time shares on resorts or real estate, and promises to surrender a child as a result of a surrogacy arrangement.

Whatever the basis for the special protection based on capacity (or statutory category) the person protected cannot waive the protection. Some statutes may vary this rule but in the common law categories it is clear. If we regard a waiver as a contract, or a transaction based on assent, you can see that this result follows from the general protective purpose of the rule. If a minor could waive the defense of his minority, for example, there would be an easy way to evade the rule relating to minors, and minors would lose the protection of the rule. Another way to see this point is to consider that a minor could promise not to assert his minority as a defense but the law would allow the minor to avoid or disaffirm that promise later.

Ability of Other Party to Disaffirm

The lack of capacity of the other party is generally not a ground for the non-impaired party to avoid contract obligations. In all these types of categories of incapacity, the person who entered a contract with the person lacking capacity bears some risk that the law will not respect the bargain. In order to protect people who lack capacity, the law allows an exception for necessaries. This means that a person who contracted with a person who lacked capacity to contract could, nevertheless, enforce a contract for necessaries. The result of this exception for necessaries is that parties who might be wary of entering a contract are more likely to enter a contract in an emergency or with people who are clearly in need of the goods or services contracted for because they have some security that such contracts will be enforceable. The rules relating to ratification also applies to incapacity as a result of mental illness or intoxication. If the incompetent regains her mental facilities and affirms the contract by words or conduct, she is bound.

Minors

Minors are people who have not yet reached the age of "majority," the age for capacity to contract. They are also called "infants" by courts and contracts commentators. Minors have the right to enter contracts, but the law treats minors differently from adults. Rather than denying minors the power to contract, the law protects minors by giving them the power to disaffirm their contracts. *Restatement Section 14* provides: "Unless a statute provides otherwise, a natural person has the capacity to incur only voidable contractual duties until the beginning of the day before the person's eighteenth birthday." This means that a minor who regrets the contract may be able to get out of it. The reason for cutting off the power to void the contract the day before the person's birthday is that he will no longer be a minor on the birthday. This rule relates to the time of entry of the contract. When the minor entered the contract prior to his birthday, the right to disaffirm can extend a short (reasonable) time after his eighteenth birthday.

Some courts refer to contracts involving a minor as voidable, meaning the minor has the power to undo the deal. Others speak of the contract being "void." It is important to note that even in jurisdictions that speak of the contract as a "void" contract do not treat such contracts as truly void in the sense of having no effect. The minor has the right to enforce the contract, and the contract is fully binding on the adult. Thus the contract has viability and is not really void. If both parties to the contract are minors, each party has the power to disaffirm. Although this power to cancel the contract is not a limitation on the power of minors to contract, it may result in a practical limitation on minors because adults will be wary of entering contracts with them. The minor's right to disaffirm continues until a reasonable time after the minor reaches the age of majority. The age of majority in most states is now 18. If, however, the minor retains and uses the goods after he reaches majority, the court is likely to see this conduct as a ratification, which will cut off the minor's right to disaffirm the contract. Thus the law provides a cushion of time after the minor comes of age as another protection for the minor. This is not an unlimited protection. If the minor affirms the contract either expressly or by conduct after she turns 18, she loses the right to disaffirm.

Because of the minor's right to disaffirm contracts, merchants often will require a co-signer with a minor. Once the merchant has the adult co-signer, it has security that it will not lose out entirely on the contract. It will have someone to proceed against if the minor disaffirms the contract. The exception for necessaries, the next point of discussion, provides some additional protection for merchants, though it does not give a merchant much certainty about a contract since the argument of necessaries may or may not be accepted by a court. The use of a co-signer is a more reliable basis for a merchant to know his interests will be protected.

The Exception for Necessaries

The Doctrine of "Necessaries" is the major exception to the rule that minors can disaffirm their contractual obligations. The rule is that a party who supplies *necessary* goods and services to a minor may recover the price for them from the minor to the extent the price is reasonable. Although you can think of this doctrine as relating to "necessities" of life, you should recognize that courts use the term "necessaries," rather than referring to necessities. The exception enhances the likelihood that people will enter contracts with minors for essential goods and services since they know they will be able to enforce such contracts. Whether particular goods or services fall into the category of "necessaries" is a fact question, making it subject to flexibility and dispute. Generally courts find food, shelter, clothing, and education to be necessaries for a minor when a parent is not providing for the minor or when the minor is in an emergency. Whether such items are necessaries in a particular case is a question of fact. If, for example, the minor has parents or guardians who are willing and able to provide these things, there is no need for the minor to obtain them directly from a third party, and thus they may not be "necessaries." If a minor is in an emergency situation or unable to get support from a parent, the court may disallow the minor's attempt to disaffirm the contract for the necessaries. The purpose of the exception is to ensure that minors who are in distress can get necessities. It is not intended to create a loophole to allow adults to enforce contracts for unnecessary items. Such a loophole would undermine substantially the rule allowing minors to disaffirm their contracts.

The exception is of particular importance to minors who are not under the care of a parent. In some states, if the minor has been freed from the relationship with a parent, the law may not consider the young person a minor for purposes of the exception. The status of the young person in this case is an emancipated minor. This status of emancipated minor results in a broader exception than the rule on necessaries since it may mean that the minor will be responsible for all of her contracts. This effect is both potentially good and bad for the minor. The benefit is that she is more likely to be able to convince adults to contract with her. The burden is the ordinary burden of enforcement of promises.

Other Cases Binding a Minor

A court may bind a minor to an obligation to a contract in other situations in addition to the category of necessaries. If the minor is found to have a legal obligation under another area of law such as tort law or restitution, a court may hold the minor for the obligation. Thus, if a minor has engaged in a misrepresentation to get the adult to enter a contract, the adult may have an action sounding in tort. Additionally statutes make certain types of contracts enforceable against minors. Contracts to enter the armed forces, student loan agreements, obligations to pay child support, withdrawal of bank deposits or payment of life insurance premiums, and contracts made with judicial approval are examples of types of contracts excluded from the power of the minor to void the contract.

When a minor disaffirms a contract, the minor must return any of the benefits of the contract that he or she possesses. If the minor has damaged or used up the item purchased under the contract, this will be a loss to the adult who entered a contract with the minor. Some state statutes require the minor who disaffirms a contract to restore the consideration to the other party.

Mental Impairment

Contract law recognizes the right of people with diminished mental capacity to enter contracts, but, like the rule relating to minority, the law recognizes the right of such people to be free of the burdens of contracts in some cases.

The rule on capacity relating to mental impairment is both more and less complicated than the rule on infancy. Section 13 of the *Restatement* states: "A person has no capacity to incur contractual duties if his property is under guardianship by reason of an adjudication of mental illness or defect." This rule is more straightforward than the rule on infancy. It simply denies capacity to people who are under guardianship. The case of people who are not under an order of guardianship is more complicated. Thus, the rule on capacity is better understood as two rules: one relating to those who have been adjudicated incompetent and another for those who have not been the subject of a court or agency adjudication.

The law seeks to protect parties who lack capacity but also to protect the justifiable expectations of those parties who entered contracts with them — so long as these other parties did not know of the lack of capacity or seek to take advantage of the person lacking capacity. Generally, in the case of a party who has not been adjudicated incompetent, the party asserting lack of capacity bears the burden of proof of establishing lack of capacity or incompetence. As with minors, if the incompetent received benefits under the contract, he must return or pay for the benefits. This concept comes from general principles of fairness; it is a restitution principle. When a party did not know that his contracting partner was incompetent at the time of contracting, he can withhold his performance upon learning of the incompetency until a guardian or parent affirms the contract. The same exception for necessaries that we discussed above relating to minors, also applies to people who lack the capacity to contract.

Adjudicated Incompetents

This is a clear rule. Thus, courts hold contracts with mentally incompetent persons are voidable when the person has been adjudicated mentally incompetent and a court has appointed a guardian for the person. This rule does not include a power of disaffirmance because no contract arises from the apparent contract with a person who is under guardianship because of a mental illness. This rule is a hard-edged, bright-line for courts. If the party has been adjudicated incompetent, the contract is voidable, even though the other party acted in good faith and without knowledge of the adjudication.

This rule puts the risk of contracting on the person who deals with someone who has been adjudicated to have a mental illness or mental defect. It can raise a problem if someone contracts with a person who is in this category but appears to be sane. This is an unusual situation since people who have been adjudicated mentally ill will be under the direct care and supervision of the guardian.

Non-Adjudicated Incompetents

When a person who is mentally impaired has not been adjudged by a court or an agency with authority, the law is more complicated. The situation clearly involves fact questions about the person's capacity, and it may be difficult for a business or person to decide to contract with a young person or someone who seems not fully in charge of their capacities. Most courts hold such contracts voidable when an individual was not capable of understanding the nature and consequences of the transaction. If the facts indicate that the other contracting party was seeking to take advantage of someone who appears to lack capacity, a court may invalidate the contract based on deceptive or unfair conduct. This issue relates to the question of unconscionable contracts. The law of misrepresentation, duress, and undue influence also play a role in cases in which a party is partially disabled. The level of duress involved may render the consent ineffective to form a contract or may create a contract voidable by the party who has been subjected to duress.

The case of the non-adjudicated incompetent presents difficult fact questions. Section 15 of the *Restatement* provides the following formulation of the rule:

"A person incurs only voidable contractual duties by entering into a transaction if by reason of mental illness or defect (a) he is unable to understand in a reasonable manner the nature and consequences of the transaction, or (b) he is unable to act in a reasonable manner in relation to the transaction and the other party has reason to know of his condition."

This rule expands on the traditional test, allowing a party (or his representative) to disaffirm a contract on the basis that even though he understood the contract his mental condition made it impossible for him to act in a reasonable manner. This expanded situation for disaffirmance is limited to situations where the other party has reason to know of the condition that impaired the person's ability to act in a reasonable manner. In the well-known case of *Ortelere v. Teacher's Retirement Board*, a schoolteacher who was suffering from a "nervous breakdown" and cerebral arteriosclerosis took a leave of absence. While she was under treatment, she changed her retirement plan to obtain a larger payout during her life. Part of this choice involved choosing to waive a death benefit for survivors. The court allowed her husband to invalidate the choice she made after she died. Although the court held that Ms. Ortelere understood the choice she made, it held that her mental illness made her unable to act in a reasonable way. It also found that the officers of the retirement plan had reason to know of her condition. Under the traditional test, a court would have accepted the contract to change the policy.

This newer test clearly expands the risk of a party disaffirming a contract. The requirement that the party seeking to disaffirm (in the Ortelere case, this was the husband of the incompetent person) provides some protection for those entering contracts with impaired people. Nevertheless, the rule has been criticized as overly protective and likely to disturb the reliability of contracts. The *Restatement* also seeks to limit this risk. It provides that if the contract is made on fair terms and without knowledge of the mental illness or defect the contract will not be avoided. This provision makes clear the power of courts to sculpt a remedy to protect both parties.

Intoxicated Persons

In some cases, a person's mental capacity may be impaired by alcohol or other substances. The standard relating to intoxication is similar to the standard for avoidance based on mental illness. Thus, when a person is so intoxicated that he or she is unable to understand the nature and consequences of the transaction, the transaction is voidable. Section 16 of the *Restatement* formulates the test with the similar language as its statement on mental illness:

"A person incurs only voidable contractual duties by entering into a transaction if the other party has reason to know that by reason of intoxication (a) he is unable to understand in a reasonable manner the nature and consequences of the transaction, or (b) he is unable to act in a reasonable manner in relation to the transaction."

Courts are often less sympathetic to the party seeking to disaffirm because he had too much to drink when the drinking was voluntary. If we look at this point as a matter of risk assessment, it makes sense to say that the party who drinks too much is taking the risk that he may not use good judgment in contracting. In most cases of drunkenness, the other party is able to enforce the promise of the drunk person, even though he has not relied on the drunk person's promise.

Formation

A good place to begin the topic of formation is to remember the Five Sequential Questions of Contract Law: Is it a valid contract? This Chapter explores dimensions of that question by looking at the mechanics of offer and acceptance and the legal requirement of the validating principle of consideration. A preliminary point of great importance is the ingredient of mutual assent.

Parties form contracts in many ways. Although formation by express words is the most obvious way to form a contract, parties can also enter a contract based on their conduct. This conduct can even be inaction or silence in unusual circumstances such as a course of dealing that establishes that the parties intended to be bound by such inaction or silence. Some contracts come from long and complex negotiations while others arise from a casual conversation. The mechanics of offer and acceptance may be clear or it may be difficult to know which party offered and which accepted. Professors sometimes put up a simple formula as an overview of contract formation. It is:

$$O + A + C = K$$

Where O = offer, A = acceptance, C = consideration, and K = contract, the formula helps us remember the elements of the classic contract. Of course each of these elements can involve difficult fact questions. For example, did the buyer make an offer? Did the seller accept? Was the agreement supported by consideration? We will explore each of these elements. Before we get to the mechanics of the transaction, let's look at the essential ingredient of voluntary assent.

The essence of the contractual relationship is its voluntary nature. Both parties must manifest the intent to be bound. Courts reject the theory of "subjective intent" as a requirement for mutual assent. Courts look to the manifestation of the parties to determine intent to be bound. This test is called "objective intent." Although subjective intent is not required to meet the requirement of mutual assent, the actual intent of a party may be relevant in determining meaning of a contract or other factual issues. Certainly if a court reaches the conclusion that the parties did intend to be bound as a subjective matter, it would enforce the promises the parties made to one another. Even when a party seeking enforcement cannot meet the high standard of subjective intent, courts generally enforce promises that manifest intent as an objective matter.

Mutual Assent

Although assent is not necessary in many areas of the law, voluntary assent is a central premise of contract law. Each citizen does not agree to be bound by the laws of the country. When we speak of the "social compact" it is not an agreement entered voluntarily by each member of society. Rather, law imposes a significant set of obligations on parties by virtue of their membership in society. You do not agree to be bound by criminal law or tort law. You are held to obligations set by criminal law, tort law, and other areas without your consent. You can be held liable for the injuries someone suffers from your negligent operation of your car without your assent to the principles of tort law. While you cannot escape the obligations created by these laws, you are able to choose whether or not to enter contracts.

Contract obligations come about because the parties to the contract have agreed to them. In this way, parties to a contract create their own law that relates to their agreement. No obligation existed between the parties until they agreed to it. The law does not require your assent to bind you to act in a reasonable way (tort law), but the law will not impose a contract on you without your assent. Thus, to make a memorable comparison, the obligation to pay damages to someone you injured by driving your car in a negligent way does not depend on your assent to tort law, but the obligation to pay damages for your refusal to pay for a car depends on a court finding that you agreed to purchase the car.

Courts refer to this requirement of voluntary assent to be bound by the memorable phrase the "meeting of the minds." At old common law, some courts required a showing that both parties subjectively agreed to the obligations of the contract at the same thing. This showing is not necessary under modern contract law. Courts do not use the requirement of assent to require subjective assent by the parties. Rather, courts determine whether the reasonable meaning of what the parties did and said created legal obligations. While courts continue to use the term "meeting of the minds," they do not require proof of subjective intent of the parties. The objective theory of assent looks to the manifestations of the parties (both words and conduct) to see whether the party with whom they communicate reasonably believed they had assented to be bound. The subjective theory of formation (if it really operated as dramatically as the term suggests) essentially gave each party an escape hatch to disavow the contract. If the subjective theory was applied literally, a party who regretted being in a deal could escape it by asserting he did not subjectively intend the contract asserted by the other party. The subjective approach undermines the certainty of obligation.

Under the modern approach of objective assent, there is a risk that a party may be bound to a contract without truly intending to be bound. This point can be understood by looking at cases in which one party may have been joking rather than seriously intending to enter a contract. In the famous case of *Lucy v. Zehmer,* the court enforced a contract for the sale of land despite evidence that the seller did not intend to sell the land and was merely joking. After several drinks, Zehmer offered to sell land he owned to Lucy for $50,000. Later Zehmer asserted that he was joking and had no actual intent to sell. Lucy accepted the offer and acted on it by securing financing to make the purchase.

A court applying the subjective theory of assent might well have rejected the purchaser's claim to require the seller convey the land if the trier of fact concluded that Zehmer was joking. That is, if the trier of fact believed Zehmer's testimony that he was joking, it might have held the promise unenforceable for lack of assent. Under the objective approach, however, the promise to sell is enforceable if the court finds that a reasonable person in Lucy's position would have believed that Zehmer was serious. If the circumstances indicate that the purchaser should have known that Zehmer was joking, there would be no contract under the objective theory of assent.

Today courts apply the objective theory of assent, looking at the manifestations of a party rather than the party's testimony (after the fact) of his own subjective state of mind. In *Skycom Corp. v. Telstar Corp.*, 813 F.2d 810, 814 (7th Cir. 1987), the court made the point in a memorable way stating that "determination of intent does not invite a tour of Walter's cranium with Walter as the guide." Judge Learned Hand also made the point in another interesting way. He stated that even if "twenty bishops" swear that the party denying the contract actually subjectively intending not to contract this testimony would not matter if the person receiving the communication reasonably believed it to be assent to the deal. Thus, in the *Zehmer* case, if Lucy actually knew or should have known that Zehmer was joking, there is no contract.

In some circumstances, the intent of the parties may seem contrary to the objective theory of assent. For example, Section 201 of the *Restatement* makes clear that if both parties hold the same meaning the court will use that meaning in interpreting the contract even if it is contrary to the ordinary meaning of a term. Section 201 states: "Where the parties have attached the same meaning to a promise or agreement or a term thereof, it is interpreted in accordance with that meaning." Thus, if the parties use the term "chicken," intentionally meaning "duck," and this point is established by evidence, the court should enforce the contract for ducks despite the apparent meaning of the contract to sell chickens.

Misunderstandings

A mistake in understanding can prevent a contract from being formed. Section 201 of the *Restatement* also explores the situation in which the parties held two different meanings and neither party knew or had a reason to know the meaning held by the other. Section 201 states:

> Where the parties have attached different meanings to a promise or agreement or a term thereof, it is interpreted in accordance with the mean-

ing attached by one of them if at the time the agreement was made (a) that party did not know of any different meaning attached by the other, and the other knew the meaning attached by the first party; or (b) that party had no reason to know of any different meaning attached by the other, and the other had reason to know the meaning attached by the first party.

Thus, if neither party knew the meaning the other intended then neither party is bound. There is no mutual assent. For example, in the past, Ford Motor Company produced a car called a Colt. If two parties discuss buying the "colt," no contract is formed if one party intended to purchase a Colt car and the other intended to sell a young horse.

Intent as to Legal Effect

There is no requirement that they intend the legal consequence of contract formation. Generally parties do intend to perform the promises they make in entering a contract, of course. Parties do not need to expressly intend the legal consequences of contracting, however. Courts generally will respect clear indications that the parties do not intend for an agreement to be legally enforceable. Such agreements are sometimes referred to as "Gentlemen's Agreements," meaning that the agreement is not intended to create legal recourse. An example of such a "Gentlemen's Agreement" is found in situations in which the parties discuss setting up a public offering of stocks to form a corporation. The parties to this agreement share information about the viability of selling the stock in the company to the public. They may intend to go forward with the public offering only if certain capitalization requirements for the company are met. If they intentionally agree that their promises to each other are given only for mutual assurance and neither will enforce the promises in a legal forum, it is likely a court will refuse enforcement of the promises. Thus, although courts do not require that parties intend legal enforcement when they make promises to each other, courts will refuse to enforce promises if it is clear that the parties expressly excluded judicial enforcement of their understanding.

Classic formation includes offer and acceptance and in some cases contract formation is clear cut. One party makes an offer and the other party accepts the offer. A contract comes into being. In many cases, the formal distinctions of "offer" and "acceptance" are not clear. Both parties talk about a deal and it is never clear who made the offer and who accepted. This lack of clarity of process does not create problems. If the substance of the matter indicates the parties intended to contract with each other, a court will enforce the agreement. Parties often reach an agreement as a result of a series of offers, and counteroffers, or "negotiations," that result in a final agreement. Precision regarding which communication is the offer is not required under modern contract law. In other words, the fact that it is not clear which communication is an offer and which is the acceptance does not necessarily prevent a contract from being formed. Courts will look to the reasonable expectations of the parties regarding whether they intended to create a commitment with each other.

Nonetheless, it is important to recognize an offer. Often it is clear that a party has accepted but it may not be clear that the party had the power of acceptance. Accepting a deal is not effective unless an offer actually was made, conferring the power of acceptance on the offeree.

Offers and Acceptance

The process of offering and accepting a contractual obligation is often referred to as the "mechanics" of contracting. This modern process is often unclear and it may be difficult to identify which communication is an offer and which is an acceptance. Nevertheless, it is good to break down the process into the steps of offer and acceptance. The simple approach is to see that the process of contracting starts with an offer. A memorable saying captures the importance of the offer:

"Offeror is master of the offer."

This statement means not only that the offer sets the initial terms of the contract to be discussed and bargained. It also means that the offer sets the terms upon which the offer can be accepted. The offer could state that no sale will occur without "cash on the barrel head," meaning that the buyer must come prepared to pay the full price. The offer can specify the method of acceptance. It can indicate that in order to accept the offeree must meet the offeror on the Empire State Building at noon on January 1 or stand on a designated corner on Bourbon Street, wearing a Dr. Seuss Cat in the Hat outfit. Or stand on a corner on your head (if you are offeree) wearing a Dr. Seuss Cat in the Hat outfit. You might question the sanity of the offeror who requires such weird acts for acceptance. You might not want to do business with such a demanding and idiosyncratic offeror. It is clearly your choice (or offeree's choice in some of these examples) not to negotiate any further with the offeror.

If the offeree wants to accept the offeror's offer, he needs to accept by the terms set in the offer, however. On the other hand, offeree could negotiate. He could talk with offeror and try to get a more reasonable form of acceptance. Or offeree might want to restart the negotiations from a new starting place, by making an offer of his own on his own terms and with his own specifications of how the other party needs to do to accept. If the offeree decides to take this route, however, he cannot close the deal with the next communication. Rather than accepting and finalizing a contract, he would be beginning the process again without certainty that the current offeror would accept his new terms. If the deal is one that offeree wants, he may simply choose to accept in the manner set by the offer despite its annoying or weird requirements.

Offers, revocations, and rejections are effective when the other party receives them. Acceptance is effective when the communication is put out of the possession of the offeree. The rule on the effectiveness of acceptance provides protection to the offeree, whose right to accept is subject to termination. The American rule is that offers can be revoked at any time. The rule on acceptance is often called the Mailbox Rule. An acceptance that is sent after a rejection by the offeree does not have the usual effect of closing the deal at the time it is sent. The universal common law rule recognized by *Restatement Section 40* is that an acceptance sent after a rejection is effective if it reaches the offeror before the rejection reaches him.

What Constitutes Acceptance

The saying "Offeror is master of the offer" captures two points: (1) the offeror sets the terms upon which the offer can be accepted, and (2) the offeror states the deal offered.

Silence Not Ordinarily Acceptance

Both parties need to assent to a contract to be bound by the obligations of contract law. Even recognizing that the "Offeror is master of the offer," we should note that this rule is not absolute. There are limits on the offeror's ability to specify the manner of acceptance. For example, offeror cannot ordinarily make silence by offeree an acceptance. If offeror had the power to make silence by the other party an acceptance, we would all need to be vigilant at all times to make sure we were not binding ourselves to contracts that we did not intend to enter. This would be an unworkable situation. Although the offeror can ordinarily specify that the offeree must do to accept, he cannot make doing nothing acceptance. A simple hypo will illustrate the problem that would result from a rule that allowed the offeror to designate silence as acceptance.

> ▶ An encyclopedia sales rep writes to Potential Customer: "I know you will like the special offer I have for you to purchase a leather bound

encyclopedia set for only $10.00 per month for 8 years. So, just sit tight and you will receive the first volume next Tuesday. If you do not wish to take advantage of this great offer, simply phone me at the number below." If Potential Customer never responds, an absolute rule of power for the offeror would find a contract is absolute, then Potential Customer's silence would bind him to the contract because the offer implies that silence is acceptance. That is not the rule. If Potential Customer never responds to the message there is no contract.

In some circumstances, however, silence may operate as consent. To take a simple example, remember the Book of the Month Club. It sets the terms of the contract so that if you receive a book and do not return it you have accepted it. This example is a bit off-center since this is an umbrella contract that sets the terms on shipment but it gives an idea of the concept of acceptance by silence. Parties who have developed a course of dealing may operate in a way that creates acceptance by silence. If a seller routinely delivers a product and the buyer accepts and pays for the delivery but never expressly accepts, the parties may have established a course of conduct (sometimes called a "course of dealing") in which they are agreeing that silence is assent to the deal.

> ▸ For five years Farmer Brown delivers hay to Rancher Black and, in return, Black sends Brown a check for the delivery. In year six however, Black fails to send the payment check arguing he did not accept the hay. A court may find Black's silence is acceptance in this case because of the parties' course of dealing. If a court finds that the parties have a course of dealing that allows silence to operate as acceptance, the offeree will need to get in touch with offeror to indicate that he is rejecting a delivery or his silence may operate as assent.

Terminating Offers

In contract law of the United States, offers are freely revocable. This means that offeror has the power to change his mind at any time. Thus, he can withdraw the offer at any time. He can destroy the offer as soon as he makes an offer, even though this means that the offeree has not had a reasonable time to consider whether he wants to accept. Sometimes commentators and scholars emphasize this point by saying that offers are "fragile." Of course some of the fact patterns used here involve difficulties of proof.

This right to revoke the offer continues until the offer is accepted. In other words, offers last until they are terminated. The corollary of this rule is that until the offer is revoked or terminated in some other way the offeree has the power to accept the offer and form the contract. When the offer terminates, the offeree can no longer accept the offer. There are five ways that offers terminate:

(1) Rejection or counter-offer by the offeree,
(2) Lapse of time,
(3) Revocation by the offeror,
(4) Death or incapacity of the offeror or offeree,
(5) Acceptance.

Section 36 of the *Restatement* notes four of these five ways listed above. It does not list the fifth way (termination by acceptance). It probably omits this method of termination because in the case of acceptance the offer matures into a contract. Nevertheless, acceptance does terminate the offer. We will look at each method of termination separately.

1. Rejection or Counter-Offer

A rejection is only made by the offeree. This is a terminology point. If the offeror calls off the negotiations, it is a revocation. When it is offeree who calls off the negotiations it is by a rejection. Clearly an offer terminates when the offeree says "no" to it. At that point, offeror is free to make the offer to someone else without fear of double liability. The same rule applies when an offeree makes a counter-offer. The rule is that the counter-offer has two functions. First the counter-offer is a new offer. Second counter-offer terminates the original offer to which it is responding.

> ▶ Seller says to potential Buyer: "I offer you my car for $10,000. You can accept by mail." Buyer calls and says: "No thanks, I am not interested."

Buyer has rejected the offer.

> ▶ Seller says to potential Buyer: "I offer you my car for $10,000. You can accept by mail." Buyer calls and says: "I will buy your car for $9,500."

Buyer's communication does two things: (1) it makes a new offer and (2) it rejects the offer from Seller. Thus, consider the following hypo:

> ▶ Seller says to potential Buyer: "I offer you my car for $10,000. You can accept by mail." Buyer calls and says: "I will buy your car for $9,500." Buyer calls back after this exchange and says "I changed my mind. I accept your offer at $10,000."

Whether or not Seller relied on the rejection by counter-offer, it is too late to accept the offer of a car for $10,000. Buyer's counter-offer rejected the original offer from Seller. Of course the Seller could write back and try to strike a deal again, since it looks like the two want to make a deal.

It is possible for an offeree to make a counter-offer without terminating the offer. Consider the following change of facts:

▶ Seller says to potential Buyer: "I offer you my car for $10,000. You can accept by mail." Buyer calls and says: "Keeping your offer under advisement, I now offer to buy your car for $9,500." Buyer has not destroyed the offer by this counter-offer since he has made clear that he is holding onto the offer. Keep in mind that offeror can always terminate the negotiations until the acceptance by simply revoking the offer. This risk continues for buyer until he accepts.

Similarly, after an offeree extinguishes an offer by a counter-offer, it is possible for the original offeror to continue or reinstate the offer. Seller can revive the offer by sending the same offer again or by simply responding in a way that is reasonably read as keeping the offer open. Consider the following change of facts:

▶ Seller says to potential Buyer: "I offer you my car for $10,000. You can accept by mail." Buyer calls and says: "I offer to buy your car for $9,500." Buyer has destroyed the offer by this counter-offer. Seller replies: "I won't go lower than $10,000 because it's a fair deal." A court may find that Seller revived the offer. This is not as clear as if he stated again he is offering the car for $10,000, but a reasonable reading of the reply is that it is still open to offeree.

2. Lapse of Time

Often the time an offer will lapse is indicated in the offer itself. When this is the case, the offer lapses at the time specified. If the offer does not state how long it is open, it will, nevertheless, terminate at some point. The exact time of termination is not known. It will never be known unless the offeree tries to accept and the offeror opposes the acceptance based on his claim that the offer has lapsed. When this happens, the dispute will go to court and the court will need to decide whether the offer had lapsed. The standard the court will apply is a rule of reasonableness.

▶ Seller says to potential Buyer on January 1: "I offer you my car for $10,000. You can accept by mail." Buyer replies by mail on December

31: "I accept your offer." The acceptance, coming on the last day of the year is nearly one year old. It is likely a court will find that the offer lapsed at some point during the year. Rather than specifying exactly when the lapse occurred, the court is like to hold the lapse occurred at some indeterminate point.

This rule creates difficult fact issues but also has the good effect of not allowing offers to extend infinitely. Offerors are free to set an indefinite period of time, but courts do not believe this means that the offeror intended to keep the offer open forever. The fact that a rule of lapse exists puts both parties on notice that the offeree does not have a limitless time to accept. This creates an incentive for the offeree to accept in a timely manner. It creates an incentive for offeror to include a time for the termination in the offer. Like so many contracts rules, reasonableness is the key. The reasonableness depends on all the circumstances. For example, in a volatile market, in which the price rises and falls quickly, the conventional wisdom is that the offer would not last very long. In a sale of land when land prices are stable and long term the offer might be said to last longer. There is a counterpoint here, however, in that courts are hesitant to impose a contract on the sale of land as compared with goods.

Lapse and the Power of Revocation

We noted above that if an offer states that it will be held open for a particular period of time or until a particular date, the offer lapses (terminates) at the time specified. A related point should be noted here. A statement of when an offer will lapse does not, without more, prevent the offeror from revoking the offer. Even if the offer states that it will remain open, the offeror may revoke that offer prior to the stated time unless there is some basis to enforce this promise to hold the offer open. A promise to hold an offer open is a promise not to revoke the offer. This promise is like other promises we have seen in that the law does not enforce promises generally unless there is a legal validation of the promise. The most common validation of a promise is consideration. In some circumstances, reliance may be a substitute for the consideration to hold the offer open. As with other promises, an action based on reasonable reliance can substitute for consideration in some cases.

▶ Seller says to potential Buyer on January 1: "I offer you my car for $10,000. This offer will lapse on February 1." On January 2, Seller writes again: "I revoke my offer to you." It may seem that seller's statement of lapse is a promise to hold the offer open. Without additional facts making clear that offeror was promising to hold the offer open, however, a court is likely to respect the revocation, however, and give it effect, cutting off the power of the offeree to accept—even before the lapse occurs. This is because the statement of lapse was not a promise to hold the offer open. Additionally, even if the statement had included a promise to hold the offer open, it was not supported by consideration.

Even when an offer includes a statement of when an offer will lapse the offeror may revoke. The offeror may revoke that offer prior to the stated time unless a court finds consideration or a reliance interest to keep the offer open. Likewise, courts will refuse enforcement of promises relating to the deal (such as an option) unless the promise is validated by consideration or a substitute. This is another way of saying that the offeror has promised not to revoke the offer. In making this promise, offeror has offered an option to offeree. A promise to hold an offer open (that is a promise not to revoke the offer) is enforceable if it is supported by consideration. In some circumstances, reliance may be a substitute for the consideration to hold the offer open. Additionally, there are some cases of statutes that recognize the powers of the parties to create an option without consideration. UCC 2-205 is the most important example for purposes of contracts classes. Under UCC 2-205, if an offeror makes a firm offer in writing to buy or sell goods, the offer is enforceable if it complies with the requirements of the statute. It provides a period of time in which the offeror cannot revoke. This provision is discussed at length later in this chapter.

Lapse in the Face to Face Setting

In the case of face to face offers, courts have held that the offers lapse when the parties leave each other's presence without striking a deal. In an employment case, an employee offered his resignation, perhaps in a heated moment. The employer did not accept. Later the employer said he accepted the employee's resignation. The court disagreed. It held that the offer to resign had lapsed and could not be accepted by the employer. This case involved an employee who had a specified term contract. If the employer wanted to discharge an employee in an employment-at-will contract, the employer would simply terminate the employee.

3. Revocation

As master of the offer, an offeror can revoke the offer at any time prior to acceptance. A revocation is only made by the offeror. This is a terminology point. When the offeror calls off the negotiations, this communication is a revocation. When offeree calls off the negotiations, offeree has made a rejection.

▸ Let's take the example used above. White sends an email to Builder: "If you will install cherry bookcases in my office, I will pay you $3,000. If you agree to finish the work in two weeks, you can accept by starting work at once." Before Builder has a chance to accept or even consider the offer, White sends a second email: "Never mind, I have changed my mind. I don't need a makeover of the offices. Disregard my prior email."

White changed his mind and communicated the change of mind in a revocation. His revocation is effective. If the builder answered back with an acceptance after builder received the revocation, that acceptance is not effective since the offer terminated when builder received the revocation. This was before the acceptance was sent. The offer terminated when White revoked and communicated the revocation to the offeree. At that point, Builder has lost his power to form a contract by accepting. The revocation of an offer is effective when it is received by the offeree. Thus, if Builder had replied as soon as he got the email and before he received the revocation, a contract would have been formed. (We will discuss the timing of the acceptance later.)

General Offers

Sometimes an offeror will make a general offer that could be accepted by any one of a large number of people. To take a clear example of a general offer, consider a posting for a reward. If offeror posts a reward and later wishes to revoke the offer, he will need to post the same type of notice to effectively revoke the offer.

4. Death or Incapacity

The death or incapacity of either the offeror or the offeree terminates an offer. The termination is immediate. Notice is not required. This creates a risk for every offeree. You might see this as a practical matter: You cannot contract with a dead man. There is an important point in terms of line drawing. If the offeree had accepted the offer one second before the death, the contract would have formed and it would be enforceable against the offeror's estate.

5. Acceptance

It may seem odd to say that acceptance terminates the offer but this is literally true. Offeror's power to terminate ends at the time of acceptance. The acceptance is the act that forms the contract. Offeror can no longer revoke the offer, and offeree can no longer reject the offer. The offer has turned into a contract. Like any contract, the parties are free to undo the deal by their joint action. They can rescind the contract. The time for terminating the offer is past, however. The only way out of the arrangement is by mutual agreement. In other words, the *offer* can no longer be terminated but the *contract* can be rescinded (terminated).

An acceptance is the offeree's expression of assent to the terms of the offer. Section 35 of the *Restatement* explains that an offer gives the offeree the "power to complete the manifestation of mutual assent by acceptance of the offer." This power continues until it terminates in one of the ways discussed above or the contract is formed by the acceptance. When the acceptance meets the terms of the offer, it binds the offeror and offeree to a contract on the terms of the offer.

Only offerees have the power to accept. When an offer is addressed to the public or a large group of people, any one of the offerees may accept. A communication is not an acceptance if it offers a different contract than the one offered by the offeror. As we discussed above, a communication that appears to be an acceptance is, nevertheless, not an acceptance if it changes the terms of the deal. Rather, such a communication is a counter-offer—even if it uses the words: "I accept." This point goes back to the introductory note that the offeror (and not the offeree) is master of the offer. Thus, if the offeree changes some term in the communication purporting to accept, he has created a counter-offer (and a rejection).

Options and Irrevocable Offers

Sometimes the offeror will indicate that the offer is irrevocable for a certain period of time. An irrevocable offer benefits the offeree because the offeree has a guaranteed period within which to accept. The basic rule is that an offer is not irrevocable even if the offeror specifically states that it is irrevocable unless the promise is supported by consideration or based on reasonable reliance.

> ▶ Seller says to potential Buyer on January 1: "I offer you my car for $10,000. I will hold this offer open until noon, February 1." On January 2, Seller writes again: "I revoke my offer to you."

This may look like an irrevocable offer. Offeror has *promised* to hold the offer open. Holding the offer open means that offeror will not revoke. Thus, offeror is promising that he will not revoke the offer. You might think the law would hold him to his word and treat the offer as irrevocable. If this were the law, it would create a special kind of promise that is not subject to the rule of consideration. The logical question is whether the offeror is bound by this offer. This is another way of saying that this promise to hold an offer open may not be enforceable. An offeree who would like to enforce this promise may not be successful unless she can show consideration or reliance. That is, the offeree who seeks to enforce the promise not to revoke must show that she gave something in return for the promise or was disadvantaged when she reasonably relied on the promise.

> ▸ For example, an owner of property offers to sell 10 acres for $500,000. He promises to allow buyer to think about the offer until the following Saturday. He even promises not to revoke the offer until that time.

The problem is that this promise not to revoke is not enforceable unless it is supported by consideration or another validation device. Remember the law will not enforce all promises — only those that it as regards meeting the requirement of consideration or some other validating principle. If a court finds this promise to hold the offer open to be a "nudum pactum," a naked promise, it will not enforce it any more than it would enforce a promise to make a gift. Accordingly, even though Seller promised to hold this offer open the promise of irrevocability is revocable. Though this may seem odd, it follows from the requirement of consideration or some other validating device. Since this promise is not supported by consideration, it is gratuitous and, thus, not enforceable. The promise not to revoke is an empty promise. If the offeree paid consideration for the promise, it would be irrevocable — so long as the consideration was bargained for.

Option Contracts

An option contract is one in which a party has the right to finalize or "opt" into an obligation. The rules on timing are different when the contract at issue is an option. An option contract is an enforceable commitment. There are different types of options in different contexts, ranging from the use of options in the securities market to making a selection under a contract. The meaning of the term in contract law often refers to the commitment to hold an offer open for a certain period of time. This means that the offeror promises not to revoke the offer during the stated time. At common law, an option was purchased for consideration. For example, a potential purchaser considering a particular plot of land might take an option to purchase the land within one year or some other specified time period. The purchaser would pay for the option, generally a fairly small price in relation to the purchase price. It is easy to see why courts would respect the right of the offeree in this setting (the potential purchaser) to enforce the promise by the offeror (the seller in this scenario) to hold the offer open. The potential purchaser has, in essence, bought a right. He has not purchased the land itself but he has purchased the right to restrain the seller for the period of time specified. In such a situation, the offer is not revocable. Moreover, the rules on rejection are also altered. This discussion on options will be revisited later in the discussion of the mechanics of offer and acceptance, after we have set forth rules on the timing of communicating offers, revocations, rejections, and acceptances. At that point we will discuss how option contracts differ from the rules on timing in significant ways.

Firm Offers under the UCC

Section 2-205 of the UCC expressly provides for enforcement of options even though they are not supported by consideration in certain circumstances. This section, entitled "Firm Offers," is not enforceable against a consumer. It is only enforceable against merchants. It can be enforced against the merchant who is offering to buy or a merchant offering to sell goods. To enforce an option based on Section 2-205, the plaintiff must show that the offer and the promise to hold it open must be made in a signed writing. It is not necessary for the writing to promise a definite time. If the writing does include a statement of time, the option is enforceable for the stated time period so long as that period does not exceed three months. This does not mean that a merchant could not make an offer that extends beyond a three month period. Rather it means that such an offer for a longer period of time would need to be supported by consideration to be enforceable. Thus, the offer that lacks consideration is, limited to a period of three months. This does not mean that the time frame for the offer might not lapse or be revocable in less than three months. If there is no time stated and the circumstances indicate that it would be unreasonable to extend the option for a full three months, the section provides that the option runs for only "a reasonable time." It caps that reasonable time at three months. The section also includes a requirement that this provision in an offer be separately signed when it is "on a form supplied by an offeree." This provision protects offerors against making an option promise without realizing it. It limits enforcement to cases where the merchant offeror signed—and thus noticed—the option.

UCC 2-205 changes the common law of this area to allow a merchant to create an option when certain requirements are met, even if there is no consideration for holding the offer open. When the requirements are met, the merchant's promise to hold open an offer is a firm offer and it is not revocable for a certain period. UCC 2-205 states:

> An offer by a merchant to buy or sell goods in a signed writing which by its terms gives assurance that it will be held open is not revocable, for lack of consideration, during the time stated or if no time is stated for a reasonable time, but in no event may such period of irrevocability exceed three months; but any such term of assurance on a form supplied by the offeree must be separately signed by the offeror.

This law allows the enforcement of an option in limited circumstances even though the promise is not supported by consideration. This rule has several requirements. First, the sale must be within the scope of the UCC. That is, it must be a sale of goods (meaning things moveable at the time they are identified to the contract). The fact that the goods do not exist at the time the parties make the contract is not a problem. The requirement that goods are "moveable" applies when the goods are identified to the contract. This means, for example, that by the time for delivery, the goods will exist. The "identification" of the goods to the contract means that parties can contract to sell animals that are not yet born or crops that have not yet been harvested. Identification must occur for delivery to be possible but it can occur prior to delivery as well, sometimes a significant time prior to delivery.

Second, the firm offer is enforceable only when it is made by a "merchant." Under the UCC, a merchant is defined as a "person who deals in goods of the kind" or who "holds himself out as having knowledge or skill peculiar to the practices or goods" involved in the transaction. The option can be either an offer to buy or to sell goods. The option (firm offer) must be made in a signed writing. The writing must gives assurance that it will be held open. If these requirements are met, the firm offer is enforceable. This means that the offeror cannot revoke the offer. This changes the usual rule that offers are freely revocable. The fact that the offeree did not give consideration for the option does not matter. The period of irrevocability conferred by the statute is limited. It is irrevocable for the period of time stated in the written offer if the period stated is three months or less. If there is no time stated in the document, the offer is made irrevocable by the firm offer for a reasonable time. Of course this raises the fact question of what is reasonable under the circumstances. This is similar to the issue discussed in the rule on lapse. The law limits the period of irrevocability established by the provision to three months. It does not, however, abolish the common law of options. Thus, if a party paid consideration for the option, the option could be effective for a longer period of irrevocability. The UCC provision contains a limit to protect offerors. It states that "any such term of assurance on a form supplied by the offeree must be separately signed by the offeror." This provision insures that the offeror will have notice that he is giving a firm offer.

Effectiveness of Communications — Timing

In this section, we will look again at the rules on offer and acceptance (the mechanics of assent). In a face-to-face negotiation, rejections, acceptances, and revocations are all effective as soon as they are stated. The default timing issues discussed here do not arise. The question of lapse is not so clear, however. It would be possible to have a question regarding when the offer lapsed. Many courts deal with this issue by a default rule that assumes that an offer lapses at the end of a face to face conversation, when the parties leave each other's presence, unless the circumstances or language of the parties alters this assumption.

Now we will focus on the issue of timing, meaning the time at which the communication becomes effective, either finalizing a contract or calling off an offer. Of course parties can start negotiations again after an offer terminates or dies. Parties can re-up negotiation indefinitely, trying multiple ways of reaching agreement. In this sense, the fact that an offer terminates is not significant. The significance of the death (termination) of an offer comes when one of the parties walks away from the deal and will not negotiate further. At that point, the rules relating to offer and acceptance have ultimate importance because one party wishes to claim a contract and the other wishes to be free of the relationship.

Thus, when there is a dispute, the rules on timing we are about to discuss take center stage. Like many rules in contract law, these rules are not needed in the vast majority of cases. The parties strike a deal and everyone is happy. When problems arise, the rules on formation are crucial to deciding whether a contract was created by the parties. The disputes that relate to formation generally concern an argument by one party that no contract was formed. This leaves the party who wishes not to be in the contract free to enter a different contract with another partner. The existence of a better deal for one of the parties is often the cause of the dispute. If the contract was formed, reneging on the contract is a breach. Parties are free to find the best deal for themselves, but one party cannot abandon a contract once it is formed to get a better deal. A more accurate way to say this is that if a party to a contract abandons the deal, he will be liable to pay damages to the other party. One of the themes of this area is that, under the American system of contracting the offer is fragile, meaning that the offeror has the power to revoke the offer at any time prior to acceptance.

Because of the importance of default rules on communication when parties dispute the existence of a contract, a list is worthwhile to keep the different defaults squarely in mind. It should also be noted that the parties could alter the defaults. The most likely alteration would occur in the offer since it sets the terms. The conduct of sending or receiving can be done by an agent and it will be effective just as if it had been done by the offeror or offeree. All of these timing rules assume a reasonable medium of communication. Thus, for example, putting an acceptance in the mail—a reasonable method of communication—makes the acceptance effective at the time it is mailed so long as it was properly mailed. Courts often call this "dispatch" or "putting the acceptance out of offeree's possession." This rule may seem puzzling because it means that the contract is formed even though the offeror has not yet received the acceptance. We will discuss this point in more detail in the discussion of acceptance. The use of the term "dispatch" in this list refers to the time the offeree puts the acceptance out of his hands. One way to visualize this is to think of offeree putting the letter of acceptance in the mailbox. This memorable visual image is captured by the term "the Mailbox Rule." Of course fact patterns can involve difficulties of proof. The facts given here are minimal, sort of a "bare bones" story to highlight the rules. Other factors in the communications could change the results. While difficult cases can arise, the general principle is the reasonable expectations of the parties. The rules you see here are built on judicial interpretation of what is reasonable. While difficult cases can arise, the general principle is the reasonable expectations of the parties.

Communication	Effective on:
Offer	Receipt (by offeree)
Revocation Direct (by offeror)	Receipt (by offeree)
Revocation Indirect (reliable source)	Receipt (by offeree)
Rejection (by offeree)	Receipt (by offeror)
Acceptance (by offeree)	Dispatch (by offeree)

Applying the Rules

Let's use the simple hypothetical of an offer to sell a car to illustrate each of these rules on timing.

Offer	Receipt (by offeree)

▶ Seller says to potential Buyer: "I offer you my car for $10,000." The power to close the deal is in Buyer's hands when he receives this offer. It is a fragile power, however, because offeror can revoke at any time.

An offer becomes effective upon receipt by the offeree. This means that offeree has the power to accept the offer and close the deal as soon as offeree receives the offer. There is a viable possibility of formation of a contract by the act of one party: the offeree.

As with most of the rules we are considering on formation, the offeror could change the time of effectiveness of the offer simply by stating the time when it is effective and when the offeree can close the deal. As a practical matter the offer will not change the time of effectiveness to anytime before the offeree's receipt of the offer since it is the receipt of the offer that gives offeree notice of the offer itself.

> *(1) Revocation Direct (by offeror)*   *Receipt (by offeree)*

> ▶ Seller says to potential Buyer: "I offer you my car for $10,000." Next, Seller sends the following revocation: "I changed my mind. I revoke my offer to you." If offeree receives this revocation before he sends his acceptance, the offer is dead. The revocation terminated the buyer's power to accept and there is no contract. It is clear that buyer cannot close the deal. The revocation has put the two parties back to the original setting of having no outstanding offer. Of course they can continue to negotiate but the stage is not set for one party to close the deal.

This effect occurs even if the revocation is less than clear.

> ▶ Seller says to potential Buyer: "I offer you my car for $10,000." Seller sends the following revocation: "I am not certain I want to sell my car. Let's talk." If Buyer (offeree) receives this communication before he sends his acceptance, he has lost the power to close the deal. Seller's statement is not clear. Nevertheless, it clearly indicates that Seller is no longer inviting buyer's acceptance. He has moved back to the preliminary discussion stage of the deal. This means that he is no longer communicating to Buyer that Buyer's acceptance is invited and will finalize the deal. There is more negotiation to be done. That means the current state of affairs is not an offer open to Buyer.

Of course in either of these two cases, the potential buyer could send a communication back to the original offeror: "I offer to buy your car for $10,000." This communication would create again the possibility of contract formation by one party (now the seller). The important thing to note here is that the offeree does not have the power to close the deal after he receives a revocation. If he writes back immediately saying "I accept your offer to sell," his communication has no legal effect since his power to accept was cut off by the revocation.

> *(2) Revocation Indirect (reliable source)*   *Receipt (by offeree)*

▸ Seller to potential Buyer: "I offer you my car for $10,000." The next day, a reliable source says to potential Buyer: "Seller sold his car to me today. This is the same car he offered to you."

In the indirect revocation situation, there has been no communication from Seller to Buyer, yet the offer is revoked. In the example given, Buyer has received what certainly appears to be reliable information that Seller is no longer interested in selling the property and that the offer to Buyer is no longer open. If in fact, Seller has sold the car to Second Buyer, the offer to the original offeree is revoked. This revocation is indirect. It does not come from Seller. Nevertheless, it is effective. It indicates to potential Buyer that he is no longer justified in believing he is invited and empowered to conclude the deal. The fact that this revocation effectively terminates the offer may seem a bit unfair to you. After all, shouldn't Seller be forced to speak directly to offeree in order to call the deal off? The law leans away from finding a deal, perhaps from reluctance to capture people in contracts that they did not desire, even if they might have desired them at an earlier time.

The rule operates only when the information of the revocation comes from a reliable source. The reliability of the source of the information is a fact issue that the trier of fact will need to resolve. If the court concludes this is a reliable source, the offer terminated at the time the potential Buyer received the information from that source. If the court concludes that the source of information was not reliable, the offer has not terminated—even if the rumor was, in fact, accurate.

From the discussion so far, it might seem unnecessary for the reliable source be accurate. Thus, it may seem that if the seller has not actually sold the car the result would be the same: termination of the offer at the time Buyer (offeree) hears the statement that the Seller sold the car. Most courts would reject such a result, however, on the basis that this is simply a false statement rather than an indirect communication of a revocation. The courts would require that the offeror do something inconsistent with the existence of the offer. *Restatement Section 43* states the rule as follows: "An offeree's power of acceptance is terminated when the offeror takes definite action inconsistent with an intention to enter into the proposed contract and the offeree acquires reliable information to that effect."

(3) Rejection (by offeree)   *Receipt (by offeror)*

▸ Seller to Potential Buyer: "I offer you my car for $10,000." The next day, Potential Buyer says: "I am not interested." The offer terminates.

The response by buyer is essentially the same as: "I am not interested; I reject your offer." Even if the potential buyer sent a new communication immediately without hearing anything from the seller, he could not accept the offer. If in a second response, the buyer said "I changed my mind. I accept your offer and will pay you the full $10,000" the response is not an acceptance because the offer was terminated by the rejection. The offeror (seller) does not need to act for the termination to occur. It occurs as a result of the rejection itself.

(4) Rejection by counter-offer (by offeree)   Receipt (by offeror)
The law treats a counter-offer as a rejection even if it does not expressly include a rejection.

> ▸ Seller to potential Buyer: "I offer you my car for $10,000." The next day, potential Buyer says: "I am interested. I will give you $9,500 for the car." The Seller's offer terminates.

This scenario seems a bit different. Buyer is clearly interested so it seems a bit odd to say that the counter-offer is a rejection. Just as noted above, however, the law treats this counter-offer as a rejection. It is just as if it had said: "I am not interested; I reject your offer and offer you $9,500." Just as we noted above, Buyer could not close the deal with a second communication immediately after the counter-offer. This is true even if Seller has not replied back, has not revoked the offer. So a letter from the offeree (Buyer) saying "I changed my mind. I accept your offer and will pay you the full $10,000" is not an acceptance. This communication cannot be effective because the counter-offer terminated the offer. The offeror (Seller) does not need to act for the termination to occur. It occurs as a result of the counter-offer (rejection) itself.

An exception to the counter-offer rule: After the offer, the offeree (Potential Buyer in this scenario) could respond in a way that could keep the offer alive. This would be a counter-offer without a rejection. It would expressly hold open the offer (take it under advisement), while making a new collateral offer. Consider the following example:

> ▸ Seller to potential Buyer: "I offer you my car for $10,000." The next day, potential Buyer says: "I will have to think about that price. Right now I will offer you $9,500. Would you consider my counter-offer while I consider further your offer?" This counter-offer does not terminate the offer. This is because it communicates to the offeror this effect. It says "I am not rejecting your offer. Rather, I am making a separate offer to you for your consideration. You can bind me at the price of $9,500 or you can wait for my acceptance." The fact that the counter-offer explicitly refrained from having the effect of a rejection does not give the offeree much power, however. This change in the

counter-offer does not alter the power of the parties much since the offeror has the power to terminate the offer at anytime.

(5) Acceptance (by offeree)   *Dispatch (by offeree)*

Seller to potential Buyer: "I offer you my car for $10,000." The next day, potential Buyer sends a letter that states: "I accept your offer." This acceptance closes the deal and terminates the offer. Offeror can no longer terminate the offer.

This effect occurs as soon as offeree puts the letter (or email) out of his hands. This is the reason for the nickname "The Mailbox Rule" for this rule. Under the Mailbox Rule, the contract is complete even before offeror knows that a contract has been formed. As *Restatement Section 63* states, the acceptance is effective "as soon as" it is "put out of the offeree's possession, without regard to whether it ever reaches the offeror." The offeror is bound to a contract even though he does not know it. Thus, if offeror sells the car to another before he receives the acceptance, he has breached the contract.

The offer could make receipt of the acceptance a requirement for acceptance. Otherwise, the offer is effective upon dispatch by the offeree. An offer is ordinarily revocable by the offeror until acceptance is sent. *Restatement 63* makes this point. However, if offeror receives a rejection sent by offeree before he receives an acceptance from the offeree, the law may estop the offeree from enforcing the contract. This is particularly important if offeror relied on the rejection that offeree sent.

Some people believe that the rule operates this way because a person cannot retrieve the letter from the Postal Service. Other scholars and the *Restatement* have noted that this is not the reason for the rule and, in fact, it is sometimes possible to reclaim a letter after it is placed in the mail. Similarly, some have speculated that the rule applies only to mail. This is not accurate; the same rule applies if the communication is delivered by other means than the mail service. It is the same if the communication is sent by courier, telegram, or FedEx or by an agent handing the communication to the offeror.

The rationale is that since the U.S. law allows an offeror to revoke at any time the offeree needs some assurance that he can get the deal he is offered. This point is often referred to by courts and others as the "fragility of offers." Since offeror can revoke, offeree needs to know that he can close the deal and it will be done. The idea is that otherwise offerees will be reluctant to deal. In other countries an offer is not freely revocable. Once made, the offeror must allow offeree a reasonable time to accept or reject. In such countries, the offeree has a dependable basis for taking the offer seriously and the Mailbox Rule is not needed.

This rule may seem strange since the offeror is bound to a contract even though he does not know it. Of course if the law required knowledge by both parties before a contract was deemed effective a party could speculate on the deal, seeking a better one while having the power to bind the other party. This would be, in effect, allowing one party to say: "you cannot bind me to the deal because you cannot prove I had knowledge of the deal before I revoked. Such a rule would limit contracting by mail and might result in a slowdown of commerce since parties would only feel completely comfortable in accepting a contract in the presence of the other party. This reality makes it necessary to have a rule that finds contract is formed before one of the parties knows a contract is formed.

The *Restatement* makes this point in a comment to Section 63: "It is often said that an offeror who makes an offer by mail makes the post office his agent to receive the acceptance, or that the mailing of a letter of acceptance puts it irrevocably out of the offeree's control. Under United States postal regulations, however, the sender of a letter has long had the power to stop delivery and re-claim the letter." A better explanation of the rule that the acceptance takes effect on dispatch is that the offeree needs a dependable basis for his decision whether to accept. In many legal systems such a basis is provided by a general rule that an offer is irrevocable unless it provides otherwise. The common law provides such a basis through the rule that a revocation of an offer is ineffective if received after an acceptance has been properly dispatched. See Comment c to *Restatement § 42*. Acceptance by telegram is governed in this respect by the same considerations as acceptance by mail.

Consider the following change of facts:

> ▶ Seller to potential Buyer: "I offer you my car for $10,000." The next day, potential Buyer sends a letter that states: "I accept your offer." If the court finds the offer was sufficiently definite to identify the car offered, Buyer's acceptance closes the deal; a contract is formed. In other words, it is clear that this is an acceptance because it says so in precise language. The only way the communication would not operate as an acceptance would be if the communication from the seller was not actually an offer. (This fact question is considered above in the discussion of offers.) Before Seller received the letter or knew of the acceptance, he sent the following revocation: "I changed my mind. I revoke my offer to you." This revocation would be ineffective. Offeree has already sent his acceptance. Contract was formed when Buyer sent the acceptance. Seller can no longer terminate the offer.

The default rule on acceptance is that the acceptance is effective on dispatch. The effect of the acceptance is to form a contract between the two parties before offeror knows the contract exists. Even if the acceptance is lost in the mail the contract was formed when the offeree sent the acceptance. This means that an offeror who does not receive a reply may want to check with the offeree before offering the deal to another party. If further steps are required by the offer, the loss of the acceptance in the mail may result in a discharge. This specific point is taken up by Illustration 4 to *Restatement § 63.*

As with many rules of contract law, the parties can vary the effectiveness of the default rules. The offeror has the power to change the applicability of the rule. Thus the offeror can choose a different time for the acceptance to take effect. The offer could declare that acceptance will be effective on receipt by offeror. Some companies alter the rule, by making the contract effective only after it is received and approved by the home office. *Ever-Tite Roofing Corp. v. Green*, 83 So. 2d 449 (La. App. 2d Cir. 1955), is an example of this practice. This case, which is included in many casebooks, involved such a form. To allow time for a credit check of the consumer, Ever-Tite included a statement that the contract would be effective upon acceptance in the home office or commencement of the work. The company form included following statement in its form: "This agreement shall become binding only upon written acceptance hereof, by the principal or authorized officer of the Contractor, or upon commencing performance of the work." The court found that the agreement by the Greens (the homeowner and consumer) did not result in a contract because this language set up formation (acceptance) by Ever-Tite. This point of law was important in the case because the Greens engaged a different roofer. When the Ever-Tite workers arrived at the home, other workers were already at work on the roof. Ever-Tite argued that the Greens breached the contract. It asserted that when its workers loaded their trucks with roofing materials and drove to the Greens' home in Shreveport to do the job the company accepted the contract. The court held that the contract was not binding on the Greens because by engaging a different company they had withdrawn their offer to Ever-Tite. The court did provide reliance damages to Ever-Tite. This point is separate from our discussion of formation. It provides an example of the way reliance can be a fallback argument to give limited protection to a party who reasonably relied on a statement.

The default rule that an offer is effective on dispatch has an exception relating to a situation that creates confusion because of the offeree's conduct of (literally) sending mixed messages. An acceptance is not effective on dispatch when offeree has already sent a rejection. If offeree has sent a rejection, offeror might rely on it. Believing the negotiations are at an end, he may seek to put together a different deal. The law respects this problem and prevents the unfairness of this situation by changing the rule on effective time of an acceptance when the offeree has created this potential problem. The exception rule is that an acceptance does not operate as an acceptance when it is sent after the offeree has sent a rejection. The communication operates only as a counter-offer unless it arrives before the rejection. If it arrives before the communication of the rejection, then it is effective.

Mailbox Rule

The following example is included to help you see how the rules stated above function. Keep in mind that the term "Mailbox Rule" is an example rather than an exception. The rule says that the contract is formed when the acceptance is sent.

▶ Seller to potential Buyer: "I offer you my car for $10,000." The next day, potential Buyer sends a letter that states: "I accept your offer." This is clearly an acceptance. It could not be interpreted as otherwise. If the letter is lost in the mail, the contract is, nevertheless, formed when Buyer puts it in the mailbox.

It is not necessary for offeror to receive the acceptance for it to be effective. Upon first consideration, this sounds like a crazy rule. Why should we hold offeror to a contract if he doesn't know that offeree has accepted it? Of course a communication can be lost either from offeree or offeror, just as an offer can be lost, an acceptance can be lost. If an offer is lost offeree does not accept it and the parties do not go forward with the transaction. There is no reliance by offeree. Offeror has no right to rely since he has merely sent an offer. The contract is lost or offeror will send a new offer or make a call. In the case of an acceptance offeror knows that it has an offer outstanding. It is not in the dark on that point. If offeror does not receive an acceptance from offeree, offeror can find out what is going on by making a call to offeree. The primary reason for this rule that seems crazy on its face is that offeree is about to rely on the deal. Because of the rule that offeror can revoke the offer at any time, the offeree who is about to accept feels vulnerable or "out on a limb." He may accept the contract and then the offeror could revoke the deal, leaving offeree without recourse. The Mailbox Rule as it is called, or the protection of offeree's acceptance is a way to provide a counter-balance protection to offeree to protect offeree from the power of offeror to revoke at any time. This is clearly not the only way to achieve a balance between the interests of the parties. Some other countries make offers irrevocable for a reasonable period of time, protecting reliance by offeree. The American rule that an offer can be revoked at any time produces notably fragile offers. To encourage offeree to go ahead and accept that offer, the American system needs a rule that will protect offeree once he has accepted. This protection is achieved by the rule that acceptance forms the contract.

Of course these rules are default rules, meaning that they can be changed by the parties. Often an offeror will protect himself by making receipt of the acceptance the time when the contract is formed. Thus, the default rule sets a protection for the offeree that can be altered by the offeror. If the offeror alters that default, offeree will know of this change. It will be stated in the offer that the acceptance is not effective until the offeror is accepted.

Exception — Although an acceptance is ordinarily effective at the time it is sent (dispatched by offeree) a rare case requires separate treatment. If an offeree sends a rejection and then later sends an acceptance, there is a risk to the offeror. Under the usual rule, the contract would be formed upon dispatch if the offeror had not received the rejection. This point follows from the two rules noted above in points (4) and (5). Remember point (4) above indicated that a rejection is effective on receipt (by offeror) and) point (5) established that acceptance (forming a contract) is effective on dispatch by offeree.

The law recognizes that the offeror is likely to rely on the rejection, which he received before the acceptance. For this reason, the law alters the Mailbox Rule slightly when a rejection is sent before an acceptance. In such a case, the acceptance does not operate upon dispatch. Whichever communication arrives first is effective. This rule is particularly important if offeror relied on the rejection that offeree sent. For example, if, after receiving the rejection, seller sold the car to another buyer, the seller's reliance on the rejection should be protected. The exception to the Mailbox Rule achieves this effect. There are other cases where the doctrine of reliance may come into play to protect a party who has relied on a communication by the other negotiating party. Consider the following change of facts:

> ▶ Seller to Potential Buyer: "I offer you my car for $10,000." The next day, Potential Buyer sends a rejection: "I reject your offer." Later that day Potential Buyer sends a letter of acceptance: "I accept your offer." Under the Mailbox Rule, the acceptance would be effective on dispatch, making it likely that the offeror-seller would be bound. The rejection would not be effective until received by seller — probably at least the next day under ordinary circumstances. Thus, the mailbox rule would operate unfairly in this context. Courts estop the party seeking to enforce in this setting.

Change of Rules on Timing for Options

Because a party who has an option has a contract right that the offeror will not revoke the offer, the rules on timing of contract formation just discussed above are different in the option contract setting. *Restatement Section 37* states that despite the general formation rules, "the power of acceptance under an option contract is not terminated by rejection or counter-offer, by revocation, or by death or incapacity of the offeror, unless the requirements are met for the discharge of a contractual duty."

The rationale for this difference in treatment between option contracts and offers is clearly that the option is a contract right and, thus, cannot be terminated by the unilateral act of the offeror. The offeree has a contract for the time specified to decide whether to accept the deal.

Similarly, *Restatement Section 63* indicates that the Mailbox Rule does not operate when a party holds the option to accept by a certain date (and offeror has promised not to revoke): "(b) an acceptance under an option contract is not operative until received by the offeror." The rationale for this exception to the Mailbox Rule on acceptance is likely that the offeree does not need the protection against the power of the offeror to revoke at will. In such a case, the offer is not fragile. A comment to the *Restatement* makes this point, using the same concept of "dependable basis" for contracting noted above: "An option contract provides a dependable basis for decision whether to exercise the option."

Unilateral Contracts

When offeree begins performance under a unilateral offer, he holds an option. Generally, when a party has made an offer for a unilateral contract, there is no need for the offeree to communicate that he or she intends to accept. This principle arises out of the nature of the unilateral contract. Since the offeror is not asking for a promise, there is no reason to require the offeree to communicate acceptance of the agreement. In other words, if no words of promise are sought, there is no need to say them.

There are two exceptions to this rule, however. The first is that the offeror making an offer of a unilateral contract can specify that she be given notice of performance, either before or after their performance is rendered. This rule follows simply from the fact that the offeror is always free to set the terms upon which acceptance should be made. The second exception, which is adopted in the *Second Restatement*, is that in a situation where the offeror has no ready means of determining whether the performance was rendered, the offeree must, within a reasonable time, notify the offeror.

The Mirror Image Rule

The Mirror Image Rule (also sometimes called the "Last Shot Rule") held that a contract was not formed if an acceptance changed any term. The title Mirror Image Rule captures well the effect of the rule. It required that an acceptance mirror exactly the offer for the acceptance to have the effect of finalizing a contract. Thus, if the offer stated: "Seller will sell to Buyer the house at 406 N. Oak Street for $100,000 with payment to be made in cash on June 1," it could be accepted only by an acceptance that mirrored this offer. If the acceptance changed any significant term, it operated as a counter-offer. Thus, if buyer responded: "Buyer accepts Seller's offer to sell the house at 406 N. Oak Street for $100,000 with payment to be made in cash on June 2," it could not close the deal. If the parties went forward with the deal after the counter-offer, the law regarded the counter-offer as the offer and, thus, the terms of the deal were those of the counter-offer. This effect is captured well by the other term for the rule: "Last Shot Rule," meaning that the final "shot" or final communication before performance was the communication of significance. It is the offer that determines the terms of the deal.

In the case of the change of the date for payment from June 1 to June 2 in the hypothetical above, the rule makes perfect sense. If the parties went ahead with the deal in accordance with the counter-offer, they clearly assented to this term. In other situations, the rule created problems. For example, suppose an offer for the sale of a house included the following among other terms: "Seller will sell to Buyer the house described in the attached description for $100,000. Seller makes no warranties of any kind with regard to the house." A letter from buyer with additional terms, states: "Buyer accepts Seller's offer to sell the house described in the attached description for $100,000." The letter also states: "Seller warrants that he owns the house free and clear of any liens and agrees to binding arbitration relating to disputes of any kind arising from this contract." In this case, if the parties go forward with the sale, delivering the money and deed, it is not so clear that they both understood and agreed to this change. Under the Mirror Image Rule, the later terms control. This is because the letter that purported to be an acceptance was not the "mirror image" of the offer. Since it was not the "Mirror Image" of the offer, it did not operate as an acceptance; it operated as a counter-offer. The counter-offer was accepted by the seller when he went forward with the deal, even though he may not have read the crucial terms. This is the current law under the common law of some states (as opposed to the UCC). The natural result is that the parties need to read carefully every communication about the contract to be sure that the other party has not changed the terms in the latest communication.

Courts moderated or softened the effect of the common law rule by limiting it to important changes. For example, if the acceptance above stated following the offer above made the following addition to the contract dealt with some fairly minor change, the court might treat the communication as an acceptance even though it was not truly a "mirror image" of the offer. For example, "Buyer accepts Seller's offer to sell the house described in the attached description for $100,000 including the wicker patio furniture," the court might decide that the communication operated as an acceptance. The court could do this by regarding the addition of the wicker patio furniture as a proposal. In other words, the court might interpret the letter including the wicker patio furniture as something like this: "Buyer accepts the offer to sell on seller's terms and would request that seller throw in the wicker furniture." This reading would mean that the buyer has purchased the house under the terms of the original offer. Thus, if the seller decides to sell to a different buyer he has breached the contract with the first buyer, and the buyer can enforce the contract. Likewise, if buyer wishes to be free of the contract it is too late for him to withdraw if the seller chooses to enforce the contract. If the court believed that the wicker furniture was a fixture somehow (because it was built into screen porch of the house somehow for example) it would likely enforce the contract with the furniture included.

Formation under the UCC: The Battle of the Forms and Abrogation of the Mirror Image Rule

The Uniform Commercial Code changed the Mirror Image Rule. The operation of the Mirror Image Rule discussed above created problems in the context of a sale of goods. This was because the practice of parties buying and selling goods is different from the practice of parties buying and selling real estate. The parties to a sale of goods rarely read the communications back and forth between buyers and sellers. The parties were likely to be caught in the Mirror Image Rule by terms they did not expect. The law dealt with this problem by changing the default of the Mirror Image Rule. Under the UCC, a communication that purports to be an acceptance operates as an acceptance even though it changes the terms of the contract. Generally the new terms are not part of the contract. A little later in the discussion we will explain the rare situations in which the additional terms may become part of the contract.

Subsection 1 of 2-207 of the UCC flips the default of the common law Mirror Image Rule. It states:

> A definite and seasonable expression of acceptance or a written confirmation which is sent within a reasonable time operates as an ac-

ceptance even though it states terms additional to or different from those offered or agreed upon, unless acceptance is expressly made conditional on assent to the additional or different terms.

The result is that a party who states new terms does not get those terms in the contract unless he clearly states there is no acceptance unless he gets the terms he wants. (He may fail to get the terms even then as we will see.) For example, an offer usually comes from a buyer. Consider a case in which we assume that Seller's communication is detailed and, additionally, indicates that buyer can close the deal.

> ▸ Seller sends a letter email to Buyer: "Seller will sell to Buyer the printing press described in the attached description for $100,000. Seller makes no warranties of any kind with regard to the product." In a long letter Buyer describes additional terms. It states: "Buyer accepts Seller's offer to sell the press described in the attached description for $100,000. Seller warrants that he owns the press free and clear of any liens. Seller also extends a life-time warranty on the press. Buyer can return the press if he is dissatisfied with its operation up to two years after the purchase date." In this case, if the parties go forward with the sale, delivering the money and the goods, Buyer would have had a good argument at common law, that his new terms were part of the contract because the parties performed after this communication with the new term. This is because any change in terms was a counter-offer and delivery of the press constituted acceptance of the counter-offer.

Under Section 2-207, Seller would argue that Buyer's terms do not come into the contract. Because Subsection (1) of 2-207 flips the default of the common law Mirror Image Rule, the Seller has a good argument that the terms of the contract are set by his offer. When the contract is formed by conduct, under UCC 2-207 Subsection 3, the terms that the counteroffer sought to incorporate do not necessarily become part of the contract. They become part of the contract only when these terms are also the gap fillers created by the UCC or when the parties expressly agree to the change of terms. In fact it may make more sense to say the terms of the counter-offer do not become part of the contract and to say that the terms that become part of the contract because they are gap fillers enter as gap filler rather than terms the offeree inserted.

Subsection (3) of the UCC makes clear that successfully sending a counteroffer does not have the effect that a counteroffer had at common law. If the offeree sends what appears to be an acceptance but actually expressly makes that acceptance conditional on a sent to additional or different terms the parties have not successfully formed a contract under Subsection (1). If the parties proceed to perform by sending and accepting goods, at that point a contract is formed. That contract is not formed, however, by the *forms* of the parties. Rather, the contract is created by the conduct of the parties of sending and accepting goods. In this case, the terms of the contract are set under Subsection (3).

Subsection (2) deals with terms when a contract is formed under Subsection (1) — by the forms. Subsection (2) states:

> (2) The additional terms are to be construed as proposals for addition to the contract. Between merchants such terms become part of the contract unless:
> (a) the offer expressly limits acceptance to the terms of the offer;
> (b) they materially alter it; or
> (c) notification of objection to them has already been given or is given within a reasonable time after notice of them is received.

The omission "different" in Subsection (2) was probably a drafting error. Most courts treat "different" terms the same way they treat "additional" terms. In other words, courts read in the term "different" into the first sentence of Subsection (2). This makes good sense because the clear purpose of this statute is to preserve terms of the original deal presented in the offer unless the offeree sends an effective counteroffer and demands and receives assent to those terms.

The second sentence to Subsection (2) makes clear that additions do not become part of the contract except in the very limited situations, which will be discussed below. Accordingly, in the situation involving contract with at least one non-merchant, no additions or changes come into the contract. Since the Code is intent on preventing "additional" terms, it would certainly make sense to be equally vigilant about preventing the "different" terms from coming into the contract.

Although UCC 2-207 has created some difficulties of interpretation for courts, the section is not as difficult as courts and students sometimes believe. The section simply switches the default rule of the common law from the Last Shot Rule to the First Shot Rule. Thus, the default under the UCC is that sending an acceptance is not effective to change the terms unless the party wishing to make the changes takes the trouble to bargain about the terms and get the assent of the other party to those terms. While some regard this as a rather burdensome thing for the offeree. In reality, it is easy for offeree to protect himself. If the offeree wishes to make changes in the contract, offeree needs to take on the issue proactively and call to the attention of the offeror the changes he wishes to make. If indeed he does not wish to enter the contract unless those changes are agreed to by the other party, the offeree can put a halt to the transaction until he gets the assent of the other party. Seller would do this by simply not sending the goods until the buyer accepts the new terms. Buyer can achieve his purpose by stating in the counteroffer that he will not accept goods and will not make payment for goods unless the additional terms are expressly accepted.

Unilateral and Bilateral Contracts

Distinction between Unilateral and Bilateral

Courts make a distinction between two categories of offers (unilateral and bilateral). The distinction is important because the responsibilities that result from these different types of offers differ significantly. Although the *Restatement* and some courts have rejected the use of the terms "unilateral" and "bilateral" as a way to distinguish contracts, some courts continue to use the terms. In fact, the distinction between the types of offers still has importance, even in the courts that have abandoned the terminology. A unilateral contract is one that creates an obligation for only one party and a right for the other party. A bilateral contract creates a right and obligation on each side of the deal.

By far the majority of contracts are bilateral. This is because most parties, in most cases, are seeking a commitment from the other party to do something in the future. (Party A will work for Party B for a certain salary. Party A will sell something — a house, or a car or diamond or a future crop of corn — to Party B for a certain amount of money.) In the ordinary case, both parties wish to have the security of the commitment from the other party.

In the unusual case, the offeror does not want a promise from the other party. This could be because the offeror does not want to invest the time necessary to talk with a number of offerees and he prefers to put the offer out and see if someone can perform. He can protect himself from owing multiple parties payment by the way he states the offer. He will want to have an obligation only to the person who is able to perform and does perform. For example, a party who wishes to incentivize a performance such as selling his house or finding a lost item may do it by setting up a unilateral offer as a reward. The person who finds the lost diamond or other property, finds a buyer for a house or acquires an interest in a business enterprise can claim the reward by following the instructions in the unilateral offer. In such settings the offeror may set up a unilateral contract, promising to pay for the desired result. The offeror — as master of the offer — creates an obligation for himself and a right for the other party. The offer creates an obligation for offeror which is conditioned on offeree performing. Thus, if offeree never performs, offeror has no duty to pay. The offer creates a right in the offeror which is conditioned on offeree's performance. Offeree has no obligation to perform. If he does not want to search for the property or try to sell the house, he can simply ignore the offer. He has no liability for not performing. However, the offeree who does perform has a right to payment from offeror.

An important note is that once the offeree begins performance, offeree holds an option. This means that the offeror cannot revoke during this time. When offeree begins performance, he has changed his position based on the promise he has received. Of course if the offeree fails to perform within a reasonable time, the option would lapse. This brings us back to the question of reasonableness.

The Key to Distinguishing between Unilateral and Bilateral Offers

Whether the contract is unilateral or bilateral is determined by the offer. If the offeror is seeking a commitment from the other party, he is putting in motion an offer to form a bilateral contract. Generally, unilateral contracts are accepted by performance and bilateral contracts are accepted by a promise. Thus, we can say that a unilateral contract is formed by a promise in exchange for a performance and a bilateral contract is formed by an exchange of promises. You should not assume, however, that every acceptance by performance forms a unilateral contract. A party may make an offer that can be accepted by performance. If the offeror indicates that beginning performance constitutes acceptance, the act of beginning performance is often a promise as well as performance and the offeree is committed to the contract to perform. Depending on the circumstances and expectations of the parties, beginning performance may be a promise to complete the job in a certain period or within a reasonable amount of time. Whether beginning performance is a promise as well as part performance depends on the offer.

The traditional hypothetical used to explain the difference between unilateral and bilateral contracts involves a walk across the Brooklyn Bridge for some sum of money. No one ever considers why an offeror would pay someone to walk across the bridge, and that point does not matter for our purposes. This is a time-honored explanatory hypo that most lawyers will remember. Like many of the stories in law school, the example is often the best way to re-member the concept. We assume for the purpose of this discussion that the walk and the payment meet the test for consideration. "I will pay you $500 if you will walk across the Brooklyn Bridge."

The traditional rule is that the offeree can accept only by rendering com-plete performance. So when Party A says to Party B: "I will pay you $500 if you will walk across the Brooklyn Bridge," Party B is offeree. If Party B does not walk across the bridge, she cannot get the $500. It is important to note that Party B (offeree) has no duty to walk across the bridge. She has a condi-tional right, which was created by the offeror. The right is that she will be en-titled to $500 if she performs. The condition is the performance. In other words, she will be entitled to $500 if she performs and she will not be enti-tled to $500 if she does not perform. Of course this point is true whether the contract is unilateral or bilateral. The right to collect the money is condi-tioned on providing performance. The difference in the two concepts does not come from this point. Rather it comes from the difference when the of-feree does not *perform.*

The important difference between unilateral and bilateral contracts is that the offeree (Party B in our hypo) has no obligation to perform. Thus, Party B has a conditional right but no duty. If she does not walk across the Brook-lyn Bridge, she has no right to the money, but she has no liability. This is be-cause she has no obligation to perform. If she begins to walk across the bridge and changes her mind she is free to go back home and will owe no obligation to offeror. Only full performance counts as an acceptance that binds the of-feror to pay.

Under the old common law, offeror was free to revoke the offer, even after offeree had begun performance. If offeror revoked, offeree had no rights. Under the more modern approach, courts recognize that when offeree begins per-formance, her reliance creates an option, making the offer irrevocable for a reasonable time in which to complete it. Under the modern approach the of-feror is not bound until performance by the other has been rendered fully. Pro-tection is provided to the performing party, however. Once the performing party begins performance, the offeror can no longer revoke the offer. The per-forming party has a reasonable time in which to fully perform. Thus the per-forming party (the offeree) has an option to complete performance and demand the promised consideration. *Restatement 45* makes this more measured ap-proach clear. Beginning performance creates an option, making the offer ir-revocable for a reasonable time in which to complete it.

In a bilateral contract situation the traditional rule is that the offer may be accepted only by a reciprocal promise. It is important to note that the promise could be expressed by beginning performance when the offer invites the offeree to accept by beginning of performance. The distinction is that the offer would need to communicate that beginning the performance will form a contract. Thus, we can change the traditional Brooklyn Bridge hypo to make it a bilateral offer: Party A says to Party B: "I will pay you $500 if you will walk across the Brooklyn Bridge. You cannot accept this offer by words but your beginning of performance will form an acceptance, making you obligated to complete performance." Again Party B is offeree. Now, however, if Party B begins the walk across the bridge, she will be liable for damages if she fails to complete the walk. This is because of the specific indication of the offer of the effect of beginning performance. Under this change of facts, the offeree has a duty to complete the walk across the bridge if she accepts the offer. She still has a conditional right, as does the offeree in the ordinary (bilateral) setting and she will be entitled to $500 if she performs. The difference is that she will be liable for her failure to perform completely, assuming the offeror can show damages resulting from her failure to complete her promised performance.

Ordinarily, when entering a contract, the parties expect and want a commitment from each other to perform. In one case included in many contract casebooks, *White v. Corlies & Tift*, 46 N.Y. 467 (1871), the court found that buying wood to begin to do a woodwork project on an office was not a clear cut indication that the builder had accepted the contract. In the *White* case, the offer stated: "Upon an agreement to finish the fitting up of offices ... in two weeks ... you can begin at once." The analysis of the court made clear that if the builder had actually started the work he would be agreeing to finish in two weeks. If the worker had done more than purchase materials that could be used in any project he would have had a better chance to have the court hold that he had accepted. As the facts of the case established, the worker had purchased materials but it was not clear that the materials were for the job at the offices of offeror.

Sometimes it is difficult to determine whether the offeror is bargaining for a performance or a return promise. The general rule is that where it is not clear what the offeror seeks, an offer may be accepted by either promise or performance. The general belief is that acceptance by either promise or performance is a bilateral contract unless the offer makes clear that the acceptance by performance does not include a promise to go forward with the performance. To extend the reasoning of the *White* case, if the worker had begun work on the office he would have been promising by beginning performance to complete the work in the two week time frame. In such a case, the offeror is not setting up a unilateral deal and offeree is not free to stop work without breaching his duty under the contract.

▸ White sends an email to Builder: "If you will install cherry bookcases in my office, I will pay you $3,000. If you agree to finish the
work in two weeks, you can accept by starting work at once."

It is likely that a court would see this offer as seeking a commitment from
offeree. Offeror is not saying "if you perform I will pay you and it is fine to
quit part way through the job." The result in the *White* case turned on the issue
of whether the offeree had begun performance, and the court held that buying materials that could be used on any job was not sufficiently clear to be an
acceptance of the job offered. This is a different point than our current point
of the distinction between unilateral and bilateral offers.

The context of the offer in the example above also helps make it clear that the
offer seeks a commitment rather than simply offering the workman the option
to begin performance without completing it. The customer did not intend that
the worker could start work and yet have no obligation to finish the work. After
all, the office will be altered once the worker begins to perform. It would make
no sense to allow offeree to come and go and work or not. Because courts recognize that parties generally want a commitment, they will view offers as bilateral, even when the offer allows the offeree to accept by either a promise or a
performance. The performance will generally be seen as including a commitment. In the *White* case, beginning performance would include a promise to
finish in two weeks. Unless the offer makes clear that offeree has no obligation
to go forward to completion once he begins, courts are likely to see offers as creating a bilateral contract.

▸ Seller says to potential Buyer: "If you will bring $10,000 in cash to me
on March 4, I will sell you my car. Your promise is no good to me. I
will only sell to you for the cash on the day stated." Potential Buyer
likes the deal. He says: "I promise to bring you $10,000 in cash on
March 4 for your car." Potential Buyer may feel he has entered a contract. This is not the case, however. Seller, as offeror, has set up a unilateral contract. If Second Buyer came along before March 4 and offered
more money for the car, Seller would be free to take that deal. Seller
will need to revoke the offer before Potential Buyer accepts by bringing the money. If Potential Buyer had second thoughts about the deal,
he could back out without liability. That is to say, offeror is free to revoke his offer any time before offeree accepts. In this example, because
Buyer did not accept in the manner called for by the Seller's offer ("bring
me the cash on March 4"), Buyer has not properly accepted. Hence, Seller
is free to revoke his offer to Buyer and sell the car to Second buyer.

Unilateral and Bilateral Offers: What Difference Does it Make?

You may have noticed from the discussion of the *White* case and the hypos above that an offeree cannot accept an offer to enter a bilateral contract by giving a promise. This is because offeror is requiring actual performance rather than a promise for an acceptance. The primary difference between the two types of contracts is the method of acceptance. In the *White* case, the court saw the offer as asking for a commitment and allowing the commitment to be communicated by starting work (a performance). If the court is convinced that this is the meaning of the offer, it will hold the offeree to its promise even though the promise was made by the conduct of beginning performance.

The Offer

Section 24 of the *Restatement* defines an "offer" as a "manifestation of willingness to enter into a bargain, made in such a way that the other party reasonably believes that his or her assent to the bargain is invited and that the assent will conclude the deal. In other words, an offer must be made in such a way that the other party reasonably would assume that simply signifying "yes" (either orally or by signing a paper) will create a contract. The person who makes an offer is called the *offeror* and the person who receives the offer is called the *offeree*. In many cases the offer is clear. A proposal to sell goods or services on clear terms will generally be an offer. For example, Henry offers to do research for his contracts professor for $10.00 an hour. The professor agrees. The parties have entered a contract.

Alternatively, the two parties might simply talk about the arrangement for research and agree to go forward together. It is not necessary to determine who is offeree and who is offeror.

Under the UCC, a contract is formed even though many terms are left open if the parties intend to form a contract and there is a reasonably certain basis for giving an appropriate remedy. The UCC also expressly provides that a court is justified in finding a contract for the sale of goods even if the moment of its making is undetermined. This approach is also used by courts determining disputes under the common law although the common law may require more certainty than the UCC, perhaps because contracts for goods generally have a good point of reference for price and reasonable terms in the UCC and the market.

Preliminary Negotiations

In a dispute over whether a contract has been formed, it may be difficult to tell whether a party's statement is an offer. Sometimes the statement is merely an invitation to receive offers or preliminary discussion or considering whether the other party has an interest in dealing. Sometimes the invitation is called an "offer to receive offers." Such communications are not offers. They do not lead a reasonable person to believe that he is invited to close the deal by accepting.

Section 26 of the *Restatement* takes up the issue an offer from the perspective of preliminary negotiations. This is a consistent but different perspective of explaining what is *not* an offer. Starting from this end of the analysis, Section 26 explains why even a communication that suggest a deal is not an offer if it is not sufficiently clear and specific. It states: "A manifestation of willingness to enter into a bargain is not an offer if the person to whom it is addressed knows or has reason to know that the person making it does not intend to conclude a bargain until he has made a further manifestation of assent."

If an owner says to a neighbor "I am considering selling my ranch. Do you think I could get $500,000?" He has not made an offer to sell. The owner is merely considering selling. The neighbor would not be justified in thinking he could close the deal by saying: "I accept."

On the other hand, if the owner gives specifics he may be getting closer to making an offer even if he continues to use some of the language associated with merely considering the possibility of selling. Here is a change of the last hypo: If Owner said: "I am considering selling my ranch. If you give me $500,000 in cash for it by Saturday the place is yours" he may be deemed to have made an offer to sell. If neighbor said "I accept," he may have concluded the deal. If a court finds an offer and acceptance, the fact that neither party has performed does not prevent the court from finding and enforcing the contract.

The offer can come from buyer to seller of course. In the above example, neighbor might say: "I have been considering making you an offer for your ranch. Would you consider $500,000." Here the initiating party is different. Just as with the inquiry from the potential seller, neighbor is making an inquiry, not an offer. Neighbor is "testing the waters" of the deal and seeking information. The fact that a party uses the word "offer" is one bit of evidence in favor of finding an offer but it is not determinative. In one case included in many casebooks, a seller responded to a letter that asked how much he would want to sell a piece of land. The owner replied with a statement that said in essence: "I would not sell it for less than" a certain sum. The court found that even in response to an inquiry the language of the response was not definite enough to be an offer. This case suggests that courts look to the total circumstances of the transaction, including the type of sale contemplated. It also suggests that courts require more certainty in a sale of land because of the unique nature of land and the regard people have for land.

Even in a sale of land, however, there is a risk for the party who sent a communication that the court may find that the circumstances justified the recipient in believing the communication was an offer. In *Southworth v. Oliver*, a court found that the amount of detail about a possible purchase of land, including the terms of payment was sufficient for the reasonable recipient to conclude that the communication was an offer. Accordingly, the court held that the acceptance of the recipient of the letter formed a contract.

In addition to preliminary negotiations, several other types of communications typically are viewed as falling outside the realm of offers. These include advertisements, price quotations, invitation for bids, and auctions.

Particular Contexts: Advertisements, Auctions, and Other Examples

Advertisements of all sorts, including fliers, newspaper ads, and broadcast ads are generally regarded as offers to receive offers or preliminary offers. This may seem odd, given the fact that you do not expect to go to a store and make a new offer to purchase the item or to actually bargain about the price. You are certain that the price in the ad is the price you will get. The store will not raise the price and it will not consider a lower price. The generally accepted reason that courts do not see ads as offers is that such an analysis would open merchants to liability for failing to have a sufficient supply to meet all the "acceptances" that might occur. This problem could be addressed in other ways. Some countries regard ads as offers with a reasonable quantity limitation. In the U.S. system ads are not seen as offers. When you respond to an ad by picking up the goods and carrying them to the clerk's station, you are making an offer to purchase. The store accepts the offer by ringing up the purchase.

In another context, the auctioneer solicits offers when he holds up an item for bids. In this context, the bidders know that the auctioneer is not intending to conclude a bargain with the first bidder's response. (This can be true if the rules of the auction are set up to mean that the first bid concludes the deal. This is the case in a type of auction called the Dutch Auction method in which the seller offers a descending price until it is accepted.) This is not the case in the usual auction in this country, however. Here, the price rises as long as bidders place new bids. Similarly, in this country, a real estate listing is seen as a preliminary negotiation, an offer to receive offers. Again, the specifics of the listing could change this effect but the starting place is that the seller is asking buyers to make an offer. When an owner calls for bids for construction, the ordinary expectation is that the opposite sort of auction is used. Of course the owner wants to secure the lowest offer as long as it is from a reputable builder and meets the specifications set by owner. The call for bids is ordinarily regarded as preliminary step, prior to an offer. It is a solicitation to receive offers rather than an offer that can be accepted by a builder. Thus, ordinarily the builder who makes a bid is making an offer, not accepting an offer. Subcontractors make bids to the contractor (builder). The builder produces its master bid by using the offers from the subcontractors (or "subs").

Checkpoints

- The classic formation of a contract is an offer and acceptance.
- Even when it is unclear which party "offered" and which party "accepted," courts will enforce the promises when it is clear the parties intended to be bound.
- Parties often reach an agreement as a result of a series of offers, and counteroffers, or "negotiations," that result in a final agreement.
- An offer is a manifestation of a willingness to enter a bargain made in a way that justifies the other party in believing that her assent is invited and will conclude the deal.
- Ordinarily, acceptance is made by an affirmative statement or action.
- The offeror has the power to terminate the offer any time before acceptance by the other party.
- The offeror can revoke the offer by words or by conduct.
- A statement or act that is inconsistent with the offer being open is a revocation.
- Termination of the offer destroys the offeree's power to accept the offer.
- The passage of time terminates the offer when the time specified for acceptance has passed.
- An offer terminates by operation of law if the offeror dies or becomes incapacitated.
- An offer can be made irrevocable for a period of time by a commitment supported by consideration.
- Offers, revocations, and rejections are effective when the other party receives them.

Checkpoints, *continued*

- Acceptance is effective when it is sent. This is called the Mailbox Rule. An acceptance that is sent after a rejection by the offeree does not operate as an acceptance. Such an acceptance is effective if it reaches the offeror before the rejection reaches the offeror.

- The common law and the UCC differ about the legal outcome when there is an offer and a counteroffer but the parties perform as if there was an agreed upon contract. This is generally called "The Battle of the Forms."

- Courts recognize both unilateral and bilateral contracts, although the *Restatement* rejects the terminology of "unilateral" and "bilateral" contracts.

- A unilateral contract arises when an offeree accepts the offeror's deal by performing rather than promising to perform.

- The unilateral contract arises when the offeror intends for acceptance to be made by performance.

- Bilateral contracts arise by assent.

- A bilateral contract involves a commitment by each party.

- Generally, the law protects individuals with a diminished capacity to understand the nature or consequences of a transaction by allowing them to avoid their contracts.

- The most common types of voidable contracts are those in which one party is either a minor or mentally incompetent.

- These classes of individuals are free to enter into contracts and the contracts are enforceable by them.

- Although these individuals are free to contract, they can avoid their contracts.

- A person's disability may cease to exist — either because the person reaches the age of majority or because the person regains his mental capacity. When the disability ceases, the individual will often be held to have affirmed the contract after a reasonable period of time.

- Because a contract is a voluntary agreement, there must be evidence that each party willingly assented to be bound by its provisions.

- Evidence of mutual assent must be found in the behavior and words of the parties (objective intent) rather than in what they allege they intended (subjective intent).

- Mutual assent means an intent to do the acts contemplated by the contract. Even if parties do not intend the legal consequences of those acts, they will be bound.

- An offer is a manifestation of willingness to enter into a bargain, made in such a way that the other party reasonably believes that his/her assent will conclude the deal and bind the parties.

Checkpoints, *continued*

- Advertisements are generally not offers. They are generally considered to be invitations to deal. But an advertisement may be so explicit that a court may find it is an offer.

- The offeror is said to be master of the offer. She not only decides the provisions of the offer but she can generally revoke (terminate) the offer any time before it is accepted.

- An offer may terminate automatically by lapse of time.

- A rejection by offeree terminates the offer.

- A counteroffer is a rejection. Thus, it terminates the offer.

- An offer may be made irrevocable for a period of time by consideration or as a firm offer under the UCC.

- Acceptance is the offeree's assent to the terms of the offer.

- Acceptance is the offeree's assent to the terms of the offer.

- Silence is generally not acceptance unless the circumstances indicate that the parties agreed to acceptance by silence or circumstances justify that result.

- Offers, rejections, revocations and counter-offers are effective upon receipt by the other party.

- An acceptance is effective (binds the other party — the offeror upon dispatch. (called the Mailbox Rule.)

- Under 2-207(1) a communication is not a counteroffer unless the offeree makes clear he is insisting upon the acceptance of the new term and is not accepting the deal without the new term.

- Under UCC 2-207(2) if both parties are merchants an additional term may become part of the contract unless the additional term is a material alteration (a significant change) or the offeror merchant objects to the term.

- Under 2-207 (3) even when offeree expressly conditions acceptance on the changes, the changes do not become part of the contract unless the terms are the gap fillers of the UCC.

Chapter 5

Consideration

Introduction: Considering Consideration

Particular attention should be paid to the legal concept of consideration. The concept is a major focus point in most contracts classes. For this reason, this book dedicates a chapter to this topic. You will notice that Chapter 4 took up the mechanics of assent and included a discussion of consideration. In this chapter, we explore additional specifics of this important concept. Consideration is the basic reason or conventional motivation for entering the contract. It is the thing transferred by the parties. It can be the transfer of a performance or a promise to perform later. It is often goods or services. Consideration includes the thing sought in a bargain: an act or a forbearance or a modification of legal relationship. It is sometimes referred to as "legal value," that is, something that the law requires to enforce promises.

At traditional common law, a party seeking to enforce a promise in court had a requirement to prove that the promise was supported by consideration. It is sometimes said that the *contract* must be supported by consideration. This is really saying the same thing: a party is seeking to enforce the *contract* by seeking enforcement of the *promise* that benefits that party. The law has developed limited exceptions to the rule, primarily by allowing enforcement based on reasonable reliance as well as consideration. The exception for reliance can be difficult to prove and the vast majority of contracts are supported by consideration. In fact, the element of consideration rarely creates a problem in enforcement. The contract will typically include money on one side and goods or services on the other. Typically each of these transfers (money on one side and goods or services on the other) constitutes consideration. Since consideration is usually a required showing, it is important to understand what is meant by this requirement. Another way to express this is to discuss what situations arise in which money or goods or services do *not* meet the requirement. Most courses and casebooks spend time on both the traditional test for consideration and the more modern approach described in the *Restatement*. As is almost always the case, courts use different formulations to describe the test for consideration.

One fundamental issue that we will need to keep in mind in this section is the terminology relating to people who give and receive promises. The party who makes a promise is the "promisor." The party who receives a promise is the "promisee." The promisee is the party in court seeking to enforce a promise. For example, if A promised to deliver a house to B in exchange for B's promise to pay $100,000 and later refused to make the delivery, B may sue A. B is the promisee of A's promise to deliver the house. If, on the other hand, it is the buyer who has failed or refused to perform, the plaintiff will be the seller (A). In this case, the plaintiff is the seller. A is the promisee of B's promise to purchase. B is the promisor of the promise to purchase the house. You can see that contracts include both a promisor and promisee on each side.

Another way to say this is that each of the two parties is promisor and promisee. On any deal both parties are promisor and promissee. In an exchange of promises, each receives a promise and each party gives a promise. When a court refers to a "promisor," it is referring to the party who made the promise that is the subject of a suit or a dispute. In other words, the promisor is the one who made the promise that plaintiff is trying to enforce. Of course, the defendant will sometimes also dispute the claim that any promise was made. After we establish that there is a promise, we need to determine whether the promise constitutes consideration.

What Is Consideration?

"Consideration" is the term courts use to describe the basic inducement or reason for entering a contract. It is the thing that each party wants from the other under the deal. As noted above, it is generally money on one side and goods or services on the other. So we could say payment is clearly consideration and the other performance paid for is also consideration. Performance simply refers to what each party promises to provide under the contract. Although the vast majority of contracts involve money for goods or services, there are other contracts that provide for money for intangibles, such as licenses, easements, stocks, bonds, and rights of all sorts—anything that could be bought and sold. Even inaction can serve as consideration. Parties can bargain for one of them to refrain from particular conduct. The most common example of bargaining for inaction is found in covenants not to compete. If you buy a business from someone, generally you do not want him to open a competing business across the street from you. Your purchase of the business would not be worth much. You would predict that you would lose business if the established business opened up across the street. So you would bargain with the owner's promise not to compete. Thus, the consideration for a payment is the inaction of not competing.

Additionally, money is not always involved in contracts. For example, by their contract parties can agree to exchange goods for other goods, or stock for other stock, or services for services, or any combination of these. The fact that no money actually changes hands does not mean there is no consideration. Transactions that involve no money may, nevertheless, involve consideration.

Consideration is similar, but not exactly the same as the old cause of action in England referred to by the Latin phrase "*quid pro quo.*" This term literally means "this for that." The old English cause of action called "*quid pro quo*" was actually a more demanding standard than the requirement of consideration. This is because the old action required a showing that the party seeking enforcement had given the something that he had promised to the other party already. Thus, the old action required a showing of reliance by the plaintiff. It was not enough to show the promise. The plaintiff had to show that he had already provided the *quid* for the *quo* of the other party and that the other party had failed or refused to fulfill its obligation under the arrangement. Despite this difference, the concept of *quid pro quo* is helpful in understanding modern contract law because it focuses attention on the thing each promised to be given and, thus, makes clear that typically contract law does not enforce promises to make gifts. You have probably heard the phrase *quid pro quo* in news reports where it would be inappropriate to have a contract. For example, a senator asserts that there was no "*quid pro quo*" between his vote for a permit and contributions that the permitted made to the senator's campaign.

In a contract, each party is normally promising to give something to the other party and to get something in return. The things given and received (goods, services, money, rights) are generally "consideration." The exception to this rule is that when the parties are merely stating conditions for giving a gift they are not giving consideration. One way to see the relationship of mutual inducement is to note the timing of the transaction. If one party has already given performance, the promise of the other to give an exchange is typically not consideration. One famous case, which is included in most case books, makes this point very well. The case is *Feinberg v. Pfeiffer Co.* In that case, Anna Feinberg had worked for many years for a corporation. The corporation awarded her a pension in a resolution that stated that her long and faithful service was the consideration for the pension. The court found that her service could not be consideration since she had already rendered the service and, thus, the employer could not be bargaining for it in the resolution to give her a pension. This case also developed the doctrine of reliance, which we will discuss later. The concept of reliance was determinative in the *Pfeiffer Co.* case. The court held that even though the promise was not supported by consideration (and thus could not be enforced on that ground), it was supported by Anna Feinberg's reliance on the promise.

Consideration need not flow to one of the parties of the contract. The bargain for consideration may be provided or delivered to a third party (an individual who is not a party to the contract). Parties may agree to deliver the consideration to anyone. In fact, it is not uncommon for parents to purchase items such as cars to be given as gifts to an adult child. The fact that the purchaser has the seller deliver the goods to a third party does not destroy the consideration.

> ▸ Father enters a contract with Car Dealer promising to pay $5,000 to purchase a car for Son.

This contract is supported by consideration. Father's promise is supported by the consideration of money. Car Dealer's promise is supported by the consideration of the car. The fact that the consideration will go directly to Son does not destroy the validity of consideration in the contract. (This fact pattern dovetails with an earlier point on gratuitous promises. If Father has promised Son to give him a car and changes his mind, that promise is unenforceable since it is a gift and not supported by consideration.)

In most contractual situations, the consideration is obvious. It does not create problems. When you buy a used car, you are bargaining for the car and the seller is bargaining for the purchase price. Your promise to pay is consideration for the dealer's promise to deliver the car. The dealer's promise to deliver the car is consideration for your promise to pay. Each party receives and gives consideration. Thus, if either party fails or refuses to deliver the consideration he promised, the other party will be able to sue and will be able to satisfy the requirement of consideration. If one party is providing what would serve as consideration and the other party is not providing consideration, neither party can enforce an obligation under the deal. Even though consideration is rarely a problem, there are cases in which the consideration element presents difficult decisions. Contracts classes focus on these difficult cases since these cases are the ones that define the line between enforceable and unenforceable promises. The history of contract law shows that the issue of drawing the line between enforceable promises and promises that fail to present a valid reason for enforcement has been around for a long time. The distinction turns on the different treatment of promises to give something and promises to make an exchange. The discussion will also deal with the deeper question of why the law refuses to enforce promises to make a gift.

Two Tests for Consideration

Two approaches have predominated in determining whether the element of consideration has been met. The older of the two tests is called the "benefit/detriment" test. The more modern approach is called the "bargain" test. The *Restatement* incorporates the bargain test. These two tests generally reach the same results, but it is worthwhile to understand the different formulations.

The Benefit/Detriment Test

The benefit/detriment test includes two different tests. Establishing either of these will meet the requirement of consideration. The plaintiff can show either that the promisor received a benefit from the deal or that the *promisee* suffered a detriment from the deal. The plaintiff does not need to show both of these. Only one is needed. It should be noted that the test is not satisfied by showing that *promisor* received a *detriment* from the deal or that the *promisee* receive a *benefit*. These tests would be met in any promise. The promisee would always have a benefit: this is the thing the promisee wants to get from the court. On the other side of the deal, the promisor would always have a detriment. To take a gift situation, if we required only that promisee have a benefit, that would mean that any promise to make a gift would meet the test. "I will give you $5,000" involves a benefit to promisee. This showing is not sufficient under the benefit-detriment test. (It also would not be sufficient under the bargain test, but we will save that issue until later. It is important to remember which party is promisor and which is promisee. On any deal, both parties are promisor and promisee. In an exchange of promises, both parties are promisor and promise. Each receives a promise and each gives a promise. To apply the test, we need to determine who promised what and whether the promise was a benefit to the promisor or a detriment to the promisee.

▶ Buyer agrees to buy Seller's house for $100,000, and Seller agrees to sell this house for $100,000.

Under the benefit/detriment test, courts enforce a promise if either of two factors is present: (1) the promisor receives a benefit *or* (2) the promisee suffers a detriment based on the promise. Of course this statement of the test requires that we identify the promisee and promisor. This may seem difficult at first glance since the typical contract includes two promises, and each promise has promisee and a promisor. The next logical question is: who are we talking about when we say promisor since each party occupies both the role of promisee and promisor in the ordinary contract? In the benefit-detriment test and in other areas when we say "promisor" we are talking about the party who makes the promise that is now the subject of the dispute or lawsuit. Thus, a seller who agrees to sell is the promisor on the promise to sell, and the buyer in that contract is the promisee on the promise to buy. Seller is the promisee on buyer's promise to buy. Buyer is the promisee of seller's promise to sell.

Buyer and Seller both made promises. They are both promisors, and they are both promisees. Whether a court refers to one or the other as "promisor" depends on which party is suing. If Seller is suing Buyer (asserting that buyer has breached by failing to go through with the purchase), Seller is suing Buyer on Buyer's promise to buy. Buyer is the promisor on the promise to buy. Seller is the promisee of the Buyer's promise to buy. If, on the other hand, Buyer is suing Seller because Seller refused to deliver the deed to the house, then Seller is the promisor in the suit. Seller is on the promisor on the promise to sell. Thus, the place to begin application of the test of benefit-detriment is to establish the following:

(1) What is the promise sued on?
(2) Who is the promisor?
(3) Who is the promisee of this promise?
(4) Did promisor receive a benefit under this exchange?
    OR
(5) Did the promisee suffer a detriment from the exchange?

Taking the example above and assuming that Seller has refused to deliver the house, the court would find the following answers:

Q1: What is the promise sued on?
Answer: The promise to sell.

Q2: Who is the promisor?
Answer: The promisor is the seller.

Q3: Who is the promisee of this promise?
Answer: The promisee of this promise is the buyer.

Q4: Did promisor receive a benefit under this exchange?
Answer: Yes, the promisor received the benefit of the purchase price.
    OR

Q5: Did the *promisee* suffer a detriment from the exchange?
Answer: Yes, promise suffered the detriment of paying the purchase price.

Clearly the test is almost too easy in the straight forward cases of exchanges of goods for money. We will see in the discussion of the bargain test that it is just as easy in similarly uncomplicated cases of transfers of goods for money. When we get to cases that are not so unambiguous, the test can be more challenging. These difficult cases require further definition of the legal terms "benefit" and "detriment" noted above.

Legal Benefit and Legal Detriment

We now need to look more closely at two of the questions in the series above. We presented the questions in a general way to explore the ordinary transaction and the designation of promisor and promisee. We presented Question 4 as "Did promisor receive a benefit under this exchange?" In fact the legal test is more precise. It is "Did promisor receive a *legal* benefit under this exchange?" We presented Question 5 as "Did the *promisee* suffer a detriment from the exchange?" In fact, the question requires the court to determine whether the promisee suffered a *legal* detriment. Paying a purchase price will meet the standard of legal detriment, but there are cases in which the detriment is less clear. We did not need this level of detail above to see the general roles of benefit and detriment and the relationship to promisor and promisee. We do need it now to see the actual application of the test of benefit and detriment. One famous case allows us to see the meaning of both terms.

To simplify and use the case of *Hamer v. Sidway* 27 N.E. 256 (N.Y. 1891), consider the following: an uncle promised to give his nephew a significant sum of money if the nephew would refrain from drinking or smoking until he reached adulthood. We simplify this case for purposes of our discussion. The actual case is more complicated than we need for the points addressed here. The party who sought enforcement of the promise was an assignee of the promise (the nephew) and the defendant was the estate of the uncle. For our purposes of understanding consideration, we can set aside these aspects of the case and treat the case as arising between the uncle and the nephew when the uncle promised to give money to encourage his nephew to stay away from harmful practices. The case involved the vices of drinking and smoking, but any vices will do for purposes of understanding this concept. The nephew is the plaintiff. He is the promisee of the uncle's promise to give him $5,000. The uncle is the promisor on the promise to pay the money. The plaintiff-nephew needs to show he (the promisee) suffered a detriment or that the uncle received a benefit. Remember, the plaintiff needs to establish only one of these facts to meet the test.

This case shows that courts applying the benefit-detriment case would not accept just anything a plaintiff deemed to be a benefit or detriment. Courts reject the idea that a psychic benefit to promisor is a sufficient benefit to meet the test for consideration. Thus, the fact that the uncle felt good about encouraging his nephew to turn away from damaging products such as alcohol and tobacco is not a sufficient basis for finding a benefit. Likewise, the case allows us to understand legal detriment. The defendant argued that giving up smoking and drinking was not a detriment. In fact, it helped the plaintiff, so it should not be seen as a basis for enforcement as a legal detriment. The court rejected this argument, holding that *legal* detriment requires only that the promisee give up something that he had a legal right to do. At the time of the case there was no statute restricting the right of young people to smoke or drink. Take the same case in a state that prohibited the conduct at issue and the test of legal detriment would not be met.

To put this case into the question sequence above we would answer the questions above.

Q1: What is the promise sued on?
Answer: The promise to pay money.

Q2: Who is the promisor?
Answer: The promisor is the uncle who promised to give the money.

Q3: Who is the promisee of this promise?
Answer: The promisee is the nephew who received the promise to pay him if he refrained from the vices noted.

Q4: Did promisor receive a benefit under this exchange?
Answer: No. Psychic benefit is not sufficient under the law.
OR

Q5: Did the *promisee* suffer a detriment from the exchange?
Answer: Yes. The nephew gave up something he had a legal right to do: smoking and drinking.

Refraining from Acting and Unilateral Contracts

An aside can be useful here. The *Hamer* case provides an example of two additional points that we discuss separately in this book: consideration can be inaction rather than action, and a promisor may seek performance rather than a promise.

First, the legal benefit and legal detriment can come from performance rather than promises. This is the concept that we explored in the discussion of bilateral and unilateral contracts. Here, the uncle did not want a promise from the nephew. Rather he wanted the performance of not smoking or drinking. As master of the offer, the uncle can set up the deal to require performance rather than a promise. If the nephew had said at the time uncle made his promise, "I promise to refrain from smoking or drinking," this would not have been an acceptance because the uncle did not seek promise. He was seeking performance as acceptance. While some courts now reject the use of the terms "unilateral" and "bilateral," the distinction between bargaining for a promise or a performance continues to be a real distinction.

A second important concept from this case is that inaction or forbearance can be consideration. Put in a funny way, the action sought by a party can be inaction. Here, the nephew's performance can be refraining from a certain thing. The most common example of this idea is found in promises not to compete. These promises generally arise in sale of businesses and in employment contracts where the employee will learn proprietary and confidential information or practices that could be used to the disadvantage of the employer if the employee went out on his own in a competing business.

Acting, Forbearing to Act, or Changing a Relationship

Although the consideration for a contract is often an act, parties may also bargain for non-action or inaction. Such inaction is often referred to in contract cases as "forbearance." Perhaps the most important examples of non-action (or forbearance) in modern business are (1) a promise not to compete and (2) a promise not to sue someone. In each case, the party is bargaining for inaction rather than action. Thus, inaction can be the performance sought under a contract. The law accepts inaction as a real thing that can be bargained for. We discussed the famous case of *Hamer v. Sidway*, 27 N.E. 256 (N.Y. 1891), to explain the legal detriment test. That case is also a good example of forbearance as consideration. The nephew's performance was forbearance (refraining from smoking or drinking until he became an adult). It constituted legal detriment. The court found the promise to refrain from vices constituted consideration.

Psychic Benefit

Courts universally reject the argument that the uncle received a benefit. We know that emotional benefits are real, but they do not meet the test of consideration under either the bargain test or the benefit/detriment test. As an example, remember the case just mentioned in which an uncle promised to pay his nephew a certain sum of money if he refrained from drinking or smoking within a certain time. Of course, as a practical matter people do receive satisfaction or psychic benefit by influencing others in positive ways. Such satisfaction does not amount to a legal benefit for purposes of the doctrine of consideration. The rejection of psychic benefit as consideration is necessary to draw the line against enforcement of promises to make gifts. This is likely the reason for the rule that psychic benefit is not legal benefit for purposes of consideration.

The Bargain Test

The more modern approach is referred to as the "bargain" test or the "bargained for exchange" test. This test achieves substantially similar results to the legal benefit/legal detriment test, although it is subtly different. These concepts continue to have power in the consideration area and in other contract areas. Under the modern test for consideration, a promise or performance is consideration for a return promise if it is "bargained for." By moving away from the benefit/detriment test and adopting the bargain focus of some early cases, the *Restatement* adopted a simplified test for consideration. It recommended to courts the bargain test as a substitute for the legal benefit/legal detriment test. Many courts have adopted the *Restatement* approach, although some courts continue to use the benefit/detriment test. Under the bargain test, the requirement of consideration is met if a performance or promise is "bargained for." This test makes it necessary to understand what we mean when we say it is "bargained for."

As an aside, we want to note this example of the way legal tests operate. Legal tests often have terms of art built into them; they are essentially tests inside of the test. You could see this with the benefit/detriment test that we discussed above. You cannot fully apply the test until you check the built-in test of legal benefit and legal detriment. Just as it was necessary to understand the concepts of legal benefit and legal detriment to apply the benefit/detriment test, we now need to understand the subtest of "bargained for" to understand the bargain test.

If a promise is "sought by the promisor in exchange for his promise and is given by the promisee in exchange for his promise" the *Restatement* test for consideration is met. So the sub test inside the bargain test is this idea of seeking an exchange of promises or performances. If the promisee's promise or performance is *sought by* the promisor, and the promisor's promise is given in exchange for what the promisor seeks, it is consideration.

The bargain test is simpler than the benefit/detriment test. Are the parties intending to make an exchange? The bargain test cuts to the chase in a sense to ask simply: did the parties each seek the exchange of the other thing that the other party provided? In a way this leaves the judgment of what has value to the parties. If the parties bargain for something, then they are attaching value to the performances they seek. They are acting in a way that indicates value and the court does not need to address the question of whether there is a benefit or detriment to the parties.

Remember the *Hamer* case discussed above as an example of the benefit/detriment test. Under the bargain test a court would not need to analyze whether the promisor received a "legal benefit" or the promisee incurred a "legal detriment." The newer "bargain" test would also find consideration because each party bargained for the thing the other could provide. The uncle bargained for the nephew's action of not acting in a certain way (refraining from drinking or smoking).

Generally, the benefit/detriment test and the bargain test yield the same result. The significance of the change in tests is that the court's inquiry is less about value and more about the desires of the parties. The bargain test is simpler and has the advantage of reminding courts that they are not in the business of determining whether the parties gave value in their promises. If a buyer agrees to pay $500 for a paper cup that Elvis drank from, the parties have bargained for the cup. Consideration exists under the bargain test. The court does not need to consider the value of the thing purchased or to confront the issue of legal benefit or legal detriment. The result should be the same under the benefit/detriment test, but it may suggest to courts that they must contemplate value in a more active way. Again, the question of consideration generally is not difficult. Both tests find consideration in the vast majority of cases and they both find no consideration when there is a promise to make a gift.

Enforcement for a Benefit Received

Courts will sometimes enforce a promise that is not bargained for on the basis that the promisor gave the promise in recognition of a significant benefit that the promisor received. This seems to be out of step with the principle that courts will not enforce contracts that lack consideration (in the sense of a bargained-for exchange). Generally, a person who has been unjustly enriched at the expense of another is required to make restitution; however, the courts are reluctant to require restitution for persons "who have had benefits thrust upon them." Courts are also reluctant to enforce promises based on past consideration. Thus, while a court might recognize an action in restitution based on a benefit received, that does not mean that the court would enforce a promise based on the same benefit received. The difference is that in the action based on restitution the court will create the promise. It is a further step for a court to enforce a promise based on the fact that restitution is appropriate. Enforcing a promise means that the court is allowing the party who received the promise to set the compensation or remedy. This result flies in the face of the general rule against enforcing promises that lack consideration.

Nevertheless, there are situations in which courts do enforce promises based on past benefits. Most jurisdictions recognize at least three well-established contexts in which this type of enforcement is common: (1) a promise reconfirmed after the promisor reaches adulthood, after earlier disaffirming the promise on the basis that the promisor was a minor at the time of the promise, (2) a promise reconfirmed after a discharge in bankruptcy dissolved the promise, and (3) a promise reconfirmed after a statute of limitations or a statute of frauds made the promise unenforceable. In each of these cases, the original promise became unenforceable and a later promise reinvigorated the enforceability of the promise.

The *Restatement (2d) of Contracts* recognized another situation in which theory of enforcement provides a legitimate basis for enforcement of a promise. *Restatement Section 86* points favorably to promises given in recognition of a benefit received by the promisor in a clear cut case of a restitutionary basis. *Section 86* provides: "(1) a promise made in recognition of a benefit previously received by the promisor from the promisee is binding to the extent necessary to prevent injustice. (2) A promise is not binding under Subsection (1) (a) if the promisee conferred the benefit as a gift or for other reasons the promisor has not been unjustly enriched; or (b) to the extent that its value is disproportionate to the benefit."

Notice that *Restatement 86* emphasizes the rare nature of this action by specifying that enforcement is appropriate only "to the extent necessary to prevent injustice." This is the traditional test for restitution. The difference between the theory recognized in *Restatement 86* and restitution is that the court proceeding under this theory grants enforcement of the promise given rather than enforcement of a remedy devised by the court in restitution. The action could be called "Promissory Restitution."

A few states generalize this line of cases by statute to allow for enforcement of such promises. Such statutes provide for enforcement of promises to pay for a benefit received. The *Restatement* rejects the argument that this is an example of past consideration. "Past consideration" is inconsistent with the definition of consideration in *Restatement §71*. Thus, promises made for past consideration or moral obligations are not enforceable on these bases without more.

> ▸ For example, Ann cares for Bob's adult son, Carl, while Carl is ill, poor, and far from home. Bob subsequently promises to reimburse Ann for any expenses incurred during Carl's care. This promise is not binding because the promise rests on either past consideration or a moral obligation to repay Ann for her services. If Bob had received the services himself, Ann would have a better argument for recovery since Bob would have received a benefit. You might think that in the ordinary sense Bob did receive a benefit since someone so closely related to him (his son) received an important (and life sustaining) benefit. The fact that the son is an adult makes it unlikely that a court would see the benefit as having a direct relation to Bob. If Bob's son had been a minor at the time Ann provided help for him, a court would see the same care and services by Ann as a benefit to Bob since Bob would have a legal responsibility for his minor son's support.

Generally, a person who confers a benefit because of mistake is entitled to restitution. However, restitution will not be required when it will prejudice the recipient of the benefit. Restitution will not be required if the value of services far exceeds what the person who received the benefit can afford.

> ▸ For example, Bob employs Ann to repair a vacant house. By mistake, Ann repairs the adjacent house, which belongs to Carl. Carl promises to pay Ann the value of the repairs; this promise is binding.

Courts are more likely to enforce promises to pay for past emergency services necessary to support life or preserve property.

> ▸ If Bob finds Ann's escaped horse and Bob cares for and feeds it, a court is likely to enforce Ann's subsequent promise to pay reasonable compensation for Bob's efforts in caring for the horse.

In a famous case, a court enforced a promise an employer made to an employee to pay a monthly stipend because the employee saved the employer's life on a job site and, as a result, suffered an injury that made it impossible for the employee to work and earn a living. The employee saw the employer two stories below as he was throwing a block from a building site. The employee fell with the block in order to divert its fall. His action saved the life of the employer (the promisor). The court enforced the promise to pay the money in support of the employee, noting that the promise was supported by theories of reliance and restitution.

If a party conferred a benefit as a gift, this basis for enforcement does not apply. The *Restatement* notes that "there is no element of unjust enrichment in the receipt of a gift" unless mistake or some other basis applies. It should be noted, however, that it is possible in rare cases for a court to find that a transfer that appears to be a gift was not intended to be a gift by the parties. In such a case, a promise to pay after receipt of the benefit could be supported by a later promise to pay.

A benefit received as a result of an unequal bargained-for exchange is not unjust. The *Restatement* explains the reasoning of this approach by reference to a promise by a person who is not a party to a bargain. It notes that "if a third person receives a benefit as a result of the performance of a bargain," between others, "the subsequent promise of the third person to pay extra compensation to the performing party" is not binding.

This theory of recovery ("Promissory Restitution" or "enforcement for a benefit received") provides for enforcement only when the promisor received a benefit. This action is like an action in restitution except that rather than seeking a reasonable amount of recovery based on the court's determination of what is reasonable, the plaintiff seeks to enforce the promise on the basis of the promise. The difference between this theory of recovery and restitution is the proof of the amount of recovery. It makes sense, then that the *Restatement* recognizes a limit to recovery based on the value of the benefit conferred. Under this approach, a court is likely to limit the recovery to the amount of the benefit received. Thus, the court may refuse to enforce the promise if the amount promised exceeds the benefit in the view of the court.

Adequacy of Consideration

An important rule of contract law is that courts do not judge the adequacy of consideration. This rule is based on the idea that parties rather than courts should determine whether a contract is worthwhile from their own point of view. The principle is basic to a free market. A contrary rule would tend to create judicial oversight of contracting. If courts rather than parties determined whether consideration is adequate, the market would be less free. Having said that, however, there are several mechanisms by which courts actually do judge contracts. The concept of consideration, thus, focuses not on the value or *adequacy* of the bargain but rather on the *fact* of the bargain. If the parties each gave a promise or performance in exchange for the other's promise or performance, courts will generally hold the element of consideration is present and the contract is enforceable absent some affirmative reason to refuse enforcement.

In most transactions the consideration flowing from both sides is roughly equal. When you buy a car, for example, the value of the car is roughly equivalent to the amount of money you will pay for it. You might get a $10,000 car for $9,000 or $11,000, but you will probably not get it for $800 or pay $120,000.

The basic rule is that the adequacy of the consideration is not for the courts to judge. This is a free market concept. In some cases the value of the things given is different than the parties understood or knew. Although the exchange ultimately is very lopsided, the test of consideration may, nevertheless, be met. In one case found in many casebooks, an American citizen trapped in a war zone offered to exchange $5,000, payable when she escapes and returns to the U.S. for $20 inside the war zone in order to buy food. The court enforced the contract despite the fact that the consideration seemed very lopsided. Courts police extreme inadequacy under the doctrine of unconscionability and by considering questions of fraud and overreaching. If a party that exercised undue influence placed the other under duress, this may be a basis for refusing enforcement. Courts reject the argument of "inadequacy of consideration" as a separate basis.

Examples of Lack of Consideration

The following discussion presents traditional arguments against finding consideration in particular circumstances.

Contracts classes often hone in on the meaning of consideration by thinking about situations where consideration did not exist. There is no legal value (no consideration) when there is a pretense of a bargain (sham). Other examples of a lack of consideration include settlements of obviously invalid bad faith claim, illusory promises, promises to perform a preexisting duty, and promises in which there is no bargain. This last example presents a situation in which the promisor did not seek to induce anything because the promisor was merely promising to make a future gift. Professor Williston's well-known "tramp" hypothetical is an example of this case. Some of the types of trouble spots are highlighted in the following sections. Although consideration is not difficult to find in most cases, there are a few standard types of cases where courts held consideration is not established.

Moral Obligation

Moral obligation is not a basis for enforcing an obligation. The rule against moral obligation exists not to diminish morality but to prevent enforcement of gifts and social promises. Most people think as a matter of morality and good conscience that people should keep their promises. The old saying "My word is my bond" may remind you of the idea that as a matter of moral action people should live up to their promises. Most people believe it is a moral failing to break a promise. Nevertheless, this moral concept is not a basis for legal enforcement of a promise. Only those promises that also meet the test of consideration are legally enforceable.

Exchanges versus Gifts

For purposes of contract law, exchanges and gifts are mutually exclusive categories. If something is a gift, it is not an exchange, and the promise to make a gift is not an enforceable promise. The key is that in an exchange parties are bargaining for the exchange of those items. With a gift, there is no *quid pro quo*, and no exchange. Courts reject suits based on gratuitous promises. The reason courts reject enforcement of promises that are gratuitous is not entirely clear. Most scholars see the exchange of promises as basic to economic activity. Gratuitous promises and exchanges, on the other hand, do not enhance the economy. The primary purpose of contract law is to facilitate the economy rather than to hold people to all conceivable promises.

This use of terms seems inconsistent with some uses of terms in the real (non-legal) world. After all, people "exchange" gifts at Christmas and for other holidays. In reality, a person who gives you a gift may expect one in return. As we noted earlier, a contract could involve the exchange of goods. You might say this is the same as the practice of exchanging gifts. Nevertheless, unless the court concludes that the parties intended to bargain for the exchange, it will not enforce a promise to make a transfer.

> ▶ Scenario #1: For example, the Nature Club provides a plaque to its outgoing chair. In the presentation, the incoming chair states that the plaque was presented "in consideration for your years of tireless service to the Nature Club."

Is the outgoing chair's tireless service consideration for the plaque? It seems unlikely that the chair served in order to obtain the plaque. The club did not bargain with the chair to serve in order to receive the plaque. This seems like a silly case in a way. The issue of consideration will never arise in this case. Since the chair receives the plaque at the time of the presentation, she will have an ownership or property claim to the plaque. She will be able to keep it.

Now, to explore the issue of consideration, let's change the facts.

> ▸ Scenario #2: In the same case as above, the Nature Club merely an-
> nounces the plaque. The Club does not have the plaque at the time of
> the presentation ceremony and later decides not to expend the money
> to buy the plaque. The speaker makes the same statement about con-
> sideration for her years of service. Weeks later the former chair learns
> that she will not receive a plaque after all. She is disappointed, of
> course. She wanted to have the plaque on her wall.

Will she be able to enforce the promise requiring that the Nature Club pro-
vide her with the plaque if she presents the statement from the presentation "in consideration for your tireless service to the Nature Club"? Will the court find that the element of consideration has been met and allow enforcement? Using the word "consideration" in the presentation either orally or in writing does not mean that the service actually meets the legal standard for consideration. The statement that the plaque is given in consideration does not mean that the chair's service to the Club constitutes consideration. It's up to the court to determine whether the element of consideration is met. The fact that the parties or the defendant used the term will not settle the matter. Absent additional facts, a court would probably find that the arrangement with the Nature Club was a charitable undertaking, given without the inducement of a plaque. One important clue on this question is timing. Since the chair's service was given before the promise to give a plaque, it is not likely that a court would see the service as an exchange for the plaque. Thus, the court is unlikely to find an unenforceable promise to give the plaque.

A second and final change of facts of this problem may show the tipping point on the issue of consideration.

> ▸ Scenario #3: At the time the Club provides the chair with a plaque
> and states it is given "in consideration of her service," it also promises
> the chair to hire her to work as a staff member for the Nature Club in
> charge of fund raising for the next nine months contract for a com-
> pensation of $20,000. The contract might even say that the offer is
> made because of the years of service the chair has given. Will a court
> enforce the promise of the $20,000?

A court is likely to enforce this contract. This is not because of the statement that the contract is based on the years of service. The consideration is not

the past volunteer work for the club. Rather, it is the promise of an exchange of future work for future salary that provides a basis for enforcement. If the Nature Club decides to save money by refusing to pay the salary, the former chair is again disappointed. This time a court is likely to enforce this exchange, finding consideration to support the promises of work and payment. The former chair is not conferring a gift of her time; she is working for the club for a salary. Each party is performing and receiving performance: money for work and work for money.

There are many different theories about why the law draws the line on enforcement to enforce exchanges but not to enforce gift promises. Most commentators recognize that the legal system cannot enforce every promise. Obviously some promises are not susceptible to enforcement. Promises such as "I will always admire and respect you," or "I will love you forever," are really beyond the power of courts to enforce. Similarly, social promises such as "I will go with you to the movies," are too numerous and burdensome for courts to enforce. No society has ever enforced all promises. It is virtually impossible. Moreover, it is undesirable to inject the legal system in all promises. Thus, we see that courts must draw a line between enforceable and unenforceable promises. The line that has developed is the requirement of consideration, which requires an exchange of promises and performances for each other.

The element of consideration serves the purpose of helping courts draw the line. It is not always easy to draw, however. To return to the case of the plaque, it might be possible to change the facts to make the plaque consideration. If the club promised the chair that at the end of the year it would award the plaque, we are getting closer to this line. A famous case that also comes close to the line is *Kirksey v. Kirksey*. The facts can be seen as either a bargained for exchange (consideration) or a conditional gratuitous promise (not consideration).

> ▶ Isaac writes to his sister-in-law who is recently a widow, saying "Antillico, if you will move here to my property, I will give you a place where you can live and raise your children." After receiving this letter, Antillico abandons her property where she had been living and moves her family to Isaac's farm. Shortly after, Isaac evicts her and the family. Should a court enforce Isaac's promise to Antillico?

The case is a good one because it can be regarded as either an exchange or a gift and, in fact, the court that decided the case included judges who disagreed on this central question. If a court sees Isaac's promise as simply trying to give a gift, then the promise is not enforceable. If Isaac is actually seeking help on the farm or is bargaining for the move for some reason, then this is an exchange. You might say it is not a gift since Antillico must do something (move to the farm). The argument is that she is giving something on her side and this something should be seen as consideration. This fact is not likely to be determinative, however, since some gifts have conditions. This may be one. Because the property cannot be moved, Antillico would need to move to accept the gift of a place to live. The case also provides a good example of how important fact development is for legal judgments. If you were the judge hearing this case, what kind of evidence would you want to have? Would it matter to you that Antillico had several sons who actually worked the farm? That Antillico had several other workers who made the transition with her to the new property? That Antillico gave up a property interest to move to the land offered? Does the motivation of Isaac matter to you? What if the evidence indicated he wanted to marry Antillico?

Conditional Gifts
(Conditional Gratuitous Promises)

The discussion above suggests an argument that is made to assert that the consideration element is not met. The question is whether a promise meets the requirement of consideration or simply is a statement of a condition on a gratuitous promise. The problem does not go away when we apply the bargain test. In the case of Sister Antillico, for example, it is possible to argue that Sister Antillico's move does not constitute consideration but, rather, is a condition of receiving the gift of a place to live.

A conditional gift does not constitute consideration. It is a gift with a condition, but it is still a gift. In the *Kirksey* case discussed above, if Isaac has no interest in Antillico moving to the property it may be a conditional gift rather than a bargain. If he does not need additional manpower to work the farm and is merely offering the property to help his sister-in-law, this may be a conditional gift. Antillico must move to accept the gift. She cannot make a home on the property unless she moves. The need of her to do something (move) does not necessarily meet the test of bargained for consideration. If Isaac simply wants to help her, this is a conditional gift. On the other hand, if Isaac wants to have her or her sons work the land for his benefit, the move may be consideration for the promise to give her a place to live. We will return to this example on the issue of reliance.

Another traditional hypothetical that contracts professors use to illustrate the conditional gift is the example of a rich man who wishes to give a suit of clothes to a tramp. Professor Williston is credited with creating this scenario to explain a conditional gift. A rich man sees a tramp walking down the street in winter and wants to help him. He says to the tramp: "If you go to the clothing store across the street, you can get a new suit and charge it to me." In this story, the trip across the street is not consideration for the suit unless there is something more to the story. If the rich man simply wants to help the tramp, he is setting up a conditional gift. It is still a gift though the tramp needs to do something to claim it. If the rich man needed or wanted to induce the walk (rather than merely suggesting the walk as a way to get the suit for the tramp) then this may be consideration. It seems a bit far-fetched but we can come up with a scenario that a court might find to be consideration. For example, if the rich man wanted to be recognized for his charitable nature and set up a photographer to capture a picture of him with the tramp we may have a case of a bargain.

As the example above illustrates, the fact that the transaction involves a condition does not resolve the question whether a promise is gratuitous. Difficult cases arise under the category of conditional gratuitous promises. A transaction that involves a condition — "if you do X, I will do Y" — Does not mean a contract is offered. Some gifts include a condition. The fact that such promises include a condition does not mean that they constitute consideration.

Illusory Promises

Illusory promises are not enforceable. The first important reality to note is that such promises are very rare. In the vast majority of cases, each party gives up and receives something of value. These are arrangements that seem to present consideration but fall short because the apparent consideration is an illusion. When one party receives an option that gives unfettered discretion to either go forward or not, this is likely to present an illusory contract. This situation is tantamount to a promise to do something if that party later chooses to do it. It is an "I will if I want to" situation. When a court finds that the agreement contains such unfettered discretion, it will find that there is no binding agreement. If one party is free to walk away without any effect, the law regards the deal as not binding on either party. Examples of such cases arise in situations such as loans. If a loan calls for repayment on certain terms but also allows the borrower to choose not to repay the loan at all this may be an illusory contract. This seems obvious but it can present a hard case. If both parties bind themselves to something, the fact that one is getting a very good deal will not prevent the court from finding consideration. For example, if the parties agree to a loan but indicate that repayment of the loan will be forgiven in certain circumstances, this may be a valid consideration. The key to determining whether a promise is illusory is to see if one party's discretion is completely unfettered. So long as the promisor's discretion is limited in some way the court will find the promise is not illusory.

In *Strong v. Sheffield, 39 N.E. 330 (1895)*, the court held that plaintiff (lender) could not recover on a promissory note because there was no consideration for the defendant's endorsement. The Defendant borrower, Louisa Sheffield, endorsed a promissory note at the request of her husband. The note had been made between her husband and the lender (plaintiff). Louisa's endorsement was given as security for a preexisting debt of the husband. The promissory note was due upon demand. The lender did not extend credit as consideration for the note. The court found that the evidence presented did not establish consideration because the lender gave nothing (neither the loan nor a promise to forebear collection). The lender could have demanded payment at the time the defendant gave the note.

An interesting case for the argument of an illusory contract is that of *Wood v. Lucy, Lady Duff-Gordon*. The Lady was a famous British fashion designer. You could think of her as the Calvin Klein of the 19th Century. If you are interested in the history of fashion, you should search for Lucy on the web. Lucy and Wood entered a contract for five-year representation under which Wood would place Lucy's clothing designs. Wood claimed the deal created an exclusive right on his part and that when Lucy began endorsing designs through other agents she breached their contract. Lucy argued that the agreement was illusory because the contract did not include an affirmative promise by Wood to distribute her designs. Lucy's defense was that Wood did not promise to do anything and, thus, his promise was illusory. Her argument was that because Wood was not bound to do anything, his promise was illusory. It is true that if one party is not bound then neither party is bound. The court disagreed, however, that Wood's promise was illusory. Justice Cardozo read the contract as a whole and found that to make sense the contract should be read as creating obligations on Wood to use his best efforts to place Lucy's designs. This is an example of an "implied" term. It is also an example of an "implied-in-fact" contract. Courts refer to such implied terms as "implied in fact," meaning the court is recognizing terms that the parties intended to include. In other words, the parties implied these terms by their words or the circumstances. We will later distinguish between the "implied-in-fact" contract and the "implied-in-law" contract, which is a restitution concept. In some cases, courts enforce a promise as result of an implied-in-fact promise that arises from the intention of the parties, as interpreted by the court.

In this case, the court recognized an implied-in-fact promise that arises from the circumstances. This is a situation which the court believes that the parties themselves implied the obligation. In the *Wood* case, Justice Cardozo notes in the carefully drafted contract the clear intent of the parties to take on a business relationship. Justice Cardozo notes that although *Wood* did not promise "in so many words" that he would use reasonable efforts to place Lucy's designs, that is clearly what the parties intended.

The following sections deal with types of situations in which early courts held that the promises involved were illusory. These are (1) contracts subject to a condition of satisfaction, (2) requirements contracts, (3) output contracts, and (4) exclusive dealing contracts. Although the traditional approach was to refuse enforcement to such contracts on the ground that they presented an illusory obligation, modern courts enforce the promises in each of these types of contracts.

Contracts with a Condition of Satisfaction

Modern law recognizes the validity of consideration in a promise that has a condition of satisfaction. Traditionally, courts held that a promise to perform to the satisfaction of one party was an illusory promise because the party could simply chose to say he was not satisfied. Early courts saw such "conditions of satisfaction" as illusory based on the reasoning that the party whose performance was conditional had unfettered discretion. Traditionally, courts viewed such a party as able to perform or to refuse to perform with impunity. These are agreements under which the promisor has promised to pay only if the return performance meets some subjective standard. For example:

> ▶ Father hires Artist to paint a portrait of his deceased child. Artist expressly promises that Father will have no obligation to pay for the painting unless he is personally satisfied with the painting. When Father receives the painting he rejects it as not a good likeness of his daughter. Artist takes the painting back to his studio and changes the painting. He presents it again to Father, but Father refuses to look at the painting and states he will not accept the painting and he will not pay for it. Should the court enforce the Father's obligation to pay?

At early common law, courts held that such promises were not enforceable because the person exercising a condition of satisfaction could simply report that he was dissatisfied and, thus, escape his obligation. At first blush, this may seem to make sense. After all, Father in the case above could just say he is dissatisfied. The modern approach is to accept the promise as consideration. Thus, modern courts reject the argument that the promise is illusory. Today courts reason that in saying he is not satisfied when he is satisfied the party is misrepresenting his true state and is breaching the duty of good faith.

You might agree with the early courts that the problem of someone simply expressing dissatisfaction in order to escape his obligations still exists. This point presents the difference between having a contract and enforcing a contract. Contracts that include conditions of satisfaction are often difficult to enforce. They are not deemed illusory by modern courts, however. While it is true that it would be difficult to prove that a person asserting he is not satisfied is actually satisfied, courts now recognize the contract and allow the plaintiff to attempt to produce the proof necessary to enforce the promise. Thus, in a free market, parties are free to enter contracts even when the type of contract entered involves difficult issues of proof. This means that the party expressing dissatisfaction may be able to withstand enforcement by asserting he is dissatisfied with performance. This analysis puts the person seeking to enforce the contract in the same difficult position as a plaintiff seeking to prove intent in tort law.

Contracts that include conditions of satisfaction are not illusory by virtue of the fact of the condition. Likewise, distributorship agreements, rental agreements where the landlord takes rent from gross profits, as well as output and requirements contracts all depend on a party using good efforts to make the business arrangement profitable for the investment side. A court may see a promise to repay with interest from profits of the business as including an implied promise to use best efforts to generate profits. The topic of conditions of satisfaction also arises in questions relating to breach. We deal with the topic in detail under the chapter on Performance and Breach.

Requirements and Output Contracts

Requirements and output contracts do not state an exact quantity of goods. Rather they set the quantity of goods committed to in the contract by reference to the measure based on need or production. The requirements contract is a contract under which a party promises to produce the quantity of goods that the purchaser requires for his business. An output contract is one under which a party agrees to purchase the entire output of goods produced by the other party. Don't be confused by thinking that these terms describe one contract from two perspectives. These are two different types of contracts. Both types of contracts deal with a measure of quantity of goods or services.

Under a requirements contract the quantity is set by the needs of the buyer, and under the output contract the quantity is set by the quantity produced by seller. For example, a manufacturer might agree to buy all of the cooking oil it needs from one supplier. This is a requirements contract. The buyer may have done studies that convince it that the oil from this seller is superior for making its own product. This is a type of exclusive dealing contract by which the seller secures a buyer for a large quantity of goods and seller secures a place to sell its goods. This reduces the transaction costs of advertising and bargaining and allows parties to develop long-standing relationship of reliance on each other as trading partners. Under the output contract, the seller agrees to sell all of a particular product it makes to the buyer.

Early courts regarded such contracts with the same sort of distrust they held for conditions of satisfaction. They saw these contracts as illusory, reasoning that the seller in an outputs contract could simply shut the doors of his factory and have no more outputs. Thus, he was seen as having unfettered discretion. Likewise, courts of the past saw the buyer in a requirements contract as having the power to choose to stop having requirements at any time. The early courts refused to enforce these contracts, reasoning that each type of contract gave unfettered discretion to one party.

Modern courts reject this reasoning. Just as with conditions of satisfaction, modern courts changed this view, ultimately finding that the duty of good faith applies and constrains the discretion of the parties, making the contracts non-illusory. Courts now enforce both requirements and outputs contracts as real, non-illusory obligations. They see the decision of the parties under these contracts as constrained by the obligation of good faith. The parties do not have unfettered discretion under this view. Under a requirements contract, the buyer is constrained to buy his full needs from the seller. Likewise, the decision of the seller to stop outputs under an outputs contract is constrained by the duty of good faith.

The UCC provides that outputs and requirements contracts are enforceable. Section 2-306 deals with the two types of contracts together. It states that a "term which measures the quantity by the output of the seller or the requirements of the buyer means such actual output or requirements as may occur in good faith." The UCC thus sets the standard of good faith as a limit on discretion, saving the contracts from the defense of illusory contracts. Similarly, the UCC used the standard of good faith to limit what a party could demand of the other under such contracts. This move also disposed of the early common law defense of an illusory obligation because it made clear that neither party had unfettered discretion under these contracts.

The provision sets a reasonableness standard as a protection against extreme quantities. It states that the quantity cannot be "unreasonably disproportionate to any stated estimate." If the parties did not state an estimate, the UCC states that only a normal or comparable prior output or requirements may be tendered or demanded. The effect of this exception is to prevent a party's attempt to enforce the contract for a quantity of goods that is contrary to an estimate the parties gave or to their prior practices. This is pretty clear-cut. If the parties enter a contract they call an output with a "cap" or "lid" on production. For example, if the parties have transferred 50,000 gallons of oil per year for some time, the seller could not require the buyer to purchase more than this amount. Parties sometimes set both a threshold and a cap. For example they might enter an output contract but specify that the quantity will never fall below 5,000 gallons per month nor exceed 70,000 per year. Such specificity gives greater certainty to both parties.

Exclusive Dealing Contracts

Exclusive dealing contracts are generally enforceable. There is no inherent problem with such contracts. Sometimes, however, an exclusive dealing contract creates an unreasonable restraint on trade. Many types of contracts restrain trade — covenants not to compete and sale of good will are two examples. Such contracts always restrain competition but courts generally hold the restraint is not unreasonable and, thus, not a violation of antitrust laws because they are related to legitimate contract purposes and, thus, are reasonable. Restraints on trade when a person has sold business (in the case of sale of good will) or restraints on competition when a person has agreed to refrain from competing with his employer are common.

Case law regarding exclusive dealing contracts centers on the question of whether these types of agreements create an unreasonable restraint on trade and, thus, violate the Sherman Anti-Trust Act. Under the *Restatement*, "a promise to refrain from competition that imposes a restraint that is ancillary to an otherwise valid transaction or relationship is unreasonably in restraint of trade if: (a) the restraint is greater than is needed to protect the promisee's legitimate interest, or (b) the promisee's need is outweighed by the hardship to the promisor and the likely injury to the public." *Restatement § 188*. Ancillary Restraints on Competition. The *Restatement* also provides examples of promises that are ancillary to a valid transaction. "Promises imposing restraints that are ancillary to a valid transaction or relationship include (a) a promise by the seller of a business not to compete with the buyer in such a way as to injure the value of the business sold; (b) a promise by an employee or other agent not to compete with his employer or other principal; and (c) a promise by a partner not to compete with the partnership." *Restatement § 188*.

Courts generally uphold exclusive dealing contracts so long as they do not restrain trade. After rejecting the argument that a particular exclusive dealing contract is an unenforceable restraint of trade, a court will need to determine whether a party breached its promise under an exclusive dealing contract. The standard courts generally apply in making this determination is one of a best efforts. Applying this standard to the alleged breach, a court would determine whether the defendant violated the exclusive dealing contract. In the context of promotion of the sale of goods, courts typically apply a standard of reasonable diligence and good faith efforts. The parties can agree to a higher standard.

The same concept as used in output requirement contracts is used in UCC 2-306(2) with sale of goods. The UCC used similar treatment for exclusive dealings contracts. UCC 2-306(2) states that an exclusive dealing contract is "a lawful agreement by either the seller or the buyer for exclusive dealing in the kind of goods concerned." The section imposes an obligation by the seller to use best efforts unless the parties agreed to a different standard. This means that the seller is obligated to use best efforts to supply the goods. The corollary for the buyer is that it must use his best efforts to promote the sale of the goods. UCC 2-306(2) requires that the parties to an exclusive dealing contract use reasonable diligence and good faith in the performance of the contract. Exclusive dealing contracts carry forward the obligation of good faith in a manner similar to output and requirement contracts. Like output and requirement contracts, exclusive dealing contracts raise questions of insecurity and the right to adequate assurance. Courts and parties use both best efforts and reasonable efforts as tests in this area. Recent case law regarding exclusive dealing contracts focus on whether exclusive dealing contracts violate the Sherman Anti-Trust Act or are impermissible monopolies.

Nominal versus Sham Consideration

While nominal consideration can serve as a basis for enforcing a promise, a sham cannot. Courts will not accept a sham or "show" of consideration to justify enforcement. Because a pretense of a bargain is not sufficient consideration, courts generally reject nominal or sham consideration as a basis for enforcement. The *Restatement of Contracts* makes this point. Sometimes courts note that the consideration provided in a contract is insignificant. It could even be "nominal," meaning it is hardly worth contracting about. We have stressed the point in this chapter that generally courts do not judge or value the deal that parties enter.

The doctrine of consideration helps keep courts out of the business of judging the value or adequacy or comparable value of the performances exchanged in contracts. An old saying that makes this point is: "A peppercorn will do." A peppercorn is worth less than a penny both now and at the time the saying was first used. The meaning of this saying is that something of almost no value can serve as consideration and courts will not judge the deal. Parties are free in a free market to make good bargains or foolish bargains. It is up to the parties what deal they will strike and courts are not there to make sure that the things exchanged are of equivalent value. Consideration is, however, required by law. Even though consideration can be small, even nominal, most courts will refuse to enforce a contract in which the parties used consideration simply as a formalism to bind themselves to a gift.

Recitation of Consideration

In option contracts, parties sometimes recite consideration without indicating the amount of the payment, asserting merely: "for one dollar and other good and valuable consideration" the parties agree to their duties. Also, in option contracts, parties often recite formal consideration but may not actually transfer the consideration. This situation raises questions for courts regarding whether they should enforce an option contract based on a merely formal (but unstated or unpaid) consideration. Courts agree that an option transfers value. Such disputes are not like promises to make a gratuitous transfer since the parties do not intend to make a gift. The option situation is clearly a commercial arrangement, and, thus, courts are likely to find consideration in this situation. A separate problem occurs when an option agreement recites consideration but the party who states he will pay the option amount never pays it. Most courts find that the situation presents consideration and also a breach of the payment obligation.

Past Consideration and Pre-existing Debts

Ordinarily courts will not respect past consideration as consideration. This is because if one party has already provided the consideration on his side the other party could not be bargaining for that thing. Remember the *Feinberg* case in which Anna Feinberg had worked for many years for a company and that company gave her a pension based on those years of past service. The court rejected the past services as consideration. Under either the benefit/detriment test or the bargain theory of contract, past consideration is not consideration. A past performance could not *induce* the new promise because it has already been provided.

In some narrowly defined exceptions to the rule, courts will give effect to past consideration. Courts recognize three situations in which a contract right that has become unenforceable is revived by a new promise. When a minor disaffirms a contract, the contract obligation is discharged. In some cases, a minor who reaches the age of majority revives the obligation disaffirmed earlier. Courts respect this revival of a promise and enforce the promise. Similarly, a debtor who has received a discharge of a debt in bankruptcy may revive the obligation by a promise to pay that debt. A court will respect and enforce the revived promise despite the fact that the consideration for the new promise is past. Finally, a debtor whose debt has become unenforceable as a result of the expiration of a statute of limitations may also revive the obligation by a new promise. In these limited situations, the fact that the consideration for the promise is past does not prevent courts from enforcing the new promise.

In each of these cases there was originally a bargained for exchange, a contract. The contract has become unenforceable by operation of law. The bar to enforcement is an extraordinary outside mechanism that destroys the original obligation. Courts allow a new promise to put the original deal back in operation.

The *Restatement* extended this concept to allow a restitutionary action on a promise when the promisor received a previous *material benefit* that was not intended as a gift. This point is discussed in detail in the section of this chapter on enforcement for a benefit received.

Pre-existing Duties and Legal Obligations

Performance by a party of an act that the party has an obligation to do is generally not consideration. If a party already has a duty to do an act, re-asserting a promise about the obligation is not a new obligation. It is already owed. Remember our discussion of the *Hamer* case, in which an uncle promised to pay his nephew a certain sum of money if he would refrain from drinking or smoking for a certain amount of time. If the nephew had no legal right to drink or smoke, his performance of refraining for doing these things would not serve as consideration. At the time of the *Hamer* case, the statutory prohibitions against smoking and drinking by young people did not yet exist. If the nephew had been subject to such legislation, neither his promise nor his performance by refraining from these actions could be consideration.

A special application of the pre-existing duty rule is the situation in which one party who owes a debt to another seeks to settle that debt for less than the agreed amount. There are two basic rules. First, where the amount of the debt is fixed and liability for it is undisputed, a modification purporting to release the debtor for a lesser amount is unenforceable for lack of consideration. When the party making the payment has an honest dispute about the debt, he may be able to bargain for reduced payment as a settlement. Similarly, if the debtor can do some payment that is earlier than due or on some different terms, a court may respect the bargained for payment as a settlement.

Claims Proved to Be Invalid

In some situations, parties bargain for something that later turns out to have no value. In some cases such dealings are analyzed under the argument of mistake, which we take up in Chapter 6. In many cases, contracts that would have been vulnerable to invalidation at early common law are enforced by modern courts. One important point that should be made here is that the time for judging a contract is at the time the parties entered the contract. The reason for this is easy to see. Often parties know that there is a risk involved in the contract. They may be drilling for oil and hit a dry hole. The fact that their hopes and expectations were disappointed does not relieve either party of their obligations under the contract. The fact that the contract failed to bear fruit does not mean that the parties are excused from their obligations under the contract. Contracts often involve risks and assumptions. One or both parties may be disappointed by the end result of the contract. This does not mean the contract is unenforceable. Generally speaking the law leaves the losses of contracts where they fall rather than saving either party from the risk set in motion by the contract.

In some cases parties argue that a court should not enforce a promise because the basis for the claim later proved to be invalid. Sometimes, a court has held the claim invalid. One party may argue that if the claim was invalid it was also invalid as consideration. This conclusion does not follow according to the law, however.

Two points will clarify the rule. First, as in all cases, consideration can be very minor so long as the parties bargained for something for each side of the deal. Second, courts judge consideration at the time the parties enter the contract. Courts measure consideration at the time of the transaction. There is also a subjective element in the test since courts will not enforce a claim when they find that the party seeking enforcement was not in good faith. In other words, the plaintiff in an action on the promise must convince the court that he held a good faith belief at the time he entered the contract that he had a legitimate claim that he could bring in a court.

Even though a claim may later be proved to be invalid, surrendering the claim may be held to be consideration for a settlement so long as the party who surrenders the claim has a good faith belief in the validity of the claim.

Rescission

The doctrine of consideration applies to a *rescission* of a contract. Generally, parties have the power to undo what they have the power to do. Since parties can create a contract they can also destroy their contract. In fact you can think of a rescission as a new contract to do away with a contractual obligation. The parties each get something and give up something. Each gives up what he would have received under the contract and each gains the right not to perform under the contract. The rescission releases each party from his obligations under the contract, destroying the obligations each owed the other. The contract no longer exists. Parties sometimes refer to this as "buying their peace."

Conclusion

The doctrine of consideration plays an important role in the analysis of contract law and the teaching of contract law. This is because it is important to be able to understand this foundational element in the area. In most cases in practice, however, the requirement is not controversial. It is easy to see that the requirement of consideration exists. Consideration is found in the bargain of the transfer of money for something. Consideration is found when the parties agree to transfer money for diamonds, money for a car, money for the haircut, and money for property, services or rights. Yet understanding the subject is important in understanding the rest of contract law. Contracts courses focus on the areas where difficulties occur and arguments arise that no contract exists. This focus and the difficulty of these unusual cases should not be taken to mean that consideration is a difficult issue in general, however. It is generally clear in practice.

Checkpoints

- The law distinguishes between agreements of exchange (contracts) and agreements to make gratuitous transfers (gifts). The tool used to do this is consideration.

- A promise is enforceable as a contract if it is given in exchange for other consideration.

- Consideration is the benefit received by the promisor, or the detriment suffered by the promisee, so long as the benefit or detriment is bargained for.

- There is no requirement that the consideration on each side be of equal value. Courts do not invalidate contracts merely because the consideration received by one party is disproportionate to that received by the other.

- Consideration that is a fake or sham will not ordinarily make a promise enforceable. An illusory promise cannot serve as consideration.

- A promise that reserves to the promisor sole discretion as to whether to perform is illusory.

- A benefit already received or a detriment already incurred cannot normally serve as consideration for a subsequent promise.

- A sense of moral obligation is not sufficient consideration to support a promise. Nor is simple love, affection, or a desire to help another consideration.

- Surrender of a claim known to be invalid cannot ordinarily serve as consideration. Surrender of a claim can be consideration when it is not clearly invalid. Courts refer to this as a "doubtful" claim.

- Performing a duty that you already have a legal obligation to do will not ordinarily serve as consideration for a new promise. Additional duties or changes in performance of the legal duty undertaken in good faith, however, can serve as consideration.

- Consideration in a contract may be furnished by or received by third parties.

Chapter 6

Defenses and Obstacles to Performance Liability

Roadmap

- Introduction
- Strict Liability
- The Pivotal Concept of Consent
- Fraud and Misrepresentation
- Negligent Misrepresentation
- Non-disclosure
- Facts, Opinions, and Predictions
- Promissory Fraud
- Duress, Force, Threat, and Other Unfair Advantage
- Threats to Prosecute or Breach the Contract
- Undue Influence
- Mistake
- Two Categories of Mistake
- Bilateral Mistake (Mutual Mistake)
- Unilateral Mistake
- Relevance of Fault to a Claim of Mistake
- Experts
- Impossibility and Impracticability
- Examples of Impossibility and Impracticability
- Relevance of Fault to a Claim of Impracticability
- Requirement of Objective Impossibility
- The Modern Approach
- Actual Impossibility or Actual Impracticability
- Impracticability under the UCC

- Change of Market Price
- Temporary or Partial Impracticability
- Duty to Notify Contract Partner of Impracticability
- Frustration of Purpose
- Failure of Purpose for the Recipient
- Existing Impracticability or Frustration
- Comparison of Existing Impracticability or Frustration with Mistake
- Insecurity, Modification, and Impracticability
- International Sale of Goods
- Economic Analysis
- Risk Allocation
- Conditions and Contingencies
- Rescission, Avoidance, and Reformation

Introduction

This Chapter takes up some of the reasons a court might refuse enforcement of a contract. Of course a court will refuse to enforce a contract if it finds defects in the formation process or other fundamental flaws. Formation is discussed in Chapter 4. This chapter focuses on types of defenses that will provide a basis for refusing to enforce a contract even when it meets the basic requirements of the mechanics of a contract (offer, acceptance, and consideration). Contracts can be found to be unenforceable for a wide variety of reasons, including fraud and misrepresentation, mistake, impossibility (impracticability) and frustration of purpose. Problems that render a contract unenforceable can result from the mental impairment or a lack of capacity of a party or from improper conduct of one or both parties. Such problems include duress, violations of public policy, and contracts that violate the law or result in a tort.

Obstacles to performance often occur after the parties enter a contract. Such obstacles may make performing more time-consuming and more costly. Thus, one party will profit less than he believed at the time he entered the contract. In fact, the obstacles could mean that the performing party actually loses money on the deal rather than making a profit. As a general rule, the fact that a contract turns out to be more difficult to perform than anticipated does not justify a refusal to perform. There are exceptions to this general rule, of course. These exceptions form the law of Excuse of Performance: mistake, impossibility (impracticability), and frustration. The law relating to all of these types of obstacles applies a reasonableness standard to the parties' disputes. If a party thoroughly investigates the costs of performing before entering a contract she reduces the likelihood of encountering obstacles after the contract is formed. It is impossible to prevent all problems that might develop, however.

It is useful to pair the concept of mistake with other bases for avoiding an obligation such as duress, misrepresentation, and unconscionability. We chose to combine coverage of mistake with the obstacles to performance because of the strong similarities between these doctrines. The three types of obstacles to performance employ similar analysis.

Obstacles may provide a basis for excusing performance in extreme cases. When the party resisting enforcement brings a successful claim for excuse, the effect is the same as a defense. Courts excuse or forgive the performance or reform the contract, relieving that party of liability for breach. Courts excuse performance under the Doctrine of Mistake when the burden is sufficiently significant and the parties (or, in some circumstances, one party) held a mistaken belief about a material fact to the contract. The related Doctrines of Impossibility and Frustration deal with unforeseen change of circumstances that also involve a basic assumption of the contract. These excuses generally arise after the parties entered the contract. The Doctrine of Frustration applies when the purpose of the contract is frustrated and has no value to the recipient. Impracticability, impossibility, and frustration are all grounds for discharging an obligation because an obstacle to performance has occurred after the parties have entered a contract. In rare cases, impracticability or frustration existing at the time of the contract may provide a basis for forgiving performance. Such cases are similar to mistake. Perhaps the main distinction between the two situations relates to the nature of the problem. The Doctrine of Mistake generally deals with a mistake relating to facts. Impracticability and frustration may relate to the expense of performing rather than actual impossibility of performance.

Strict Liability

The general rule of contract liability is Strict Liability. This means that when someone fails to perform under a contract that party is liable for damages without regard to fault. Thus, a person can be in breach of contract even though he was not negligent or wrongful in his conduct. The *Restatement (Second)* of Contracts introduction to the topic of Impracticability of Performance and Frustration of Purpose makes this point with reference to the Latin phrase associated with this foundational point:

Contract liability is strict liability. It is an accepted maxim that *pacta sunt servanda*, contracts are to be kept. The obligor is therefore liable in damages for breach of contract even if he is without fault and even if circumstances have made the contract more burdensome or less desirable than he had anticipated.

Accordingly, courts ordinarily do not remake the deal for the disappointed party or protect the disappointed party from his failure to allocate risks. In other words, a court should hold the parties to their deal except when extraordinary circumstances justify a departure from this general rule. The exceptions to this view constitute the law of mistake, impossibility, impracticability, and frustration.

The Pivotal Concept of Consent

In some situations, the law recognizes that a party's expression of consent does not constitute true consent. A clear example of the lack of true consent is found in cases of fraud. The party who agreed to the deal in the case of fraud did not agree to the actual deal but, rather, to the misrepresented bargain. In cases in which a court finds the party resisting enforcement did not truly give consent, it may excuse the party from the obligation. Generally this result occurs because the party resisting enforcement established a defense to the contract. Ordinarily defenses are raised by defendants. The defendant wishes to escape the consequences of the contract after they have been sued by plaintiffs. Defenses may also be raised by plaintiffs who seek to undo a particular transaction and get their money or property returned. We will explore some of the numerous grounds for and defenses that exist for invalidating a contract or refusing enforcement of a contract. When parties with capacity to contract enter an agreement that is supported by consideration, we can say that they have entered a contract. Defenses to enforcement may mean that one party cannot enforce the contract or that neither party can enforce. This state of affairs leads some courts and scholars to treat the situation as one in which no contract exists even though the structure of a contract is present. Others view the situation as one in which the contract is unenforceable. In other words, the contract is formed but one or both parties are not able to enforce the contract in court. Parties may raise a defense to enforcement of a contract, or they may fail to raise it. They may fail to bring it simply because they did not think about it. In such a case, a court is likely to enforce the promise. Also, when defects in the contracting process are present, they may be insufficiently important to amount to a defense to enforcement. In other words, matters of degree do matter in contract law. Not every shortfall in disclosure of information or every case of unequal bargaining power will relieve a disadvantaged party of the obligations created by the deal. Parties often accept contract terms that are less than desirable and that they dislike because they want the overall deal. Whether it is an overpriced soft drink at a football game or an outrageously high price for a work of art, one option to terms that are onerous to one party is to reject the deal. Unless the court asked to refuse enforcement sees the disadvantaged party as being essentially without recourse in an important matter or fundamental need, it is unlikely to hold that the contract is unenforceable.

In some consumer contracts the point seems particularly hard to accept. If you want to take a cruise, you may have to agree to a forum selection clause. This means that you would not be able to bring a claim against the cruise company except in the forum (jurisdiction or court) it has selected. If you purchase a computer with an arbitration clause in the terms of the sale, you probably will not be able to bring a claim against the manufacturer in court. You will need to bring your claim in the arbitration setting indicated in the contract. The arbitration agreement forecloses the opportunity to litigate claims before a court. The fact that you need a computer and cannot get one without giving up the right to litigate claims in court has been insufficient to convince most courts that the terms agreed to in the contract should not be enforced. Insurance companies sometimes also include arbitration clauses in their policies. Typically, courts hold that the disadvantaged party could have rejected the deal and entered a contract with a different provider. Of course, as a practical matter, no other vendor or provider may have offered the service or good without an arbitration clause. Economists say that if this creates a significant problem for consumers the market will respond, making it possible for people who want to be able to litigate claims to pay a premium and retain the right to bring a claim in court rather than in arbitration. Parties may not have an alternative without the offending clause, however. In contracts that are the subject of actual bargaining, both parties to the transaction have the same right to insist on terms. Agreeing to the other party's particular terms unwillingly does not affect the fact that the party's consent is deemed to be voluntary. Courts have extended this point to form contracts. Form contracts are ones that are set by the vendor or dominant party by offering a form to each customer. This means that the consumer will either do without a computer or accept the terms offered in the marketplace. Thus, customers will need to accept the price or do without the computer. Likewise, it follows that customers will need to accept the inclusion of terms such as arbitration or go without the computer. This analysis follows from the application of the bargain principles to the consumer context even though true bargaining may not exist in this context.

When the party's consent was obtained by force, threat, or other compulsion courts will set aside the contract and will not enforce the obligations against the party who was deceived or influenced. These include the defenses of duress and undue influence. When a party induced the consent of the other party by lies, misrepresentations, or failures to disclose important information, the court may accept the defense to enforcement on the ground of fraud, misrepresentation, or non-disclosure. In some situations one or both parties were operating under a significant mistake of fact. These are the defenses of mutual mistake and unilateral mistake. Additionally, a court may accept the defense of unconscionability even though no compulsion or misrepresentation or mistake was present. The defense of unconscionability may apply when the transaction is patently unfair as a matter of the process or substance of the deal.

Fraud and Misrepresentation

A court may refuse to enforce a promise if the party seeking enforcement knowingly made a false statement of fact, intending that the other party rely on the statement. Indeed, even the fact that the party made the statement without intent to mislead will not necessarily mean the claim of fraud will fail. Even innocent and unintentional misrepresentations may serve as a defense. When a misrepresentation is intentional, it may serve as a defense even when the fact misrepresented is not material to the transaction and even if there is no injury to the other party. Additionally, the party harmed by the misrepresentation may have an action in tort as well as contract. From a contract perspective, the party who relied on a false statement did not truly consent to the deal since he did not have true knowledge of some important aspect of the deal. If someone is induced to enter into a contract based on deliberately false statements by the other party, he did not truly consent to the transaction. The defrauded party therefore has a right to escape liability under the contract. The statement may be literally true and yet the basis for a defense if the defendant was reasonable in relying on a misleading statement that was material, meaning that it related to some significant aspect of the contract.

The distinction between a misrepresentation that results in no formation of a contract, and a mutual mistake, which provides a ground for avoidance of a contract or reformation of the contract, can be found by comparing *Restatement Section 20* and *Restatement Sections 152* and *153*.

A false statement may be made with no intent to mislead. Nevertheless, even such an innocent misstatement may provide a basis for a defense to an enforcement action.

► Buyer of a house asks the seller if the house is infested with termites. The seller says there are no termites. Even if seller believed that this was true, the law of the state may create an obligation on the seller to inspect for termites and to respond to questions about termites knowledgeably. In such a case, even if the seller did not know the statement was false, a court may allow rescission of the contract on the basis of the false information.

As in the case of fraud, the party alleging the misrepresentation must have believed the misstatement, and must be relied on. If the party resisting enforcement on the basis of fraud or misrepresentation did not believe the statement and entered the contract anyway, the court will not rescue that party from the deal. It really cannot be said that the party was mislead or lacked sufficient information to consent in that situation.

Negligent Misrepresentation

For some purposes, even a non-intentional misrepresentation may have legal consequences. For example, at common law some jurisdictions established that either an intentional or negligent misrepresentation of fact may be a basis for estoppel. We will discuss estoppel and its relation to the modern action based on reliance. Some courts have rejected the concept of negligence in this context as contradictory to the intentional nature of misrepresentation. Other courts have recognized negligent misrepresentation in various contexts. The elements required for the tort of negligent misrepresentation include a showing that the defendant owed a duty of care to plaintiff. Defendant made a false statement negligently to the plaintiff, intending that plaintiff would act on the statement and knowing that plaintiff was likely to rely on the statement. Of course the plaintiff must also show that he did act in reliance on the statement and as a result suffered a loss.

Courts have accepted negligent misrepresentation as a way around the lack of privity of contract between the plaintiff and the defendant. For example, the absence of a contract between a real estate agent and a sublessee of property may not bar the sublessee's claim for negligent misrepresentation against the agent when the agent gave detailed information about the property to the sublessee. The claim of negligent misrepresentation often accompanies a claim of non-disclosure, our next topic of discussion.

Non-disclosure

The failure of a party to disclose a fact may also provide a defense to a contract. If a court finds that a party had a duty to disclose information and failed to disclose facts, it may allow a remedy for the party harmed for the failure to disclose. The traditional common law rule is that a party to a contract has no duty to disclose information to the other party unless the other party asked a question that elicited an answer. Statutory requirements and other changes in the law trump the traditional principle of caveat emptor ("let the buyer beware"). While the general rule relating to disclosure remains the same, courts recognize significant exceptions to this rule.

This duty to disclose can arise from the relationship between the parties or from the law. An example of the duty to disclose arising from law occurs in some jurisdictions that require a seller to disclose the presence of termites. The terms of the statute control in this setting since the statute sets forth the duty and the method for fulfilling the duty. For example, many states (particularly states in the southern part of the country, in which termite problems are common) have statutes that require disclosure of termites and of termite treatments and contracts with termite companies such as Terminex. An example of a relationship that might give a basis for a court to refuse to enforce the contract might be the case of a guardian and a ward of the guardian. The court dealing with this situation might find that the guardian had a duty to advise the ward of everything he knew about the property. This is because of the relationship of trust that exists between a guardian and his ward.

Another significant exception is concealment. Where a party not only fails to disclose the problem but takes active steps to disguise it, the party will be liable for non-disclosure. For example, if Seller knows his house has termite damage and, rather than revealing the problem to a potential buyer, Seller covers the evidence of termite damage, he has taken active steps to deceive the buyer. For example, Seller might move a chest to cover the damage or cover it with wallpaper. By covering up evidence of the problem Seller is misrepresenting the true nature of the house.

Courts also recognize half-truths as a type of misrepresentation. Even if a party's statements are true from a literal standpoint, the choice of giving some information and omitting other information can create a misimpression and can be held by a court to amount to a misrepresentation.

> ▸ Seller and Buyer are negotiating over the sale of Seller's house. Buyer inquires whether there is a termite problem with the house. Seller says, "We had a problem several years ago, but the problem was treated and

everything was repaired." This is, in fact, true. What seller does not say is that there has been a second infestation and termites are currently present in the house.

Here, what Seller says is literally true, but the words fail to give a full picture. Thus, the response is misleading. If Seller had remained silent, there would not be a misrepresentation. Of course if Seller remains silent, the Buyer would be concerned that he did not receive an answer. Seller's statement, while literally true, implied that there were no present problems with the house, which is not accurate.

> ▶ While he is showing a house to a prospective buyer, Seller, pounds on the interior wall of the house and states: "This is cedar, the most termite resistant wood in the world." Even if Buyer has made no inquiry and the statement about cedar is true, a court may see it as a half truth and thus, a misrepresentation if in fact the house has a termite problem. Seller created an impression in Buyer's mind that the house did not have termites when in fact it did have a problem.

Misrepresentation may arise in another situation where a party has made a true statement but subsequently discovers information which makes that statement false. For example, if Seller truthfully tells Buyer that the house has never had a termite problem and that it is currently free from termites, a court may find that Seller has a duty to correct this misstatement if he later learns that the house does in fact have a termite infestation. The court's decision would not change based on whether the termites had infested the house at the time the Seller made the statement or the infestation occurred later.

The starting place of the concept of discovering information is that each party has an obligation to do its own research and due diligence and to seek out information relating to the deal. Most of the research will simply be questions asked by buyer of the seller. If the seller has a continuing economic interest in the enterprise, it is likely the seller will also ask questions.

The general rule that each party is responsible for seeking information rather than simply expecting the other party to deliver all the relevant information still exists in today's legal world; it is by no means the end of the analysis, however. Modern courts are more likely than courts of the distant past to find that a seller had an obligation to reveal information about defects that a buyer could not be expected to see in the ordinary course of inspection. Thus, modern courts may find a duty to reveal "latent" defects in property or goods. The difficulty of discovering the defect and the gravity of the danger posed by the defect are factors that may influence a court. Defects that are apparent or are discoverable with casual or easy investigation are less likely to give rise to a duty of disclosure.

Some state statutes require disclosure of certain defects such as the existence of termite infestation, radon, and lead paint. In such cases, the duty to disclose information is clear. In buying real estate today, most states require formal disclosure statements by sellers. Failure to make a required disclosure may constitute misrepresentation as well as a violation of the statute.

> ▸ Manufacturer of a popular car states that problems arising from the braking mechanism of the car are not the result of a faulty computer but, rather, are the result of a sticky mechanical systems. In such a case the car company failed to live up to its legal obligations to reveal dangerous conditions. Knowingly hiding a dangerous defect can also result in liability under applicable regulations as well as under contract law.

Facts, Opinions, and Predictions

Generally, courts require a showing that a misrepresentation involves a statement of fact, rather than a statement of opinion or a prediction. This rule has exceptions and flexibility, however, and you should not assume that this defense will be effective. Opinions reflect a party's own estimate of such things as quality and value. Different parties will have different opinions as to the quality or value of any particular item. Your intuition will tell you that the following statements lack substance or factual value: "This house will make a lovely home for your family." "This car is a honey." "You could not do better than this price in this neighborhood." Such statements are mere opinion and do not amount to actionable misrepresentation. Similarly, predictions are estimates of the likelihood that certain events will occur in the future. Since the future is inherently unknowable, a prediction is not ordinarily regarded as a misrepresentation.

Statements of law are not usually regarded as representations that give rise to an action for misrepresentation. It is often said that everyone is charged with knowing the law. Since everyone is assumed to know the law, a statement like, "The Zoning Rules would allow you to build two more lots on that property," will not ordinarily form the basis of a misrepresentation claim.

Opinions, predictions, and statements of law may sometimes be treated as statements of fact, in some circumstances. For example, when the person making the representation is an expert in the field, a statement of opinion as to the quality or value of the property may be viewed as a statement of fact. Where the party making the misrepresentation has superior access to the facts on which the opinion is based, the opinion may be treated as a statement of fact.

A lawyer's opinion about the law generally will not be protected within the category of "statement of opinion" exception. If the lawyer provides an opinion of the law that is inaccurate, he will not find protection from a claim that everyone is charged with knowing the law. After all, the lawyer's legal opinion is the precise thing the contracting party bargained for in retaining the lawyer. Another important principle comes into play here and provides some help to lawyers. It is that lawyers ordinarily do not guarantee a particular result. Rather they contract to render competent services.

Promissory Fraud

Ordinarily, a statement of what a party intends to do in the future is merely a statement of opinion or a prediction and, thus, does not support a claim of fraud. People routinely change their minds. Moreover, in every contract that involves a promise of future conduct, the promissor is representing that she will carry out the promise. It is possible that a person making a promise is also engaging in misrepresentation. An English judge explained the cause of action: "The state of a man's mind is as much a fact as the state of his digestion."

Not every breach amounts to promissory fraud, of course, and the area of promissory fraud presents difficult cases, often because of the issue of intention.. The question in determining whether a breach also amounts to promissory fraud is whether the promisor intended at the time of the making of the promise to refuse to perform. Because this fact involves intention, it is inherently difficult to establish. If the plaintiff is able to prove the intent not to perform, the court may also find the defendant guilty of a misrepresentation. In other words, a statement about current intentions can be found to be a fact and a misrepresentation.

> ▶ Giant Corp. signs a contract with Steelco Inc. under which it promises to buy all of Steelco's steel output for a period of five years. At the time it signs the contract, Giant intends to breach the contract as part of plan to prevent its competitor, Acme Products, from getting access to steel. Acme goes bankrupt, and Giant breaches the contract.

If plaintiff Steelco can establish that at the time Giant made the promise it knew that it did not intend to carry through with it, it misrepresented its intentions and engaged in promissory fraud.

Duress, Force, Threat, and Other Unfair Advantage

Despite the general rule that parties are accountable for the deals they enter into, courts will sometimes invalidate an obligation because of the improper influence or improper advantage-taking by a party. Duress, force, threat, and other unfair advantage are all types of conduct that courts sometimes find sufficient to overcome the general principle that parties are accountable for their promises.

Duress deprives the person who is the subject of the duress of free will. Thus, his acts are not voluntary. Since contract law requires that agreements be voluntary, courts will not enforce promises given as a result of duress. A party who assented to a contract in a state of duress should be able to avoid the contract by petitioning a court for this effect. Of course, the decision regarding whether the promise was the result of duress is a judgment that the court must make. It is not sufficient that a party asserts that he promised under duress. If the rule worked in this way, parties would have a free card to avoid any deals they later regretted by asserting they did not act with free will. The classic choice of "your money or your life," made by a robber clearly qualifies as duress. Courts deal with claims of duress in much less dramatic and clear-cut situations, however. Traditional courts have held that to constitute an instance of duress a threat must be the kind of statement would "overbear the will of a person of ordinary firmness."

Modern courts are more likely to look at the full relationship and circumstances involved in the case. They recognize people are susceptible to threats based on circumstances. Thus, courts have avoided contracts based on duress when it seems understandable to the court that the party's consent was induced by the threat—whether or not the threat would overcome a person of ordinary firmness. Modern courts continue to look for wrongful conduct by the person claimed to have engaged in duress. Such wrongful conduct generally will involve the illegitimate use of power. Thus, merely hard bargaining generally will not qualify as duress. The art dealer who says "take it or leave it" when offering a work of art at a very high price is generally within his rights and, thus, not engaging in duress, no matter how badly a collector wants a work of art. A seller who threatens to withhold performance on a different contract unless the buyer accepts an additional contract at an unusually high price may be engaging in business duress, however. Courts find business duress when one party takes advantage of the other because of circumstances of exigency.

Threats to Prosecute or Breach the Contract

Threats to prosecute a breach can create a basis for refusing enforcement of a promise. Although it may seem without risk to threaten to do something you have a right to do, some caution in the area of threats is in order. Courts find that threatening criminal prosecution is improper. Courts also find that threatening to use bring a civil suit is improper when it is made in bad faith. Courts treat such threats as a breach of the duty of good faith and fair dealing. The result of such a judgment by a court could mean that the party who made the threat is in breach of contract. If there is an element of coercion in the threat, the lawyer or party making the threat may be subject to prosecution as well as invalidation of the contract. Threats of legal action can constitute duress, particularly when the party threatening legal action uses a threat as a way of pressuring the other party into modifying the contract or complying with unusually burdensome terms. In one case, officials from a school district met with a teacher after office hours to insist that the teacher resign.

In *Austin Instrument, Inc. v. Loral Corp.*, 29 N.Y.2d 124, 272 N.E.2d 533 (N.Y. 1971), the court found a threat by a subcontractor to default on contractual commitments resulted in economic duress to the government contractor who needed parts from the subcontractor to meet commitments under a sale to the government. Loral, a manufacturer of precision machinery, had a contract with the U.S. Navy to produce radar sets. The contract included a schedule of deliveries, a liquidated damages clause for late deliveries and a cancellation clause in case of default by Loral. Loral entered a contract with Austin Instrument for precision gear components needed to produce the radar sets. As time for delivery of the radar approached, Austin threatened to cease deliveries of the parts unless Loral consented to substantial increases in the prices under the agreement. Austin's demand for increases related to both parts already delivered and parts not yet shipped. The court held that the threats by Austin constituted economic duress. The court noted that Loral faced a genuine possibility of substantial liquidated damages. Loral was under strict delivery requirements for its delivery to the U.S. Navy and had little opportunity to find an alternative source of supply for the parts.

A party who refuses to release another person's property until an agreement is reached is similarly at risk. For example, a landlord who retains property of the tenant in order to coerce a settlement or the shop that retains goods that have been repaired could run afoul of this doctrine. The old common law action relating to this conduct was called duress of goods. Like threats of criminal prosecution, the party using this tactic may face significant risks.

A troublesome type of duress involves threats to breach a contract. When one has an undisputed contractual obligation, a threat to breach the contract is wrongful. Thus, when a party refuses to carry out an existing contract unless it gets more money, and the other party is in a position where it has no real choice but to agree, a subsequent agreement is invalid for duress. Even a threat to breach a contract can create risks for the party making the threat. The party who seeks to renegotiate a contract to obtain benefits not secured under the original contract bears the same type of risk of being judged to be coercive. The party who seeks a modification when there is no change in circumstances to justify a modification is engaging in risky conduct. It creates the risk of being found to be in bad faith and acting in a coercive manner. On the other hand, when a court finds that there was a reason to renegotiate, it is not likely to penalize the party seeking a change in terms of the contract.

Undue Influence

The distinction between duress and undue influence is a wavering and fine-line. This defense to contract enforcement focuses on the relationship between the parties and the conduct that one party used to influence or persuade the other to enter a contract or to modify a contract. Courts often pay attention to the relationship of trust between the parties and the problem of one party taking advantage over the other party. When one party is a trusted adviser, such as a lawyer, teacher, physician, banker, or a guardian, courts are apt to be particularly protective of the party who relies on the judgment or advice of that party. Each of the roles named includes an actual fiduciary relationship or at least an air of a fiduciary relationship, which makes the court scrutinize the relationship and the actions of the dominant party. In a case found in some books, a couple purchased a horse from another couple who had been in the business of buying, selling, and training horses. The purchasers turned down a possible purchase of a different horse because of advice of the sellers. Purchasers and sellers became friends during their association based on sharing of information and experiences with horses. The purchasers intended to breed the horse, which they learned after purchase was lame. Though not based on a formal relationship such as a guardian and ward or a teacher and student, the court took into consideration the relationship of trust that had developed between the buyers and sellers in this case. Even a family relationship, such as husband and wife or parent and child may cause special scrutiny of a transaction by a court.

Not surprisingly, courts are particularly protective of someone who lacks full mental capacity. Even if that person is adjudged to be competent, his reliance on advice of a trusted adviser (a lawyer, doctor or guardian) may mean that a contract entered by the dependent party with the adviser is subject to avoidance or alteration by the court. If a dominant party takes advantage of the dependent or impaired party (or even appears to do so) the court may determine the transaction is voidable. A housekeeper comes into the home of her aging relative at the request of the relative. After a year or so of serving as a caretaker, the housekeeper convinces the aging relative to change her will to give all of her property to the housekeeper. The will or contract may be challenged on the ground of undue influence. Additionally, criminal charges against the dominant party are also a possibility.

Mistake

A mistake is simply as "a belief that is not in accord with the facts." The first illustration to *Restatement (Second) of Contracts Section 151* makes this point. Both courts and the *Restatement* use this simple definition. The Doctrine of Mistake provides a basis for excusing a party from an obligation under a contract without payment of damages. Successfully asserting mistake achieves a kind of defense to a claim of breach of contract. The doctrine deals with unknown or unallocated risks when some obstacle to performance existed at the time the parties entered the contract. A party (generally the defendant) seeks to be relieved of the duty to perform on the basis of mistake. The mistake can be mutual or unilateral, depending on the circumstances and evidence.

The importance of the meaning of the term is that it does not refer to a mistake in judgment or to disappointment. While it is not unusual for people to regret having entered a contract or to regret some terms in the contract, "buyer's remorse," or "seller's remorse" is not the issue dealt with by the law of mistake. "Wow, entering that contract was really a mistake!" is not the kind of mistake that provides a basis for excuse under contract law. The first illustration to *Restatement (Second) of Contracts Section 151* makes this point.

▶ A contracts with B to raise and float B's boat which has run aground on a reef. At the time of making the contract, A believes that the sea will remain calm until the work is completed. Several days later, during a sudden storm, the boat slips into deep water and fills with mud, making it more difficult for A to raise it. Although A may have shown poor judgment in making the contract, there was no mistake of either

A or B, and the rules stated in this Chapter do not apply.... If, however, the boat had already slipped into deep water at the time the contract was made, although they both believed that it was still on the reef, there would have been a mistake of both A and B.

In this illustration, the parties may have made a mistaken judgment about the likelihood that the ocean would create an obstacle to performance of the contract. If the boat is in the water at the time the parties enter the contract, they are contracting with reference to a belief that is not in accord with the facts and the Doctrine of Mistake may apply. If the obstacle arises after the contract, the Doctrines of Impossibility (Impracticability) or Frustration may apply. To succeed under a mistake theory, the defendant must show a mistake of fact. It is a mistake about the state of affairs rather than a party's mistake in judgment. These arguments arise when the party who resists enforcement of a contract argues that a mistake was not his fault. Essentially, the mistake is so significant to the contract that the contract should not be enforced. It was something outside his control. Defendant argues that if he had known the true state of affairs he would not have entered the contract. In a sense, the defendant who asserts the defense of mistake is arguing that he did not assent to the contract because he did not know some important fact upon which the provisions of the contract rely. To put it another way, his assent was actually to a contract that does not exist because that state of affairs that he assumed is not based on reality.

> ▶ In the famous case of *Sherwood v. Walker*, 33 N.W. 919 (1887), the parties entered a contract for the sale and purchase of a cow named Rose that both parties believed was infertile or barren. In that case, the plaintiff purchased the cow for $80 but before delivery, the seller learned that Rose was "with calf" or pregnant. Seller refused to deliver the cow, arguing that the cow he sold was a cow different in kind than the one that actually existed. Thus, the mistake in the transaction is that the facts did not comport with the beliefs of the parties. The Court agreed with this analysis and voided the contract, excusing Seller from his obligation on the basis of mistake.

Two Categories of Mistake

The Doctrine of Mistake is, in reality, two separate doctrines: 1) Unilateral Mistake and 2) Bilateral Mistake. Bilateral Mistake is also called "Mutual Mistake." These defenses are dealt with separately in *Restatement (Second) of Con-*

tracts Sections 152 and *153*. Unilateral mistake is a mistake made by only one party to the contract. Bilateral mistake occurs when both parties hold an incorrect assumption about some material fact or facts relating to performance.

When both parties misunderstand the material facts in negotiating a deal, it is possible for their misunderstanding to prevent a contract from being formed. Section 20 of the *Restatement (Second) of Contracts* sets forth the rule on this issue, indicating that a misunderstanding can result in the failure to form a contract when the parties attach materially different meanings to their manifestations and neither party knows or has reason to know the meaning attached by the other. The different meanings do not need to be a mistake of fact for this effect to occur. Such a misunderstanding of the meaning the parties hold could also arise from mistakes about material facts that the parties believe apply to the contract. The old common law used the phrase "meeting of the minds" to express the assent of the parties to a deal. Although that phrase is nowadays regarded as misleading in the sense that it suggests a subjective agreement, it can help you remember that it is possible for parties to fail to have a contract because the parties have fundamentally different deals in their minds. Don't let the use of the term "meeting of the minds" mislead you into thinking that contract law requires a subjective "meeting of the minds," however.

Bilateral Mistake (Mutual Mistake)

The Doctrine of Mutual Mistake allows a party to avoid an obligation when both parties held a mistaken belief at the time of contracting. Section 152 of the *Restatement (Second) of Contracts* sets forth the doctrine:

> Where a mistake of both parties at the time a contract was made as to a basic assumption on which the contract was made has a material effect on the agreed exchange of performances, the contract is voidable by the adversely affected party unless he bears the risk of the mistake under the rule stated in § 154.

Parsing this statement reveals four elements that defendant must establish to avoid a contract obligation on the basis of mistake: (1) The mistake existed at the time the parties entered the contract, (2) The mistake related to a basic assumption that the parties held, (3) The mistake has a material effect on the agreed exchange of performances, (4) The adversely affected party did not bear the risk of the mistake under the rule stated in § 154.

The first element means that the issue of mistake is limited as a matter of time. If the mistake did not exist at the time the parties entered the contract, one of the other doctrines relating to excuse of impossibility or frustration may apply, but the Doctrine of Mistake does not. The second element means that the mistake cannot relate to a trivial or attenuated issue. It must be a basic or foundational fact of the bargain. This element allows significant subjective judgment by courts deciding a claim or default of mistake. The third element, the material effect on the agreed exchange, is similarly subject to different interpretations. This element involves line-drawing by the court. Although the term "material effect" is not susceptible of precise definition, it is clear that the test anticipates that only significant mistakes should be the basis for excuse of performance. The risk of a trivial mistake is borne by the party that suffers the adverse effect of the trivial mistake. The fourth element, that the adversely affected party did not bear the risk of the mistake, is explained more fully by Section 154 of the *Restatement*:

> A party bears the risk of a mistake when
> (a) the risk is allocated to him by agreement of the parties, or
> (b) he is aware, at the time the contract is made, that he has only limited knowledge with respect to the facts to which the mistake relates but treats his limited knowledge as sufficient, or
> (c) the risk is allocated to him by the court on the ground that it is reasonable in the circumstances to do so.

Thus, Section 154 sets forth the possible ways that a risk may be allocated: (1) by contract, (2) by circumstance, and (3) by the court. One also might think of (1) and (3) as contractual and judicial allocation of risk, respectively, and of (2) as the adversely affected party's assumption of risk. The *Restatement* discussion of allocation follows the traditional approach that has resonance in other areas in addition to mistake. This breakdown of the reasons for which a party may bear a risk will remind you of ways that conditions may be created. The first situation comes out of the power of contracting. Certainly if the parties bargain about a particular risk and agree that one of them will bear that risk, a court will respect this allocation. The second situation employs common sense about risks. A party who knows that he does not have all the important facts relating to his contract naturally should recognize that he may be assuming a risk. The third situation relates the second in a way, noting that the court will decide the question based on a reasonableness approach.

Unilateral Mistake

In some cases, mistake may be a basis for excusing an obligation when only one of the parties entered the contract on the basis of a mistaken belief. You may wonder why bilateral mistake is ever argued when a mistake by one party can be a basis for excusing an obligation. Why, you might ask, would a defendant take on the additional task of showing that both parties held a mistaken belief if he could simply establish his own mistake? Since the showing for unilateral mistake will always be encompassed in the showing for mutual mistake, why not simply plead unilateral mistake and present evidence on one party only? The answer is that the standard for judging unilateral breach includes additional difficult elements, which are not included in the showing for mutual mistake. The standard for proving mistake is higher when the claim is unilateral mistake rather than mutual mistake. In addition to the elements required to show bilateral mistake, the party seeking to be excused on the basis of unilateral mistake must also prove one of the following: (1) that the other party knew or should have known of the mistake, or (2) the contract as it stands is unconscionable.

Restatement (Second) of Contracts § 153 states:

> Where a mistake of one party at the time a contract was made as to a basic assumption on which he made the contract has a material effect on the agreed exchange of performances that is adverse to him, the contract is voidable by him if he does not bear the risk of the mistake under the rule stated in § 154, and
> (a) the effect of the mistake is such that enforcement of the contract would be unconscionable, or
> (b) the other party had reason to know of the mistake or his fault caused the mistake.

As you can see, the basis of Unilateral Mistake is different from the basis for Mutual Mistake. It includes the difficult factual showing that the other party knew or had reason to know of the mistake.

Relevance of Fault to a Claim of Mistake

Although lawyers do not want the court hearing a case of mistake to find their client at fault, a finding of fault will not necessarily undermine the client's case. *Restatement (Second) of Contracts § 157* notes that "[a] mistaken party's fault in failing to know or discover the facts before making the contract does not bar him from avoidance or reformation ... unless his fault amounts to a failure to act in good faith and in accordance with reasonable standards of fair dealing." This section recognizes the significant leeway courts have in deciding claims of mistake. This is largely a matter of line-drawing. A comment to § 157

notes: "in extreme cases the mistaken party's fault is a proper ground for denying him relief for a mistake that he otherwise could have avoided." At any rate,
a court determination that the mistake should have been apparent to the party
seeking to avoid a contract is likely to deny that party relief.

Experts

In considering claims of mistake, courts may take into account the relative
knowledge and expertise of the parties. Thus, it seems likely that a court will
not excuse a mistake when the mistake relates to judgment in the area of expertise of the party claiming excuse. This intuition will not always prevail,
however. Remember that the excuse based on mistake is not about a bad judgment but about a mistake of fact.

> ▸ In *Beachcomber Coins, Inc. v. Boskett*, 400 A.2d 78 (1979), a coin
> dealer brought an action for rescission of its purchase from the de-
> fendant of a counterfeit rare coin based on mutual mistake regarding
> the genuineness of the coin. The trial court refused to grant rescis-
> sion, holding that the dealer had an obligation to investigate the gen-
> uineness. The appellate court reversed, on the basis of mutual mistake.
> Here, even though the purchaser was an expert, he was ultimately able
> to prevail on the basis of mistake. The difference of views of the two
> courts gives a sense of the difficulty of determining issues of mistake.
> When the parties include one expert and one consumer, the allocation
> of risk may be affected by this fact. Mistakes by experts are likely to
> be the basis of undoing the contract. This is not a case of courts pro-
> tecting the "little guy" in a contest with the dominant party or "big
> guy." Rather, it is an example of allocation of risk based on the presumed
> knowledge of the parties. In the case of a consumer who actually works
> a fraud on an expert, courts will rescind the contract on that basis.
> Of course, making the case that someone engaged in a fraud involves
> the difficult element of intent. This point gets us into tort law, and
> thus, outside our topic.

Impossibility and Impracticability

When parties make a "basic assumption" about their contract that is fundamental to their commitment, they may be excused from their obligations if
some supervening event destroys that basic assumption. This discussion treats

impossibility and impracticability together, noting the similarities and distinctions.

Note on Terminology—The terminology in this area has changed over time. Older cases refer to discharge of a duty on the basis of "impossibility." More recent cases use the term "impracticability" instead of the term "impossibility." By the time of the first *Restatement of the Law of Contracts*, the defense of impossibility had expanded to include impracticability based on "extreme and unreasonable difficulty, expense, injury or loss involved." In other words, courts began giving a "practical rather than a scientifically exact meaning" to the term a generation ago. Scholars and courts sometimes lump discussion of the related claim of frustration under the general category of impossibility as well.

A court has the power to discharge a contract obligation on the basis of impracticability. *Restatement (Second) of Contracts § 261* notes the discharge of a party's performance when it is "made impracticable without his fault by the occurrence of an event the non-occurrence of which was a basic assumption on which the contract was made." The most frequent cases of discharge involve death or incapacity of a person who is necessary for performance, the destruction of something necessary for performance, or a change in the law that prohibits the performance. The law does not require absolute impossibility. Like mistake, this question also involves line-drawing. "Mere unanticipated difficulty" is not enough. While courts sometimes dispute the idea that the issue of impracticability turns on a matter of degree, the question is ultimately one of line drawing. We can get a sense of this line-drawing by realizing that the degree of loss must be significant—as the comment to Section 261 of the *Restatement* puts it—it must be "well beyond the normal range" of loss that one should accept as part of the risk of the deal.

Examples of Impossibility and Impracticability

A typical example of impossibility occurs when the parties name a specific person to provide the performance, assuming that that person would be alive to provide the performance at the time specified. If that person dies before performance is due, the defense of impossibility may apply. Thus, if I promise to represent you in a lawsuit and argue in court on your behalf, I would be excused from this obligation in the event that I die before the date set for the trial. Other typical cases include (1) the sale of an item which is destroyed prior to the date of delivery; (2) the destruction of something assumed to be in existence in order for the contract to go forward; and (3) a change in the law that prohibits the performance.

You may think that this is a silly doctrine. It seems not only obvious but also irrefutable that the person cannot perform if he is dead. Certainly it is true that the dead person cannot perform. However, the legal consequences of this situation are our focus. An additional point is important as a matter of contract law. This is whether the failure to perform is a breach. Although dead people cannot perform contracts, their estates can be held for damages if the contract is not excused.

> ▶ For example, if a talent agency contracted to provide a singer for a wedding, the contract may be excused if it called for performance by a particular singer who is dead or sick at the time set for performance. If the contract did not name the singer, the agency will need to find a replacement singer in the event the intended singer died. If the singer himself entered the contract to sing personally at the event, it seems clear that the agreement included as a basic assumption that the singer would continue to live and have the ability to sing. Thus, in the contract with specific performer to sing, the death of that performer pretty clearly presents a case of the excuse of impossibility.

Relevance of Fault to a Claim of Impracticability

Unlike the area of mistake, the issue of fault plays a pivotal role in impossibility. An element of the claim of discharge by supervening impracticable is that the party's performance is made impracticable without his fault. If the party seeking a discharge based on impracticability or impossibility is shown to be at fault, a court will not accept his argument. As Section 261 of the *Restatement (Second) of Contracts* explains, discharge is appropriate when a party's performance is "made impracticable without his fault by the occurrence of an event the non-occurrence of which was a basic assumption on which the contract was made."

> ▶ Changing the facts of the English case of *Taylor v. Caldwell*, 122 Eng. Rep. 309 (Kings Bench 1863), provides a good hypothetical on the issue of fault. There the court discharged the duties of the parties under a contract for the rental of a music hall when the hall burned down before the time for performance. The Taylor case did not involve arson; at least the facts do not indicate it was arson. If the fire had been the result of arson by a party, the court would not have excused performance by the party at fault. Criminal law would come

into play when the fault of the party is also a crime, such as arson. There would be a case of arson against the party who burned the hall down.

Requirement of Objective Impossibility

Courts often note that to merit a discharge the impossibility asserted must be objectively (rather than merely subjectively) impossible or impracticable.

▶ For example the following dialogue presents a clear losing case for the party claiming impossibility as an excuse:

> Buyer: "I'm sorry I can't perform the contract because I have no money. I lost my money due to no fault of my own so you see it is impossible for me to pay."
>
> Seller: "See you in court."

Failing to have the money to pay a contract is clearly a risk assumed by the buyer who accepted the obligation to pay under the contract. Of course this does not mean that inability to pay is irrelevant to the analysis of a case. Parties who are insolvent are typically not worth suing. They will not be able to pay the judgment by the court any more than they could pay the original purchase price. It is important to note that the decision not to sue an insolvent purchaser is not an indication that the impossibility to pay provides an excuse under contract law. Rather, it is simply recognition that if the party has no money and no assets it won't be worth the expense to bring an action against him to get a judgment that will ultimately be suitable only for framing.

▶ Switching the parties in terms of who is begging off the obligation does not alter the point:

> Seller: "I'm sorry I can't perform the contract. I am over-extended. I have taken on too many jobs and it is impossible for me to do the work."
>
> Buyer: "See you in court."

Comment (e) to Restatement *(Second) of Contracts § 261* gives a softer stance on this point than is sometimes seen in decisional law. It states that "if the performance remains practicable and it is merely beyond the party's capacity to render it, he is ordinarily not discharged." While the *Restatement* rejects the use of the terms "objective" and "subjective" in this area, it continues to reflect the rationale of the common law.

The Modern Approach

"Impracticability" is the modern version of impossibility. While the shift of terminology from "impossibility" to "impracticability" reflects a more relaxed approach, do not allow this change to lead you to think that impracticability is now an easy case to make out. "Impracticability" may sound like a fancy legal term for simply saying that something is impractical. That is not the case. Performance could be impractical in the sense of being unwise or too burdensome and still fail the more rigorous test of impracticability. This test requires more than impractical performance. It requires a failure of a basic assumption of the parties. The word "impractical" (unwise or unrealistic) actually means something different from the word "impracticable" (not capable of performance), though lawyers and courts sometimes confuse these terms.

Modern courts consider whether performance has been made extraordinarily difficult or costly and whether the problem is created by the occurrence of an event the non-occurrence of which was a basic assumption on which the contract was made. This idea of non-occurrence of a basic assumption may seem like a tangled test. In reality, the rule gives a basis for courts to balance the interests of the parties and relieve a party of the contract in rare cases. The rare case in which the claim of impracticability is met includes the showing that an event has occurred that contradicts a basic assumption of the contract.

> ▶ An illustration to Section 261 of the *Restatement (Second) of Contracts* indicates that a contract to sell and deliver at a designated port that is later closed by quarantine regulations during the time set for delivery meets the test of impracticability if no commercially reasonable substitute performance is available. The result is that the duty of seller is discharged. Additionally, the duty of buyer is also discharged.

The modern version of the excuse of impracticability does not require true or actual impossibility. Courts sometimes excuse performance that has become unreasonably costly. Although the modern view (referred to as "impracticability") is a softening of the test, the softening does not relate to the requirement of the objective nature of the difficulty, however. "I cannot do this thing" remains an insufficient defense.

Actual Impossibility or Actual Impracticability

The preceding section of this chapter dealt with the fact that a court may excuse performance despite the fact that the performance may not be literally impossible. A related point taken up here is that the fact that something is actually impossible does not mean that the defendant will be excused from performance. Thus, we see that actual impossibility is neither necessary nor sufficient in all cases to prevail on this theory.

Under either the test for impossibility or impracticability, a court can award damages even if it is beyond the power of the court to require actual performance. This area of law is about who should bear the loss, not whether a contract performance can actually be rendered.

> For example, assume that Seller enters a contract to sell a unique diamond necklace to Buyer. Before delivery, Seller sells and delivers the necklace to another party for a higher price. Whether Buyer #1 can recover the necklace from Buyer #2 is not the issue for purposes of the doctrine of impossibility. That issue deals with the question of whether Buyer #2 is a bona fide purchaser. Whether or not the necklace can be reclaimed or found, Seller can be held answerable in damages for the breach of failure to deliver.

Impracticability under the UCC

The Uniform Commercial Code (UCC) provides for excuse based on impracticability. It uses slightly different terminology, calling the rule "Excuse by Failure of Presupposed Conditions." UCC 2-615 states the test for when a party's duty to perform is excused or modified. It notes that the party seeking not to perform may be relieved of the duty to perform under this section either in whole or in part. The section makes clear that the rule it announces can be altered by the parties if they contract for the seller to accept a greater obligation. This section states:

> (a) Delay in delivery or nondelivery in whole or in part by a seller who complies with paragraphs (b) and (c) is not a breach of his duty under a contract for sale if performance as agreed has been made impracticable by the occurrence of a contingency the nonoccurrence of which was a basic assumption on which the contract was made or by compliance in good faith with any applicable foreign or domestic governmental regulation or order whether or not it later proves to be invalid.

The core of this test is substantially the same as the common law test of impracticability. It could be said that the common law is substantially similar to the statute. The *Restatement (Second) of Contracts* introductory note indicates that its analysis adopts the approach of the UCC rather than the analysis of some courts that analyze the issue as one of implied terms. The defendant who is seeking excuse must establish three elements to be eligible for excuse: (1) his performance is not practicable; (2) it has been made impracticable by the occurrence of a contingency; (3) a basic assumption of the contract was the nonoccurrence of this contingency.

A separate ground for the Excuse Doctrine is that by not performing the defendant is complying in good faith with a foreign or domestic governmental regulation or order. The statute insulates the defendant from a later action that could come about if the government regulation or order is later found to be invalid. This means that the defendant is not in breach even if the regulation or order turns out to be invalid. If the party makes these showings, the result under the provision is that his non-performance or partial performance is not a breach. The statute uses essentially the same language as the common law, stating that the party is not in breach of his duty when performance "has been made impracticable by the occurrence of a contingency the nonoccurrence of which was a basic assumption on which the contract was made."

Subsections (b) and (c) note related duties of the party who meets the test of impracticability. Although that party is excused from performing, he must act reasonably in the context. If some goods are available, the excused party must allocate these goods among the buyers.

Change of Market Price

Ordinarily a change in market price will not be a basis for a successful claim of impossibility or impracticability. This is because the reason for entering a contract is generally to lock in an agreed price. In fact, allocating the risk of shifts in market price is one of the basic purposes of the contract. In rare circumstances, however, a change in price may be involved in a successful claim of impracticability. If the parties assumed facts that turned out not to be true and that influenced the market price, the situation may present a successful defense.

The comment to UCC 2-615 gives the following illustration:

> A severe shortage of raw materials or of supplies due to a contingency such as war, embargo, local crop failure, unforeseen shutdown of major shutdown of major sources or the like, which either causes a marked increase in cost or altogether prevents the seller from securing supplies necessary to his performance, is within the contemplation of this section.

When the contract is silent about the allocation of the risk, a court may find a basis for the defense of impossibility or impracticability. The comment's reference to a case being "within the contemplation of this section," means that the examples meet the test of impracticability. While a price rise is not by itself a basis for impossibility, the party suffering a significant financial loss as a consequence of a price shift may be able to make out a defense of impracticability in situations like those noted in the comment.

Temporary or Partial Impracticability

Subsection (b) of UCC Section 2-615 states the duty of a party to allocate goods fairly when he faces temporary or partial impracticability. The section gives specific guidance on fairness in this context, giving significant leeway and protection to the seller. It specifically allows the seller to include regular customers even though they are not in the contract at issue. It also recognizes his right to allocate some goods to himself to meet his own requirements for further manufacture: "Where the causes mentioned in paragraph (a) affect only a part of the seller's capacity to perform, he must allocate production and deliveries among his customers but may at his option include regular customers not then under contract as well as his own requirements for further manufacture."

The seller has leeway to allocate quantities of goods when circumstances create impracticability.

Duty to Notify Contract Partner of Impracticability

Subsection (c) of UCC Section 2-615 describes the excused seller's duty to notify the buyer of the situation of impracticability and the fact that there will be a delayed delivery, partial delivery, or non-delivery. It states: "The seller must notify the buyer seasonably that there will be delay or nondelivery and, when allocation is required under paragraph (b), of the estimated quota thus made available for the buyer."

Frustration of Purpose

The Doctrine of Frustration gives the court the power to relieve the defendant of the promise to pay for a performance when that performance no longer has value for him. The loss in value must be fundamental to an assumption of the parties. Frustration of purpose is an even more difficult basis for excuse than impossibility or impracticability. Like the Doctrine of Impracticability, the Doctrine of Frustration of Purpose is an exception to the rule that contracts are to be performed: *pacta sunt servanda*. This narrow exception to the general rule that promises are enforceable is the argument for the party who promises to pay for a performance under the contract. At this point in the analysis of this argument it is good to remember that the fact that a contract obligation is more burdensome than anticipated is not a basis for refusing to perform. This is true when the party seeking release from a contractual obligation is the one providing performance (building the house for example). It is also true when the party seeking to be excused is the one paying for the performance (the purchaser of the house, for example). Likewise, the fact that the value of the performing is less than anticipated does not destroy the obligation. The fact that the builder of the house will make less profit than anticipated does not mean he can walk away from the contract with impunity. Likewise, the fact that the purchaser of the house no longer wants the house is not a basis for walking away from the contract with impunity. One way of understanding this doctrine and its narrow range is to consider the fact that the party who no longer wants a performance or says it has no value to him assumed the risk that he would have a change of mind by entering the contract.

Failure of Purpose for the Recipient

A review of the cases in this area reveals that the defense is one used by the recipient to the contract (the paying party). Frustration cases present a situation when the party who promised to pay for the performance seeks release from the contract. As we have seen above, courts are reluctant to relieve either party of the promised performance. This reluctance is strongest in the area of frustration. The recipient's duty to pay is clearly a risk that the recipient accepts. The defense of frustration does not permit inability to pay as a reason for excuse of performance. Rather, the party defending on the basis of frustration is arguing that performance is of no value to him. The performance of the contract has no value for him because of the failure of a basic assumption of the contracting parties. In other words, after contracting, something happened that made the contract worthless and the recipient did not bear the risk of such occurrence.

The exception of frustration of purpose applies when the court is convinced that something has occurred that makes the contract valueless to the party seeking excuse.

▶ The English case of *Krell v. Henry* illustrates the situation and the argument. In that case, the plaintiff hired a flat (an apartment) that was located along the parade route for the coronation of Edward VII. Unfortunately, the coronation was postponed because Edward fell ill. Mr. Henry, the recipient of the contract (the party who promised to pay) no longer wanted the apartment. Mr. Henry refused to pay. He argued that the entire purpose for the contract was to watch the coronation parade. Now there would be no parade and, thus, the contract was of no value to him. Clearly there is nothing impossible about performance here. The party who had rented the flat could still rent it and the recipient can pay. There is no obstacle to performance at all. Rather, the performance is merely of no value to the recipient.

The basic goal of this defense is to convince the court that it makes no sense to hold the parties to the contract, because the purpose of the contract no longer exists. Just as in the case of the defense of impossibility or impracticability, if the parties allocated the risk of the nonoccurrence of a basic assumption of the contract, the court will accept that allocation. The court's decision regarding whether to forgive performance involves an interpretation of the contract. As with impracticability, simple unprofitability is not the test for frustration. In fact, significant losses will not necessarily make out the case for excuse.

▶ Illustration 6 to Section 265 makes the point powerfully with a case about A:

6. A leases a gasoline station to B. A change in traffic regulations so reduces B's business that he is unable to operate the station except at a substantial loss. B refuses to make further payments of rent. If B can still operate the station, even though at such a loss, his principal purpose of operating a gasoline station is not substantially frustrated. B's duty to pay rent is not discharged, and B is liable to A for breach of contract. The result would be the same if substantial loss were caused instead by a government regulation rationing gasoline or a termination of the franchise under which B obtained gasoline.

Such cases are not unusual since cities do make changes in traffic regulations, which can have significant impacts on nearby businesses. A change in the facts affecting the reason for the loss does not necessarily change the result. The fact that it was a government regulation that makes the performance difficult does not necessarily provide a basis for excuse. A government prohibition is more likely to set the stage for the excuse, unless a party guaranteed that no change in the law would occur.

> ▶ Illustration 4 gives a clear case:
> A leases neon sign installations to B for three years to advertise and illuminate B's place of business. After one year, a government regulation prohibits the lighting of such signs. B refuses to make further payments of rent. B's duty to pay rent is discharged, and B is not liable to A for breach of contract.

Comparing these two illustrations can help clarify the point and may also emphasize the lawyer's role of advocacy. The principal purpose of the contract in Illustration 6 is assumed to be the ability to make a profit. The illustration demonstrates that a change that destroys the profit is not necessarily sufficient to release the party who is hurt by the change of affairs. Perhaps this is because the risk of doing business in this way included such changes. In Illustration 4, by contrast, the purpose of the contract for the sign was to have a sign. When the regulation prohibits the sign, that purpose of having a sign is clearly lost completely. In both cases the bottom line is that someone will bear a loss, but the illustration involving a government prohibition is more definite. Additionally, the specific duty to pay in the case of the sign relates clearly to the prohibition.

Existing Impracticability or Frustration

The cases in this area generally arise because of some change that occurred after the parties entered the contract. In some cases, however, the performance is already impracticable or a party's principal purpose is already substantially frustrated at the time they enter the contract. This difference in timing of the basic assumption does not necessarily destroy the claim of excuse. The same relief of excuse of contract available for supervening impracticability and frustration is also available to a party who can show that the situation arose without his fault and without his knowledge prior to contracting. Just as with supervening impracticability and frustration, the party seeking to be excused from his obligation needs to establish for the court that he did not know or have reason to know of the fact that created the situation of impracticability or frustration and, further, he must show that the non-existence of the occurrence was a basic assumption of the contract.

Comparison of Existing Impracticability or Frustration with Mistake

The comment to Section 266 to *Restatement (Second) of Contracts* indicates that the party seeking relief from the duty to perform has the option of proceeding under the theory of mistake as well. The two areas are similar. Remember, however, that the Doctrine of Mistake is different. It is limited to situations in which the parties hold a "belief that is not in accord with the facts." This argument generally arises when the belief is one about facts. By contrast, the Doctrines of Impracticability or Frustration are not about facts relating to the contract. Rather, they relate to the nature of the performance under the contract. They focus not on facts *per se* but rather on the nature of the performance. In these cases, performance is problematic; the performance is extremely and unreasonably difficult because of expense or likelihood of injury. A separate basis for the claim is that the performance is without value to the recipient and the recipient does not know this fact at the time of contracting.

Insecurity, Modification, and Impracticability

When an obstacle to performance arises, it will generally create a sense of insecurity in the party who still believes the contract should be performed. An assertion that the parties were contracting on the basis of a mistake or that performance is impracticable means that the party who expected performance now sees that there is a significant risk that he will not receive the expected performance. When it appears unlikely that the other party will perform — whether the failure to perform arises from personal whim or from circumstances that make performance unprofitable or burdensome, the party who is made insecure may have a right to seek assurances from the other party. Section 268 reflects the view of cases that a prospective failure of performance may discharge the other party's duties or allow suspension of those duties. Such circumstances may provide a situation in which the parties will choose to modify the contract. We discuss modification in detail in the next chapter.

International Sale of Goods

Some contracts professors now include coverage of the Convention for the International Sale of Goods (CISG) because of the growing importance of international transactions in today's market. Although the Convention uses different terminology than the UCC, it presents an inquiry that is substantially similar to the question of excuse of performance under the common law and Article 2 of the UCC. The common law speaks of obstacles to performance while the CISG deals with the similar question of "impediments" to performance. Article 79 of the CISG deals with the question of excuse of performance by discussing situations in which a party will be exempt from liability despite a failure to perform. It states:

> A party is not liable for a failure to perform any of his obligations if he proves that the failure was due to an impediment beyond his control and that he could not reasonably be expected to have taken the impediment into account at the time of the conclusion of the contract or to have avoided or overcome it or its consequences.

Article 79 requires that the party seeking to be excused "give notice to the other party of the impediment and its effect on his ability to perform."

Economic Analysis

Economists suggest that in order to determine whether performance should be excused courts should consider which party is the primary risk bearer. UCC provisions on mistake and impossibility present a template for weighing the performing party's need for a change in the contract against the needs of the recipient. Thus, while these doctrines place a burden on the party seeking to change the contract, they provide judicial leeway to protect parties from unforeseen and unallocated contingencies. In this area, courts assess "the ever-shifting line, drawn by courts hopefully responsive to commercial practices and mores, at which the community's interest in having contracts enforced according to their terms is outweighed by the commercial senselessness of requiring performance." *Transatlantic Financing Corp. v. United States*, 363 F.2d 312 (D.C. Cir. 1966.)

Risk Allocation

Risk allocation is at the heart of many issues in contract law, including not only areas such as mistake and impossibility but also other areas such as modification, performance, and even interpretation. It is of such importance that it deserves separate discussion here.

Allocation of risk can be either express or implied. If the parties express the allocation of risk relating to particular contingencies in their bargain, a court will ordinarily apply the allocation set forth by the parties. However, cases that come to court almost invariably do not present an express allocation by the parties in relation to the dispute. This is true because parties who take the time and trouble to allocate risk do not litigate the matter in the event the contingency occurs. They know the outcome in court would be the agreed-upon allocation. Thus, litigating the issue would be a waste of time and money.

> ▶ *Florida Power & Light Co. v. Westinghouse Elec. Corp.*, 517 F. Supp. 440 (E.D. Va. 1981), provides a good example of this point. There the court rejected the defenses of impossibility, impracticability, frustration or mutual mistake, holding that the contractor assumed the risk of difficulty of performance. In this case, a utility company brought a claim against a contractor for breach of contract for the sale of nuclear steam supply systems for generation of electric power. The contract stated that the contractor assumed the risk of difficulty or impracticability of performance as to its obligation to remove and dispose of spent fuel. The court upheld this provision, finding no reason to alter the determination of the parties.

When a case comes to trial and the parties have not allocated the risk, the court supplies the implied allocation of risk that is most reasonable under the circumstances. As in other areas we cover in this book, courts create allocations that they believe the parties would have agreed to if they had expressly dealt with the issue. If a party accepts a particular risk as a matter of bargaining, then he should expect the loss to fall on him if it occurs. In such a case, he has accepted the allocated risk. *Restatement (Second) of Contracts § 261* includes a caveat for allocation of risk. It states the rule of discharge of a party's performance on the basis of impracticability when the elements for discharge are present "unless the language or the circumstances indicate the contrary." The Comment to Section 261 of *Restatement (Second) of Contracts* reiterates the point, indicating the court's decision to discharge the duty "yields to a contrary agreement by which a party may assume a greater as well as a lesser obligation." This is a strong statement of the respect courts accord allocation of risk in this area. Likewise, UCC 2-615 notes the power of the parties to allocate risk. The introductory language of UCC 2-615 carves out the exception to its terms by the language "except so far as a seller may have assumed a greater obligation," to make clear that the parties' allocation of risks trumps the remedy of UCC 2-615.

When a party contracts to achieve a particular result without regard to supervening events the party is, in a sense, providing insurance as well as a promise to perform. A case that is less clear but also a problem for a party exists when he knows that he does not have all the relevant information. In the words of the *Restatement*, he knows he "has only limited knowledge with respect to the facts to which the mistake relates." When parties do not expressly allocate a risk the court may determine who should bear the risk or cost. A party to a contract that is the product of mutual mistake can void an adverse contract unless that party bore the risk of the mistake. Arguments in this area turn on the issue of who should bear a particular risk when the parties have not indicated in their contract the risk and the risk bearer.

One might argue that the failure to allocate a risk should mean that the risk simply rests with the party who experiences that risk. Nevertheless, when the impossibility relates to a basic assumption of the parties, a court may help the party who encountered the problem by excusing (forgiving) the obligation.

> ▶ The English case of *Taylor v. Caldwell*, 122 Eng. Rep. 309 (Kings Bench 1863), involved such a case. The plaintiff rented a music hall for four performances. Before the time for the performances, the hall burned down. The court held that the parties could have made an express stipulation in their contract to allocate the loss. Such a term would be dispositive, but its absence would not preclude the court from finding an implied term to accomplish the same result. The court held that when performance depends on the continued existence of a given person or thing, a "condition is implied that the impossibility of performance arising from the perishing of the person or thing shall excuse performance."

Courts often consider the issue of the foreseeability of the loss or the risk in the context of a claim of impracticability or impossibility. For example, in *Sunflower Elec. Coop. v. Tomlinson Oil Co., Inc.*, 638 P. 2d 963 (Kan. Ct. App. 1981), the court rejected the argument of impracticability because it found the risk foreseeable. It also held that the contract indicated that the seller assumed risk of a price rise.

Students sometimes see the failure to allocate a risk as foolish on the part of the parties. Hindsight is 20/20, of course. Sometimes parties decide (consciously or unconsciously) not to allocate risks. They leave such problems for later bargaining or, if necessary, judicial resolution. The value of a contract is reduced to the extent that parties spend time allocating every risk. Abraham Lincoln once said that he wrote a beautiful $100 contract (a substantial sum of money in his day) for the sale of a chicken house. Unfortunately, the chicken house itself was worth less than the cost of contracting. This story indicates the problems parties face if contract law required them to foresee and expressly allocate all possible risks.

Conditions and Contingencies

Many of the cases that arise in the area of mistake and impossibility would not go to court if the parties had made their contract contingent on a particular fact. For example, if the price of Rose (the cow in the Sherwood case) had been contingent on her being barren, then the seller could have avoided the contract when it became clear that she could reproduce. It is virtually impossible to foresee and deal with all contingencies before they occur. Contracts have become more complex and deal with more contingencies than in the past, especially when the money involved is significant. The *Restatement (Second) of Contracts* makes the point that parties can control the extent of exposure they take on in their contracts by reference to common clauses to limit liability in the introduction to this chapter on Impracticability of Performance and Frustration of Purpose:

> The obligor who does not wish to undertake so extensive an obligation may contract for a lesser one by using one of a variety of common clauses: he may agree only to use his "best efforts"; he may restrict his obligation to his output or requirements; he may reserve a right to cancel the contract; he may use a flexible pricing arrangement such as a "cost plus" term; he may insert a force majeure clause; or he may limit his damages for breach.

Of course the court's perspective will play an important role in decisions, such as whether a party's action of taking chances without allocating risks should allow him to seek relief from problems that arise in the performance stage of the contract.

▶ For example, in the case of *Watkins & Son, Inc. v. Carrig*, 21 A.2d 591, 594 (N.H. 1941), the court rejected the excuse of mistake when a contractor who was excavating a cellar unexpectedly hit rock below the surface of the soil. The contractor could have controlled the issue if he had included in his bid for excavation a contingency relating to subsurface conditions. The price for excavation could have been stated with a condition attached, such as so long as "no subsurface conditions make it unduly burdensome to excavate to the desired depth." The difficulty with this approach is that it requires the parties to invest the additional time to identify the risks. Thus, parties recognize that they might deal with contingencies ahead of time, but often they do not invest the effort and money to do that.

Rescission, Avoidance, and Reformation

Although most cases involving mistake, impracticability or frustration deal with the remedy of avoidance of a contractual obligation, courts have the power to do more than avoid the contract. Courts can also reform a writing to make it express the agreement that the parties intended to express. Neither the Parol Evidence Rule nor the Statute of Frauds bars such reformation to correct a mistake or prevent injustice that would result from impracticability or frustration. *Restatement (Second) of Contracts Section 155* notes the power of courts to provide the remedy of reformation in this context. In *Aluminum Co. of Amer. v. Essex Group, Inc.*, 449 F. Supp. 53 (W.D. Pa. 1980), the court reformed the agreement on the basis of the Doctrines of Impracticability and Frustration. The basis for the court's holding was that after the execution of the long-term contract, the seller's non-labor production costs rose beyond the foreseeable limits of risk. The objective pricing formula was tied to wholesale price index for industrial commodities. Without judicial relief, the seller was likely to lose more than $60 million out of pocket during the remaining term of contract.

CHAPTER 6 · DEFENSES AND OBSTACLES TO PERFORMANCE LIABILITY   153

Checkpoints

- Remedies of rescission, avoidance, and reformation may be available to the plaintiff in obstacle cases.

- Courts sometimes find a mistake of fact that prevented formation of the contract when both parties were mistaken regarding a material fact that relates to a basic assumption of the contract.

- A defendant seeking to convince a court to excuse his performance based on a unilateral mistake about a material fact relating to a basic assumption must establish that the plaintiff knew or should have known of the mistake or that the contract is unconscionable.

- Defendant may seek to prove that a temporary or permanent situation of impracticability makes it unfair to require him to perform.

- Has the defendant-recipient proved that his purpose in the contract has been substantially frustrated, making the contract essentially valueless to him because the basic assumption of the contract failed?

- When parties modify a contract after recognizing that it was made unenforceable because of the doctrine of excuse, a court is likely to uphold the modified contract.

- Courts often consider which party is more likely to bear the risk regarding the material fact that relates to a basic assumption of the contract. When courts identify the logical risk bearer, that party is likely to lose the court battle over a contractual obligation.

Chapter 7

Modification

Changes to a Contract

A modification is a change in the contract after parties have entered the agreement. You can think of it as an amendment or adjustment of a deal. Parties decide to change a contract for many different reasons. Modifying a contract can be a beneficial mechanism for changing an agreement either in response to altered circumstances in the performance stage or because of new information that changes the burdens of the contract. Some modified contracts facilitate an efficient allocation of resources, saving a deal that would otherwise have ended in breach. In other cases, a modification may undermine the reasonable expectations of the parties. For example, a modification could be the product of deceit, economic coercion, or the initiating party's ability to dictate changes to secure a better deal than he had under the contract. Courts face a difficult decision in determining whether to enforce a modified promise.

A good place to begin our discussion of modifications is to consider two questions. First, why might a party or parties to a contract want to modify a contract that they have entered? Second, what situations would convince a party to a contract that a modification sought by the other party is justified? Of course, these two questions do not define the full extent of the issues raised when one party seeks a modification or seeks to enforce the modification in court. While an infinite number of particular circumstances exist, these questions help establish a general framework and set the stage for discussing modifications in a meaningful way.

On the first question, a party may want to modify because the burdens of performance have changed. Alternatively, a party may simply be unhappy with the deal struck in the original contract. A seller may regret the contract because he thinks he should be paid more money by the buyer than the contract provides. A buyer may want a modification because he regrets the price he agreed to pay. He wishes he could pay a lower price for the performance agreed to or he thinks he should get more for his money, enhanced performance by the other party.

The second question is at the heart of the judicial inquiry regarding modification. Like other contract disputes, this one involves issues of the reasonable expectations of the parties. If the court sees a modification as an understandable response to changed circumstances, it is likely to give effect to the modification. Getting a better deal after the contract exists is sometimes referred to as "recapturing foregone benefits" because the party gains back an advantage given up in the contract. If the court regards the party seeking to enforce the change as taking advantage of the other or recapturing benefits it gave up in the original contract, it is likely to refuse to enforce the modification. Courts consider the circumstances on a case-by-case basis to decide who bears a particular risk and whether the parties are acting in good faith.

Modification cases involve a typical pattern. The plaintiff is generally seeking to enforce a new promise that modified the original agreement. The defendant is typically the promisor who made a new promise but refused to perform the modification. The modification can be a change in the contract terms of either the performance or consideration.

A Change on Each Side

Sometimes a modification involves a change of performance on both sides of the deal. In these instances, it is more likely that a court will enforce the contract as revised. For example, if the contractor of a house promises to build an additional room on the house for the promise from the purchaser to pay an additional sum of money, the change on each side presents a situation more likely to pass judicial scrutiny and earn enforcement. This is because each party appears to have consideration for the modification. A court will not enforce mutual modification, however, if the party resisting enforcement shows that the other acted coercively. Modified contracts that benefit only one party are less likely to be enforced. Because courts will typically not disrupt a party's right to receive the benefit of his bargain, courts refuse to enforce modifications in which a party recaptures a benefit he gave up in the original bargain.

A hypothetical case can set the stage in terms of seeing how the modification issue arises.

> ▶ Montana County (Buyer) and Glass Perfect (Seller) entered a contract for Seller to manufacture glass panels for Buyer to use in the construction of a stadium. Before the first delivery, Seller called Buyer and stated that, because of an increase in the price of fuel used in the manufacturing process, Seller wants Buyer to agree to pay a higher price. Buyer, doubting it could obtain a substitute contract, agreed to the changed price. Despite agreeing to the modification, Buyer refused to pay the additional price after delivery, claiming the change was unfair, coercive, and unenforceable. Seller sued for the balance of the higher price due under the modified contract. Whether the modified promise is enforceable depends on several factors we will discuss.

It is possible for the modification question to arise in the reverse setting as well. For example, a Buyer may demand a lower price for the goods, or seek other concessions such as an increased quantity of goods, higher quality goods, accommodations relating to payment terms or delivery terms, or other matters advantageous to Buyer. In our hypothetical, if the request for a modification made by Seller was based on an unforeseen and unallocated increase in the market price of glass that gave rise to a good faith belief in Seller that it had a basis for refusing to perform, Seller's circumstance seem to present a reasonable ground for seeking modification. Likewise, when performance falls within a force majeure clause, the parties may revise the contract to change the obligation to address the circumstances. On the other hand, if no price increase had actually occurred or if the Seller accepted the risk of the price increase at the time of contracting, the court may hold that the modification was unreasonable and unenforceable.

The new promise in a modified contract may make performance either more burdensome or easier. It may alter the amount or timing of the payment so that it is greater or lesser. For example, in the hypothetical case above, the promisor on the modified promise, Montana County, promised to pay more for glass than the price of the original contract. If the glass company sues, it will be seeking to enforce the modified (second) promise. In its defense, Montana County will allege that the second promise should be held to be unenforceable because no second promise ever occurred, or, if it did occur, the promise was defective for some reason (e.g., it was coercive, or amounted to economic duress).

Enforceability of Modified Contracts versus Original Contracts

The core difference between a modification promise and an original promise is that in the modification case the parties have an ongoing relationship in a contract already established prior to the modification. Both parties have invested in the current deal and will lose that investment if the deal falls apart. When the parties entered the contract together they rejected other potential parties to the deal. A buyer may have taken bids on a building project from twenty general contractors. It will be difficult and time consuming for Buyer to go back and review the offers from the other nineteen contractors to try to revive the offers. This burden and uncertainty pushes Buyer toward accepting a modification request by the initial general contractor rather than reopening the process of bidding a second time.

Who Are the Parties to the Dispute?

The plaintiff is generally the initiating party who wanted the new promise that modified the original agreement. The defendant, the resisting party, is typically the promisor on the new promise. For example, in the original short hypothetical case at the beginning of this chapter, the promisor on the modified promise to pay an increased price is Montana County (Buyer). If the county refuses to pay the increased amount, the promisee on that new promise to pay more may sue the county on the newly modified promise.

How the Issue Arises

Typically, the issue of modification arises when a party refuses to pay a higher price than originally agreed despite an alleged change of the price. Courts inquire whether the modification is a good faith change or whether it resulted from coercion.

What Does Plaintiff Argue?

Plaintiff will typically argue:

(1) The parties voluntarily modified the contract
(2) The circumstances justified the modification
(3) The modification was made in good faith, and (perhaps)
(4) Each party received consideration for the new deal.

Generally, plaintiff will make the first three arguments together.

What Does Defendant Argue?

Defenses raised by the defendant generally fall into three categories:

(1) There was no modification
(2) The party had no right to modify
(3) The modification was made under coercion or by overreaching.

These arguments may be raised singly or together. Each defense raises credibility issues. If the parties put the modification in writing, the first defense is not likely to be a winner. In the first category, the defendant denies that the parties agreed to a modification. He may even argue that plaintiff did not seek a modification.

The second defense — that there was no reasonable ground for seeking the modification — presents difficult questions of credibility when interpreting the facts. This involves issues of allocation of risks and foreseeability suggested in the contract examples above. As we've established, the fact that performance was more difficult than the parties anticipated at the time the parties entered the contract, does not necessarily provide a reasonable ground for modification. Thus, if the parties agreed to a result (excavating a basement for example), it is more likely that a court may see the allocation of risk of unanticipated difficulties as more likely to fall on the performing party because he promised a particular result. An easy case would be presented if one of the parties created or allowed a change of circumstances; for example, if the seller gave a raise to employees and then later claimed a change of circumstances based on the higher price of labor, then the court is likely to agree that this change in circumstances was not a reasonable ground for seeking a modification because it was within the control of the initiating party. The range of possibilities in this area is large. Accordingly, the range of judgment regarding what is of reasonable ground is just as broad.

The third defense (coercion) is similarly difficult. If the alleged coercion comes from circumstances outside the control of the plaintiff, then the defendant's claim is weakened. When the defendant claims that the plaintiff coerced the defendant's assent to the modification, the court should consider both evidence of the reason for the change and also the type of communications involved. One party may view something as coercive that is viewed by another as merely difficult circumstances. For example, a seller may say that he is unable to perform because of a rise in the cost of raw materials. Nevertheless, if there has been a rise in the cost of raw materials, the defendant may see this as a risk that seller bore and, thus, he may see the demand for a modification as coercive. The sense of coercion is heightened if seller knows of buyer's particular need for the performance from seller within a particular timeframe. If a party threatens to retaliate in some way other than non-performance, the court is more likely to find coercion. If the party seeking a modification threatens to cease performance under another contract between the parties unless the modification is accepted, a court is likely to see this kind of conduct as coercive.

A Sample Matrix of Changes of Modifications

The following matrix of the types of changes that a party may seek presents generally predictable changes. The changes in the buyer column are ones you would expect to see the buyer demand. This matrix is not exclusive or entirely predictable. Particular circumstances could alter these presumptive positions, and the changes a party seeks might even be different than the ones noted here. These changes are likely ones because they are generally helpful to the party seeking the change.

Buyer	Lower Price	Greater Performance	Higher Quality	Change in Timing of B's Payment (Later)	Change in Timing of S's Performance (Earlier)
Seller	Higher Price	Less Performance	Lower Quality	Change in Timing of S's Performance (Later)	Change in Timing of B's Payment (Earlier)

The matrix suggests that requests to make a change by a seller or buyer are likely to be related to their predictable interests. When the party seeks a change in the timing of his own performance it is likely to seek a later time. For example, paying later gives that party the additional benefit of using the money longer. Money has a value relative to time and, thus, a later payment gives the paying party a benefit that is typically equal to the interest rate value of the money over the time extension. Alternatively, the modification could present a reduced price rather than an increased price. In such a case, the buyer would be the party that sought the seller's promise to accept a lower price — probably on the basis that buyer encountered greater than expected costs in some related aspect of the contract.

Of course, a modification may relate to issues other than price. It could be an enhanced performance, or reduced performance from that of the original contract. For example, taking the illustration above of a modification with a change on both sides, the contractor promised to build an additional room in exchange for purchaser's promise to pay additional money. Similarly, a contractor may promise to add a small feature, such as a patio to the promised construction, even with no additional payment on the other side. On the other hand, the party on the performance side of the contract may have extracted a promise from the recipient of the performance to accept less than was originally promised on the contract without changing the price of the contract. When the party seeking a change in time is the performing party (the one who will build a house or produce goods for the buyer), he is also likely to want to obtain a later date for his own performance. When the party who seeks a change of contract terms relating to time seeks to change the timing of the other party's performance, it is likely to seek an earlier time. Most modern courts enforce modifications without consideration if the modification is reasonable under the circumstances. *Restatement 89* provides cases on this point.

It is important to note who is requesting the change in performance and how it affects the original deal. A modification to the performance side would occur when the contractor promises to give more in the construction. He might agree to add a feature, such as a bay window for example, to the promised construction with no additional payment from the owner. By contrast, the performance side of the contract may be modified to make it less burdensome. For example, a contractor might extract a promise from the buyer-owner to accept less performance than was originally promised on the contract without changing the price of the contract. For example, the contractor or builder may demand that the buyer to accept the construction with a smaller square footage or to accept the construction without a bay window that was in the original plans.

Tests for Enforceability of Modified Contracts

Traditionally, the Law of Modification focused on the Doctrine of Consideration. This approach brought a formalistic structure to the Law of Modification that made it difficult to enforce a change. The modern approach to the Law of Modification has moved to a focus on the fairness of the change (rather than the formalistic concept of consideration). The traditional approach to enforcement of modifications started from a presumption against allowing the modification unless the parties had rescinded the original contract and entered a new one. The traditional approach is generally regarded as stricter: making modifications more difficult to enforce than the more modern approach. The modern approach focuses on the fairness of the change in the deal in light of developments after contracting or in recognition that the parties relied on false assumptions about the performance in their contract.

Modern courts, legislatures, and scholars have developed several different lines of analysis for addressing whether the modified contract should be deemed enforceable. The law seeks to balance the interests of the parties' reasonable expectations, to give effect to reasonable modifications and to refuse unreasonable ones. Who should bear the burden of demonstrating good faith or the lack thereof? Should a court enforce a modification only if the plaintiff demonstrates a valid commercial reason for his request to modify, or should the defendant bear the burden of proving that plaintiff lacked a reasonable basis for modifying? The following tests continue to play a role in this area of contract law:

(1) The Pre-Existing Duty Rule and Rescission
(2) The UCC
(3) The *Restatement* Test
(4) Bad Faith or Coercion
(5) Reliance on the Modified Promise

1. The Pre-Existing Duty Rule and Rescission

The Pre-Existing Duty Rule is a common law rule that precludes enforcement of a promise when a promise modifies an existing contract by changing only one side of the contract. The concept behind this rule is that there is no consideration for the new promise when that promise changes an obligation that is "pre-existing." This means that once parties are in a contract, modification of one duty under the contract is not enforceable unless there is new consideration for the change on the other side. The Rule presents the common law recognition of the potential for coercion in the modification context.

Under this rule, a party could defeat enforcement of a modification unless the plaintiff established that the modification was supported by consideration.

▸ The case of *Alaska Packers Ass'n. v. Domenico*, 117 F. 99 (9th Cir. 1902), is frequently examined for this point. Fishermen in a remote area in Alaska demanded an increase in compensation for their work in harvesting salmon during the salmon run. The employer agreed to the modified price. The court refused to enforce the modification, holding that the promise of additional compensation to the fishermen lacked consideration and thus was unenforceable under the Pre-Existing Duty Rule.

This traditional common law rule required consideration to enforce a modification. If the parties had rescinded the first contract or changed both sides of the deal, a court could find the Pre-Existing Duty Rule was not violated. The Rule required the party seeking enforcement to satisfy the doctrine of consideration as a way of protecting against coercion. If the evidence shows that those parties destroyed the original contract, thereby rescinding the original agreement, but after that rescission entered a new agreement, the court is likely to find that the party seeking enforcement of that new agreement is in a better position than if the agreement was simply modified. The Pre-Existing Duty Rule does not apply when the parties rescind the original contract and enter a new contract to achieve a change. Because the parties have rescinded the contract containing the original duty, the second contract does not change a pre-existing (and currently existing) duty. Thus, the new contract would not violate the Pre-Existing Duty Rule. This theory is called "mutual rescission." In his article, Contract Modification under the *Restatement (Second) of Contracts*, Professor Robert A. Hillman, 67 Cornell L. Rev. 680, 685 (1982), noted that this argument is the "most frequently invoked exception to the pre-existing duty rule." Even in the case where the original contract is destroyed, the party resisting enforcement is not without arguments. He may argue that the destruction of the first contract and creation of the second was a product of duress. If the court is convinced that economic duress or coercion was the basis for the parties' actions, the court will not enforce the new contract. Whether it will regard the original contract as enforceable is a separate question.

The modern approach means that when a modification request is reasonable and the party agrees to the change, the doctrine of consideration (The Pre-Existing Duty Rule) will not nullify the enforcement of the new promise.

▶ In the case of *Watkins & Sons v. Carrig*, 21 A. 2d 591 (N.H. 1941), the court rejected a strict consideration test for a modification. The performance side of the contract was a promise to excavate a basement. The contractor found subsurface conditions of solid rock, a difficult and expensive situation. The court noted that requiring new consideration for the promise "clothed" consideration with too much importance. Thus, the court applied a new test that related to the fairness of the new contract. The Watkins case is an early example of the modern approach to modification. It looks to the substance of the modification rather than the formality of whether the parties rescinded the first agreement.

2. The Standard of UCC Section 2-209

UCC § 2-209 dispenses with consideration in the modification area, enforcing modifications made in good faith. UCC § 2-209 (1) provides: "An agreement modifying a contract within this Article needs no consideration to be binding." This provision changed the common law of modification in the goods area by dispensing with the requirement of consideration. By imposing a requirement of good faith, the drafters of the Code discarded the test of consideration in modification disputes The common law did not test good faith directly for modifications. The common law did include such considerations under the policing mechanism of duress, coercion and unconscionable contracts. The requirement of good faith appears in the official Comment 1 to UCC § 2-209. The comment illustrates this standard with an example of intentional flexibility..Comment (1) to UCC § 2-209 limits the provision to "all necessary and desirable modifications." It expressly rejects "the technicalities which at present hamper such adjustments," apparently referring to the Pre-Existing Duty Rule. The second sentence of Comment (2) provides the clearest focus on the good faith requirement, stating that modifications "must meet the test of good faith." This suggests that the plaintiff seeking to enforce a modification must establish good faith to enforce a modification. The third sentence of Comment 2 flips the standard. It states "The effective use of bad faith to escape performance on the original contract terms is barred, and the extortion of a 'modification' without legitimate commercial reason is ineffective as a violation of the duty of good faith." This sentence states an example that clearly does not meet the standard of good faith. Obviously the test of good faith is not met when the court finds the promise was extracted by bad faith. Some courts have read this sentence to require defendants to establish the initiating party's bad faith.

Sentence 4 of this Comment to UCC § 2-209 rejects "mere technical consideration" to support a bad faith modification, emphasizing the Code's rejection of consideration as a test in the modification area. The Comment notes that "an objectively demonstrable reason for seeking a modification," may be required in some cases. Thus, the Comment suggests a lot of leeway. Like many tests in contract law, the test presents "bookend" cases and leaves a lot of room for judicial discretion in between: A good faith modification should be enforced. A bad faith modification should be denied enforcement. Figuring out which rule applies and what the facts establish in a given case is for the courts to decide in individual cases. As an example, the comment provides, "Such matters as a market shift which makes performance come to involve a loss may provide such a reason even though there is no such unforeseen difficulty as would make out a legal excuse from performance under UCC §§ 2-615 and 2-616." This indicates that a market shift in the cost of performance that does not present a legal excuse may provide a basis for enforcement of a modification. The drafters may have intended to include cases in which the initiating party may fail to establish the legal excuse of impracticability although he acted in good faith.

While the UCC refers to a duty of good faith in modifications, it does not elaborate on what constitutes good faith in this context. Thus, courts must decide whether a modification was demanded in good faith based on general standards. The UCC does not explicitly state which party has the burden of proving good faith.

3. The *Restatement* Approach to Modification

Section 89 of the *Restatement (Second) of Contracts*, states the test for an enforceable modification based on the fairness of the modification, considering circumstances that arose after the parties contracted or in view of circumstances not known by the parties at the time of contracts. It discarded the formalistic approach noted above. It provides:

> A promise modifying a duty under a contract not fully performed on either side is binding (a) if the modification is fair and equitable in view of circumstances not anticipated by the parties when the contract was made; or (b) to the extent provided by statute; or (c) to the extent that justice requires enforcement in view of material change of position in reliance on the promise.

Unlike the UCC, the *Restatement* § 89 test does not use the vague test of good faith. Rather, it specifies the ingredients of good faith in the modification context, requiring that to be enforceable the modification must be "fair and equitable in view of circumstances not anticipated at the time by the parties when the contract was made." Although the "fair and equitable" test is also subject to significant flexibility, it has more substance than the term "good faith" alone. It points to the central issue of what the parties knew at the time they entered the contract, indicating that fairness and equity are to be judged "in view of circumstances not anticipated by the parties when the contract was made." This test makes clear that a court would be justified in enforcing a modified contract based on a statute (including the UCC). Additionally, the test gives reliance as a separate basis for enforcement of the modified promise. Thus, this more detailed test is more helpful than that of the UCC approach in two ways. First, the standard focuses on the modification itself. It draws attention to the event of modifying the contract. Second, it gives meaning to the terms of fair and equitable by focusing on the ground for a modification, noting the context relates to "circumstances not anticipated by the parties." The requirement of the section "goes beyond absence of coercion and requires an objectively demonstrable reason for seeking a modification."

> ▸ In *Angel v. Murray*, 322 A. 2d 630 (R.I. 1974), the Rhode Island Supreme Court approved (the then-proposed) Section 89 of the *Restatement (Second) of the Law of Contracts* and delineated the test for modification, requiring that circumstances "which prompted the modification were unanticipated by the parties, and the modification is fair and equitable." Other courts focus on whether changed circumstances at the time of the modification justify a change in the contract.

4. Bad Faith and Coercion

Courts often consider bad faith in the modification context. A court will not enforce a modification if it concludes that the party seeking enforcement extracted a promise based on coercion or in an attempt to recapture benefits he gave up in the original deal. If a party obtained a modified promise simply to get a better deal, it is likely to have used coercive methods or exploited the situation of the other side. This discussion tells us that one thing lawyers will argue when asserting that a modification should be enforced is that there was some kind of motive for suggesting the change. When circumstances changed in some significant way before performance was complete, the plaintiff has a good argument.

> ▸ For example, if the party building a bridge cannot hire workers at the rate both parties anticipated at the time of contracting, the contractor may have a good argument for modifying the contract. Even in such a circumstance, however, the argument should fail if the contractor assumed the risk of higher construction labor charges.

In some cases, defendant establishes bad faith or coercion by the initiating party who is objecting to the modification.

> ▸ For example, in *Ralston Purina Co. v. McNabb*, 381 F. Supp. 181 (W.D. Tenn. 1974), the court held that a modification resulting in compounding Seller's damages was not a good faith modification. The court refused to enforce the modification because the purchaser knew or should have known that seller would not be able to complete the contract at the time the purchaser sought the change. Courts also refuse to enforce modifications that a party entered as a result of economic duress or coercion. This is true whether the contract is subject to the UCC or the common law. For example, in *Roth Steel Products v. Sharon Steel Corp.*, 705 F. 2d 134 (6th Cir. 1983) the court held a modification ineffective because seller failed to comply with the requirement of honesty in fact.

Courts look at the entire situation of the parties to determine who is more deserving of protection.

> ▸ In *Jamestown Farmers Elevator v. General Mills, Inc.*, 522 F.2d 1285 (8th Cir. 1977), a seller of grain brought an action to recover the difference between the market price at the time of delivery and the contract price, claiming it was compelled to deliver under the contract because the buyer, a large corporation, threatened to put the seller out of business and to institute criminal or regulatory proceedings. The court found the seller had failed to establish duress, stating that establishing business compulsion requires "more than a mere threat which might possibly result in injury."

If a court holds that the party seeking a modification engaged in coercion, the court should refuse to enforce the coerced promise. This point really is broader than the modification context. It applies to contracts in general. Some courts have held that a rescission of part of the agreement occurred by implication when the parties changed a term in the agreement. In other words, changing a term rescinds the old term that is displaced by the new term. Some jurisdictions continue to apply the Pre-Existing Duty Rule, but it appears to be of decreased importance. Even so, the theme of protecting a party when coercion is present in a modification continues to play a role in assessment of modification cases.

In the comments to UCC § 2-209(1), the drafters of the UCC endorse this view. The distinctions between the good faith and bad faith standard often affect the burden of proof. In *Wisconsin Knife Works v. National Metal Crafters*,

781 F.2d 1280 (7th Cir. 1986), Judge Posner noted that the UCC drafters "took a fresh approach" to the issue of modification. He looked to the doctrines of duress and bad faith as protection "against exploitive or opportunistic attempts at modification."

> ▸ In *Austin Instruments v. Loral Corp.*, 272 N.E. 2d 533 (N.Y. Ct. App. 1971), the New York Court of Appeals refused to enforce a modification on the basis that the seller unfairly coerced the buyer to increase the price of component parts the buyer needed for a contract with the Navy. The court focused on the buyer's inability to obtain the goods from other dependable suppliers. The defendant manufactured sophisticated military machinery for the Navy to the "strictest engineering standards," and, thus, maintained a list of approved suppliers. The court found it would be unreasonable to require the buyer to cover with parts from other dealers not on its approved list because of its need for precision parts to fulfill its contract. The absence of an objective commercial reason for demanding a modification may also provide a basis for refusal to enforce. Likewise, in *T & S Brass and Bronze Works v. Pic-Air, Inc.*, 709 F. 2d 1098 (4th Cir. 1985), the court refused to regard a delay in production as a legitimate commercial reason for the seller's modification that shifted air freight charges to the buyer.

5. Reliance

A plaintiff's reliance on the other party's promise modifying the contract may provide a separate basis for enforcement of a modification in some cases. *Restatement § 89* endorses reliance as a basis for treating the modification as binding "to the extent that justice requires enforcement in view of material change of position in reliance on the promise." In *Wisconsin Knife Works v. National Metal Crafters*, 781 F.2d 1280 (7th Cir. 1986), the court required a showing of reliance by the plaintiff to enforce an oral modification. Reasonable reliance may arise from circumstances in which a party relies on promises of his contracting partner to give some additional benefit not included in the original bargain.

> ▸ For example, if Seller agreed to modify a contract by promising to provide reinforced packaging for shipping the glass panels in the Montana County hypothetical discussed earlier, a court could hold the Buyer to its promise, at least to the extent of its reliance damages. If a seller relies on a buyer's promise to pay the higher price by continuing to manufacture the goods and ultimately delivering the goods to

the buyer, a court may enforce the buyer's promise to pay the higher price if it finds the reliance was reasonable.

Changes in Circumstances

If the Seller encounters a significant change, and the risk of the contract did not allocate the risk to Seller, a court is likely to enforce a modification as long as Seller did not engage in coercive tactics.

> ▶ In the case of *Angel v. Murray*, 322 A. 2d 630 (R.I. 1974), the Rhode Island Supreme Court enforced a modification of a contract between the City of Newport and a company under contract to haul city waste. It held that the modification was justified because changed circumstances made the modified contract fair and equitable. It also noted that the circumstances giving rise to the modification were "unanticipated" by the parties.

Up to this point, we have considered the tests and elements of modification. The balance of the chapter takes up issues of perspective that have not been fully developed. Modification can be a double-edged sword. While each party to a contract is vulnerable to demands for modifications by his contract partner, each is also vulnerable to a hard-nosed refusal to modify a contract despite a justifiable reason for modifying. At the time a party seeks modification, the other party has a right to insist on the original agreement. He can enforce the agreement in court unless the initiating party convinces the court that his performance should be excused under the doctrine of mistake or impossibility, or some other basis for excuse.

The right of refusal to modify may seem to protect the non-initiating party. If he needs the goods and does not wish to grant a concession to the party seeking a modification, he should simply refuse the modification request and demand performance as originally agreed. In many cases, the option of refusal is not a realistic choice, however. When the non-initiating party needs the goods or services offered by the contract, he may be forced to agree to the modification or face a lawsuit for his own failure to perform on another contract that depended on the contract at issue.

For example, in the case of *Austin Instrument, Inc. v. Loral Corp.*, 272 N.E. 2d 533 (N.Y. 1971), the court held that the buyer had no choice but to agree to demands for modification because the buyer had entered contracts to provide products to the Navy on schedule. Inability to obtain the goods from Seller harms not only Buyer but also those subsequent purchasers of goods and services further along in the stream of commerce. To consider fully this point, take the perspective of the non-initiating party.

> ▸ Suppose you run a catering service and you entered a contract to deliver and serve a dinner for 80 people. You agreed to prepare fresh salmon. In a separate contract, your seafood supplier agreed to sell you salmon for $6.90 per pound. However, one day before the dinner engagement, the supplier calls you and says he must increase the price by $2.00 per pound. While you could go look for other salmon, you still need to arrange the flowers and polish the silver and set up the beautiful white canvas tent for the party. Maybe you could ask your partner to hunt for other salmon, but she is busy meeting with another potential client. You think about bargaining or driving to the next town, but eventually you decide you should simply pay the price and get on with your work. In other words, circumstances matter.

Refusal to Modify

You may wonder why the issue of enforcement ever arises. To establish a modification, the plaintiff must show both that he sought a modification and also that the other party agreed to it. A party has a right to refuse any requested modification and/or demand performance and then sue if performance is not forthcoming. In such a case, the rule on modification has no application because there was no modification—i.e. the request to modify was denied. The party can also urge the initiating party to perform. You might assume that the party hurt by a suggested modification simply refused to modify since that is his right under the contract. However, a party may agree to a modification that reduces its rights under the original contract. The reasons a party would agree to such a request vary. When circumstances have changed significantly as a result of an unexpected occurrence, it may be fair to both parties to make the change.

> ▸ Example One: Suppose a storm wiped out a farmer's entire crop of peanuts. The Farmer (Seller) had promised Buyer a certain quantity of peanuts at a set price. Farmer may seek to modify the agreement to obtain an increase in price. This would be an especially convincing case if the net result for seller is a loss or a significant loss in profit. In *Agroindustrias Vezel, S.A. de C.V. v. H. P. Schmid, Inc.*, 15 F.3d 1082, (9th Cir. 1994), the court held that the modification by a supplier of sesame

seeds was not made in bad faith under the economic duress doctrine. The supplier contracted with the defendant for the sale of seeds at a price of $28.50 per 100 pounds. Before shipping, the supplier contacted the defendant and requested that the contract be modified to increase the price to $29.50. The reason for the change was that floods had destroyed forty percent of the sesame seed crop. The defendant agreed to the price increase under protest. After rumors that the supplier was not fulfilling other contracts, the defendant withheld part of its payment and demanded assurances of performance. The supplier refused the defendant's demands and sued for the modified contract price. The court rejected the defendant's claim of bad faith, noting that supplier's "request for a less than four percent price increase in the wake of severe crop damage from natural forces was not bad faith."

▶ Example Two: A legal researcher entered a contract to write an annotation of a federal environmental statute for a set sum ($2,000). Because the time that this project took was significantly longer than expected, this author spoke with the project coordinator and asked for an increase in the contract price to $3,000. Both parties agreed that the work merited a higher rate. In this example, no dispute ever arose. Both parties agreed that the modification was fair. Of course, courts only address the issue when the parties ultimately disagree and one party brings a lawsuit.

Relationship of Modification to Consideration

While the Doctrine of Consideration provides a minimal test for enforcement of bargains, it does not include a fairness test. Thus, a court does not need to judge a contract to be fair in order to enforce it. The test for modification is a bit more demanding. After parties enter a contract, they stop the search for a contracting partner and prepare to perform. If courts merely applied the consideration doctrine without concern for fairness, it would be fairly easy for a party to enter an agreement and then modify it. This could be accomplished by simply demanding a change for some minimal consideration. A party might even insist on reinstating terms that the other party had rejected in the original bargain. To combat this possibility, the good faith standard for modifications requires that a new agreement meets a minimum fairness test. The difference in treatment of these two situations reflects the judgment by the courts that the situations differ in significant ways.

Modification and Risk Allocation

When parties expressly allocate a risk of a contingency, courts typically respect that allocation. If parties do not expressly allocate a certain risk that ultimately is a subject of a dispute, courts will decide the most natural allocation of risk. Enforcing the new promise by permitting the modification may seem contrary to the basic idea that parties allocated and accepted risks in the original contract. Nevertheless, courts enforce modifications when the circumstances indicate a good faith reason for the change.

Parties recognize that events sometimes make a contract less beneficial than expected. In that case, the party who bore a risk of a particular contingency absorbs the cost of that contingency. Courts typically allocate the risk of a price increase to the seller and the risk of a price decrease to the buyer. In the event of a price increase, Seller regrets the contract, wishes he had not agreed to the lower sales price (i.e., lower than that he could obtain after the price rise). Conversely, in the event of a price decrease, Buyer regrets the contract, knowing that he now could obtain the same goods for a lower price. In either case, however, the change of affairs does not provide a basis for a refusal to perform. Contract law allocates the risk of such market changes to each party. If a price change provided a basis for nonperformance, the reason for entering contracts would be significantly diminished. Exceptions to this allocation are found in the doctrines of mistake, impracticability (also called impossibility) and frustration. When a court finds the state of affairs operates unfairly under these doctrines, it may excuse performance.

Many contingencies are allocated either expressly or implicitly. Other types of risks include the risk that an employee will quit, making it more difficult or more expensive to perform on the seller's side. Buyer also bears the risk that he may run out of money and have a hard time paying for the performance. Even when an unforeseen or unforeseeable event makes a contract better for one party, this change does not necessarily lead to a modification or even a modification request, especially when the burden of that risk was previously allocated by the contracting parties.

Economic Analysis and Public Policy

In one type of modification case, the cost of performing is higher than the performing party expected. In another type of case, seller's performance itself does not cost more but the seller has an opportunity to do better in another contract than in the current contract. For example, a seller who can handle only one job at a time is presented with a significantly more profitable contract. Thus, Seller has an offer to use his time more profitably, and his offer to modify can be seen as giving the non-initiating party the option of seeking damages or deciding to pay a higher price to compensate for the raised opportunity costs to seller. From the point of view of the other party (the defendant who now refuses to pay for the performance), this seems like a "hold up."

In the raised-cost situation, by contrast, the party seeking to modify may be in a losing situation. His costs are higher than believed at the time of contracting. In these instances, if a modification allows parties to save the contract, then it serves a good purpose. However, when a modification simply gets a better deal for one party than was first negotiated, it undercuts the original purpose for contracting. This situation is also referred to as a "hold up." Thus, these two possibilities present competing views of the situation in the modification context: (1) changing an unfair contract, or (2) an unfair "hold up" in which one party extracts an unfair advantage after the deal is completed. The view that a contract is unfair, and thus a good candidate for modification, can be based either on unknown unfairness that existed at the time the contract was entered into, or on a change of circumstances after the parties entered the contract.

"Not Fully Performed" Limitation

The *Restatement* test limits modification to a "contract not fully performed on either side." The text and comments do not explain the reason for this limitation. This limitation may mean that a dispute regarding a contract that is already fully performed on one side presents a dispute for settlement rather than a case for modification. A party who has performed can no longer modify his performance. Accordingly, he lacks leverage in negotiations to change the contract.

> ▶ For example, consider our previous example of a contract to excavate a basement. Upon hitting rock, the excavation company seeks an increase in the price. If the buyer of services has already paid the full contract price (say, $10,000), he is worse off than if he has not paid anything. If he chooses not to go forward with the modification, he will need to seek return of the payment in addition to finding a substitute deal. Likewise, a seller who has fully performed before receiving payment is also vulnerable. In a scenario where Buyer is holding the money and Seller has invested reliance costs in performing, if the Buyer demands some additional effort from Seller before

paying, Seller would find it difficult to refuse to give the additional work. The rule that the modification doctrine applies only to contracts not fully performed on either side means that if one party has fully performed the parties could enter a settlement but it is too late to modify the deal.

No Oral Modification Clauses

Can parties to a contract prevent themselves from changing a term in the future? Many parties have tried to limit their power to make changes in their contract by requiring that changes be in writing, but courts often enforce changes in contracts when both parties agree to the change as long as it meets the tests of honesty and good faith. Suppose parties want certainty at a new level, or, more likely, one party wants such certainty. The parties may include in the contract terms that a written document is required to make any future change enforceable. This term is essentially a "private statute of frauds." The term is also called an "NOM" clause (no modification except in writing). The party who includes an NOM wants certainty that the contract could not be modified in the future.

Parties should put modifications in writing as a matter of good practice. In some cases, the parties agree to put future modifications in writing. Often parties will include this promise in their written contract. UCC § 2-209(2) states that a modification of a contract for the sale of goods is unenforceable unless the modification is in writing when the parties agree to modify only by a written promise. However, courts frequently enforce oral modifications even when the parties have agreed to modify only in writing. Parties have a general right to contract, and this general right includes the right to contract about the contract. Thus, later on parties can agree (contract) to discard the requirement that they create a writing to modify the contract.

What Should a Party Do When the Other Party Seeks a Modification?

A party faced with a request for modification from the other party has a difficult choice. He can refuse the modification, insist on performance and sue for breach if the other party does not perform. In cases where the excuse doctrine will forgive performance, nonperformance is not a breach. Thus, the party who rejects a modification offer runs the risk of bringing an unsuccessful suit, if the court forgives the performance.

▶ To return to the introductory hypothetical, if Montana County (Buyer) rejected Seller's request and Seller then refused to perform, a court will not force the modification on the parties, even if Seller had a reasonable ground for requesting the change. If Buyer rejects the modification and Seller does not perform, Buyer may seek damages for the Seller's breach by nonperformance. If the court finds that Seller had reasonable grounds for a modification that constituted legal excuse under the doctrines of mistake or impossibility, a court will excuse Seller's performance. Thus, the initiating party who seeks a modification based on a reasonable ground (such as mistake or impossibility) has protection against the recalcitrant party's refusal to modify. Refusing to perform is, nevertheless, a second best choice because ordinarily the parties will prefer to continue with the contract in a modified form. If a court finds that Seller's request, though reasonable, did not amount to legal excuse by mistake or impossibility, it will grant Buyer (injured party) damages for Seller's refusal to perform.

Modification and Freedom of Contract

Parties are free to enter contracts of their own choosing. They are also free to enforce new contracts and discard old ones. Modification is, in a sense, just a new contract. Thus, it is an example of the freedom to contract. Nothing in contract law prevents changes. Both parties can make new agreements that change part but not all of an old agreement. The plaintiff can argue that freedom of contract requires enforcement of the new contract. He will say that the parties have the power to modify the contract and that the court should accept their bargain on the modification unless the defendant can show coercion or bad faith. In other words, the new promise is a contract and deserves the respect of the court. Defendant will argue that judicial resistance to modification is well-placed because courts should honor the original deal. Entering the first contract created a real obligation and freedom of contract will be undermined by giving effect to the modification. Unless both parties received new consideration and the second contract is fair and reasonable, the modification should have no effect. Otherwise, a contract would merely start a process of modified changes.

Relationship of Modification and Obstacles to Performance

The party who refuses to modify the contract when some significant change has occurred gambles on the court's judgment about the other's obligation to perform. Various grounds for non-performance exist, including mistake, impossibility, impracticability, and frustration of purpose. It has been said that the enforceable modification is a substitute for the doctrine of frustration. This is because a party who has a successful claim for forgiveness of performance can refuse to perform without incurring damages. Under the law of excuse, a court may allow a party to avoid an obligation under a contract. This avoidance is sometimes referred to as an excuse for non-performance. Of course, parties who are negotiating a modification do not know whether a court would forgive or excuse the nonperformance. This situation of uncertainty pushes the parties toward keeping the deal alive because neither knows for sure who would win the argument on the doctrine of excuse.

The Doctrines of Mistake, Impracticability (Impossibility), and Frustration define the situations in which a court will excuse or forgive performance of a contract. This means that a party does not need to perform his contractual commitments (paying money or delivering goods, services, licenses, or some other performance) when the court finds that one of the doctrines of excuse applies. Nonperformance is not a breach in this circumstance. Chapter 6 deals with obstacles to performance and the remedy of excuse of performance.

Accord and Satisfaction

An Accord and Satisfaction is another legal agreement parties sometimes use to resolve their obligations. A debtor party in a contract who is unwilling or unable to pay the full amount of money to satisfy his obligations under the contract may seek to pay less than what was agreed to in the initial contract. Under the Doctrine of Accord and Satisfaction, payment of the lesser amount may discharge the debtor from the original obligation. This doctrine provides the party asserting it with an affirmative defense to a suit on the original debt when that party has made the second (lesser) payment.

▸ Law Student goes to Stereo Dealer and purchases a new stereo system from Dealer for $900. As part of the agreement, Student takes the stereo home. He agrees to pay Dealer the amount owed on March

30 (thirty days after making the contract). Law Student has recently finished exams and decides to celebrate with friends. After a lengthy celebration, Law Student realizes he does not have the money to pay his debt to Dealer on the due date. He contacts Dealer and negotiates a new agreement. Deciding that some payment is better than none, Dealer agrees to accept $800 on March 15 in satisfaction of the original $900 debt. Student pays Dealer $800 cash on the due date. By the agreement and payment (Accord and Satisfaction) the original contract for $900 is satisfied and discharged.

In the above example, the new agreement Law Student made with Stereo Dealer is called an "accord." A "satisfaction" occurred when Student paid the amount due on the second agreement, thus, the debt is "satisfied" and discharged. The "accord" is the contract, and the "satisfaction" is the performance. Thus, the "Accord and Satisfaction" encompasses both the second agreement and the performance of the second agreement. If Stereo Dealer sues Law Student on the debt, Law Student has the burden of raising the affirmative defense of Accord and Satisfaction.

An Accord and Satisfaction bears some similarity to a Modification or a substitute contract in that all three doctrines provide mechanisms for altering obligations. There are important differences among the doctrines, however. In an Accord and Satisfaction, the original contract is still enforceable. If the debtor fails to perform under the second contract, the original contract is not discharged. It applies only when the debtor has *performed* (not merely promised to perform) the second agreement. In the example above, if Law Student failed to pay the $800 amount, Stereo Dealer could sue Law Student for the entire $900 due on the original contract. In contrast, if the parties had agreed to a modification of the original contract, and Student failed to pay the $800 amount when due, then Dealer would have a right to pursue only the $800 due on the modified contract—assuming the court found the modification was enforceable; i.e., the original contract was superseded by the second, and Dealer has rights only under the second contract.

In some cases it is not clear whether the new agreement is an Accord and Satisfaction or a Modification. In ambiguous cases, courts consider the facts and circumstances to decide whether the new agreement was intended to completely replace the old agreement (modification or substitute contract), or whether the parties intended to suspend the original obligation until performance of the modified obligation (accord and satisfaction).

A common type of dispute arises where one party issues a check that has a printed line that says "paid in full" or equivalent language. Generally, when the original debt is not disputed and not supported by new consideration, courts decide that "paid in full" language on a check is not sufficient to create an accord. To restate this point, courts respect an accord based on the "paid in full" assertion only when the obligor establishes a good faith dispute or consideration for the second agreement. The party claiming Accord and Satisfaction has the burden of proof. See *Kilber v. Frank L. Garrett & Sons, Inc.*, 439 P.2d 416 (Wash. 1968).

> ▸ Debtor owes Creditor $2000 on a contract. Debtor issues a check for $900 that has a line printed on it that says "Paid in Full." Creditor takes and cashes the check. Debtor claims that by cashing the check Creditor has agreed to an Accord and Satisfaction.

Whether the argument of Accord and Satisfaction will succeed in this case will depend on whether the court sees the circumstances and communication as creating notice of a good faith dispute and an expectation that the lower payment is full payment. The validity of an accord is governed by the same principles that apply to contracts generally. If the original duty is doubtful or if the substituted performance differs significantly, then the obligee's promise to accept the substituted performance may be supported by consideration. *See Restatements § 73 and § 74.* The promise may also be sufficient without consideration when a substitute basis for enforcement exists, i.e., reliance by the obligor in this case. *See Restatement § 90.* Finally, standard defenses applicable to contracts generally are available as a defense to the accord. These defenses include absence of consideration, lack of good faith and fair dealing, unconscionability, and fraud.

Checkpoints

- A modification is a change in a contract.

- A party may want to modify a contract because conditions have changed. If the modification responds to a change of conditions that would have provided a basis for refusal to perform based on mistake, impossibility (impracticability) or frustration, a court is likely to enforce the modification.

- A party may want to modify a contract because he is unhappy with the deal struck in the original contract. If the modification arose merely because of dissatisfaction with the contract, a court is unlikely to enforce the modification.

- A court is more likely to enforce a modification that involves a change of performance on both sides of the deal.

- The plaintiff in a suit based on a modification is generally the party who wanted the modification.

- The defendant in a suit based on a modification is generally the party resisting the new promise.

- Courts inquire whether the modification is a good faith change.

- Plaintiff is likely to argue that the circumstances justified the modification.

- Defendant is likely to argue that the initiating party had no right to request a modification.

- Defendant is likely to argue that the modification was made under coercion or by overreaching.

- The Pre-Existing Duty Rule denies enforcement of a promise if it modifies an existing contract by changing only one side of the contract.

- The Pre-Existing Duty Rule has declined in influence in modern times.

- UCC § 2-209 dispenses with consideration in the modification area, enforcing modifications made in good faith.

- The *Restatement* approach to modification focuses on the fairness of the modification.

- Courts consider reliance interests in modification cases.

- The party presented with a request to modify may refuse the request and demand performance under the contract.

- The party presented with a request to modify may also urge the initiating party to perform.

- The party presented with a request to modify should consider whether the party seeking a modification has a right to refuse to perform based on doctrines of excuse, such as mistake, impossibility (impracticability), and frustration.

- When parties expressly allocate a risk of a contingency, courts typically respect that allocation.

Checkpoints *continued*

- Courts often refuse to respect a modification if it modified a contract fully performed on one side.

- The Parol Evidence Rule does not prevent modifications.

- "No Oral Modification" Clauses seek to limit the power to modify the contract.

- A "No Oral Modification" Clause may be ineffective if a court finds that the parties actually agreed to a modification.

- Parties sometimes resolve an obligation by a performance that alters the original agreement under the doctrine of Accord and Satisfaction.

- Courts respect the discharge of the original contract when parties enter "accord" (the new contract) and follow through with the "satisfaction" (performance of the new contract).

- To be effective, the accord must arise from a good faith dispute on the original obligation or be based on new consideration.

- The original contract obligation is discharged upon performance (satisfaction) of the new accord.

- The doctrine of Accord and Satisfaction differs from modification in that it suspends obligation of the first contract rather than discharging it.

- An Accord and Satisfaction is distinguishble from a modification because the duty owed under the original contract can be enforced if the debtor does not perform (satisfy) the terms of an alternative agreement (accord).

Chapter 8

Exceptions to Bargain Theory: Contracts without Consideration

---

Roadmap

- Enforcement without Consideration
- Historical Note: Equitable Estoppel
- Contracts under Seal
- Charitable Subscriptions
- Restitution (Quasi-contract)
- Modifications to Sales Contracts
- Estoppel and Promissory Reliance
- Reliance as a Basis for Enforcing a Promise
- *Restatement 90 (First) of Contracts*
- *Restatement 90 (Second) of Contracts*
- Application of the Doctrine
- Preliminary Negotiations and the Intent to Be Bound

Enforcement without Consideration

Now that you fully accept the importance of consideration in contract law, it is time to explore exceptions to the general principle that a promise is not enforceable unless it is supported by consideration. The law of Promissory Estoppel provides an exception to Sequential Questions we have been examining as a structure for understanding contract law. You remember that Sequential Question #1 is "Is there a valid contract"; that is, a contract that evinces a mutual assent to be bound by an offer, an acceptance and consideration. Sequential Question #2 states "Even if there is a valid contract, are any of its terms enforceable?" As we have already seen, a contract may be valid but unenforceable because (as examples): its terms are illegal or its terms may be required to be in writing.

Is there any way a party can secure a remedy if he cannot prove a valid contract supported by consideration? The short answer is "yes," under the Doctrine of Promissory Estoppel. The related Doctrines of Promissory Estoppel and Promissory Reliance are the subjects of this chapter. The law of Promissory Reliance provides an exception to Sequential Questions we have been examining as a structure for understanding contract law.

Historical Note: Equitable Estoppel

The history of the development of these doctrines is a fascinating example of how the common law evolves. Understanding the variation in the doctrines is also important because some jurisdictions follow different formulations of the doctrines. We will begin with a discussion of the doctrine described in the first *Restatement*, which many jurisdictions have followed.

In some cases, courts grant enforcement of a promise even though the plaintiff does not establish consideration. For example, at common law, courts enforced promises made under seal even without a showing of consideration. This basis for enforcement has fallen out of favor with courts. In fact, many state legislatures have passed statutory bars against the use of the seal. Also, Courts sometimes use the basis of restitution to enforce promises that were never made. Such enforcement is called enforcement in "quasi-contract." The cause of action in such a case is referred to as "Restitution." The most common theory for enforcing a promise when a party fails to prove consideration is the theory of law called "Reliance." This basis for enforcement grew out of an older cause of action referred to as "Promissory Estoppel." Under the Doctrine of Promissory Estoppel, a party could be estopped (barred) from denying the existence of a contract when he had created a situation that gave rise to a belief in the contract. Promissory Estoppel was based on an inaccurate fact which created a misunderstanding. While it is possible for a party to seek Promissory Estoppel today, the modern approach is more likely to be an action in reliance. This section describes the reliance cause of action.

The influence of history in the law is sometimes dramatic. This area of contract law provides a good example of the importance of history in the law. The older cause of action referred to as "Promissory Estoppel" actually grew out of an even more ancient legal theory know as "Equitable Estoppel." Equitable Estoppel is premised upon plaintiff's reliance on a misstatement of facts by the defendant. In either case, where similar elements of the tests are met, the promisor is bound to ("estopped to deny") his assertions. The Doctrine of Promissory Estoppel uses the same legal mechanism, stopping the defendant from asserting a defense, but it adapts this mechanism to a new setting. The plaintiff using the action of Promissory Estoppel argues that he relied on a promise rather than on a misstatement of fact.

> ▸ Suppose Depositor goes to the Bank and asks Teller for the account balance. Teller reports to Depositor a balance of $1,347.99. Depositor believed the Teller and wrote a check for $500 on the account. If a court finds that Depositor's reliance on this statement was reasonable, it could award the Depositor the damages suffered as a result of fees imposed on the overdraft. In this case Depositor relied on a Misstatement of Fact. Accordingly, the older doctrine of equitable estoppel is applicable.

Contracts under Seal

Traditionally, an agreement under seal did not require consideration to be enforced by a court. The "seal" had its basis in the formality of a real seal, a wax impression affixed to a formally executed document by impression of a ring or symbol. If a promise were made in writing, sealed, and delivered to the promisee, it was enforceable whether or not there was any consideration for it. Before the 19th century, most wealth in England and America was tied up in land. It was common at this time to make promises using a seal (an impression made with a metal seal on wax). The seal formally declared the effectiveness of a promise, even a promise not supported by consideration. With the passage of time, it became common to simply write the word "Seal" on the document—or even have it on a preprinted form. Many jurisdictions abolished the use of seals. The Uniform Commercial Code makes seals ineffective in sales of goods transactions.

Charitable Subscriptions

Historically charitable subscriptions were also enforceable without consideration. Today the rule on this point varies from jurisdiction to jurisdiction. In some states voluntary promises made to charitable institutions continue to be enforceable without consideration. The *Restatement (Second) of Contracts Section 90* retains the rule that a promise to make a charitable gift is binding even without proof that the promise induced action or forbearance. For example,

Donor promises to give $1 million to the law school her father attended to create a scholarship fund in her father's honor. Subsequently, and before paying the pledge, Donor learns that the law school Con Law professor published a controversial article about the original intent of the drafters of the Constitution and informs the school that she is withdrawing her pledge. This promise may be enforceable. Courts traditionally recognize that the work of charities relies on a stream of donations, making it difficult to identify which particular project was taken in reliance on which particular donation. This may be part of the reason that courts historically do not require a showing of either consideration or direct reliance on a particular pledge for enforcement of a pledge. In some cases, a pledge card used by a charity does not include a promise, raising a question whether the pledges is enforceable under any theory.

Restitution (Quasi-contract)

Restitution is the oldest ground for recovery within the domain of contract law classes. Sometimes restitution is included in the topic of contracts without consideration. The quasi-contract is clearly without consideration. Indeed it is without all the elements of a bargained-for exchange since it is also without offer, acceptance, or any true assent. It is important to note the existence of quasi-contract and restitution because it continues to play an important role in the law. We cover the topic of restitution more thoroughly in the remedies section. You may wonder if it amounts to a remedy without a right since the remedy and the right in this case is so intimately intertwined.

A quasi-contract is not a contract in the sense we generally use the term "contract." A contract is generally a bargained-for exchange. It usually includes assent between the two parties. A quasi-contract or implied-in-law contract is a contract created by the court to prevent unjust enrichment. Quasi-contract and restitution are intimately connected to the historical evolution of contract law. Some scholars have pointed out that the restitutionary claim is the strongest of all the interests protected in contract law. In the introductory section we talked about the three interests protected by contract law: (1) expectation, (2) reliance, (3) and restitution. The claim for restitution is the strongest from an economic perspective. The claim in restitution essentially rests on the idea that defendant has something that belongs to plaintiff. Historically, the claim to recover money loaned to defendant was based on the idea of restitution. If the transfer of money was a loan, with the expectation of repayment, and not a gift it was the property of the plaintiff. The court did not need to find a promise to require defendant to return the money to the plaintiff. It was his money.

The importance of restitution both historically and currently can be understood by recognizing that in the past restitution occupied a major place in law school and in legal analysis. There is a *Restatement of Restitution* which catalogues the well-defined principles of recovery and a rich body of case law about restitution. The subject is no longer taught as a separate course in most law schools, however. This does not mean that the concepts are no longer important in the law. Restitutionary claims continue to be brought, and nearly every law school course includes coverage of restitution as a basis for contract claims.

We sometimes talk about the swinging pendulum as a metaphor for the way things change in law and society. A less elegant but more accurate metaphor for changes in the law is the lava lamp. This home décor item of the 1970s presents some kind of petroleum product, rising and moving in a mass that reconfigures itself. Restitution, like the colorful mass of the lava lamp, has been subsumed within the (now) larger topic of contract law.

From one perspective this makes no sense. Restitution does not rest on assent or promises. From another perspective, however, restitution follows the same concepts and same interests for protecting parties as contract law. Thus, quasi-contract is a fictional contract, an implied-in-law contract. This means that it is a contract constructed by the courts to prevent unjust enrichment. As with reliance, it is not enough that the world will be a better place or justice will be served if a particular interest is protected. Rather, the state of affairs must be *unjust* unless the court acts to correct the status quo. The following example will make clear the distinction between quasi-contracts and contracts made by the parties.

> ▶ Mr. X has just been injured in a streetcar accident. His life is in peril. Doctor arrives on the scene and administers medical care. The man is taken to a hospital where he dies. The doctor makes a claim on the estate of the man.

Obviously Mr. X made no promise to the doctor. He was unconscious when the doctor arrived on the scene and never regained consciousness before he died. Nevertheless, the court enforced the claim on the ground of unjust enrichment or quasi-contract. This is a contract created not by the parties but by the court. It is an implied-in-law contract. You might say that the man was not enriched by the doctor's services — after all, he died. Services from doctors (like services from lawyers) are not generally conditioned on a promise to secure a particular result, however. Thus, courts see the rendering of medical care as enriching a patient even when the medical care is not ultimately successful. In the case of *Cotnam v. Wisdom*, 104 S.W. 164 (Ark. 1907) the court created the promise between the doctor and the unconscious patient. In such cases the award is not based on a bargain since there is no bargain. The court creates the promise and also the measure of recovery. The theme of restitution is carried forward in the *Restatement* enforcement of a promise for a benefit received. This merging of the concept of benefit and promise is set forth in *Restatement 86*. Under this claim, a Plaintiff's basis for recovery is a benefit (in the *Cotnam* case, this would be the rendering of medical services). The difference between a pure restitutionary claim and the enforcement of a promise for benefit received is that the measure of damages is different. In both cases the reason for enforcing the claim is the restitutionary. The measure is drawn from contract law, enforcing the promise made by the defendant.

Modifications to Sales Contracts

Traditionally, two parties who entered a contract and later agree to modify their contract faced the same consideration requirement that they did when they entered into the original contract. A modification is, in fact, a new contract. Early courts held that, unless the parties gave new consideration for the new contract, that new contract (the modification) was not enforceable. UCC Article 2 changed this rule to allow contracting parties to modify their contracts even where the modification advantage only one side as long as the modification is reasonable under the circumstances. A party which has a right to insist that goods be delivered by Tuesday may agree to accept goods late. The buyer in such a case may simply be trying to accommodate. It is not uncommon, for example, for a party that has agreed to buy a good or service to agree to a price increase even when it gets nothing additional in return.

While consideration is not necessary for a modification to a contract for the sale of goods, the absence of consideration may suggest that there are other problems with the transaction. Lack of consideration may in some cases suggest that the modification was the result of some overreaching or other improper conduct by the other party.

Estoppel and Promissory Reliance

The following discussion takes up the modern theory of enforcement called "an action in reliance" and also looks at the predecessor theories of "Promissory Estoppel" and "Equitable Estoppel." The fact that Reliance has evolved as a recognized field does not mean that courts now refuse to consider the older

theories of recovery. Rather, it simply means that the more common and expected basis of reliance is the lawyer's primary tool for seeking enforcement of
a promise when the element of consideration is not present in a case.

Reliance as a Basis for Enforcing a Promise

The most likely basis for enforcing a promise despite the absence of consideration is the theory of reliance, in which one party has relied on the promise to its detriment when the court sees that reliance as reasonable. In such
cases, courts enforce the promise as a way of protecting the reliance interest of
the plaintiff, but only when the court sees the plaintiff's action of relying on
the promise as reasonable. The flexible elements of a reliance claim make it
difficult to be confident about prevailing in a case based on reliance.

The theory of reliance is similar to the older doctrine of "Promissory Estoppel." Courts enforcing on the theory of reliance may find a promise to be enforceable even though it is not supported by consideration. Typically courts
require the following showings to enforce a promise on the basis of reliance:
(1) the promisor knew or should have known that the promisee was likely to
rely on the promise; (2) the promisee did in fact rely on the promise; (3) the
promisee's reliance was reasonable; (4) the promisee suffered a detriment as a
result of her reliance; and (5) injustice can be avoided only by enforcing the promise. Such cases are an exception to the usual theory of consideration or a bargained-for exchange.

> ▸ Mr. Rich knows that his granddaughter Louisa would like to quit
> her job to stay home with her young children. Mr. Rich promises to
> convey a substantial amount of money to his granddaughter. He notes
> that his other grandchildren do not need to work and can spend time
> with their kids. Louisa did not promise to quit her job and Mr. Rich
> did not ask her to promise to quit.

The elements are open to debate and interpretation. The element of injustice absent enforcement is also open to debate. Some courts suggest that they
will enforce a promise to create justice. Others require a showing of injustice
in the status quo. The most common statement of the elements includes this
orientation: that injustice exists unless the court enforces the promise. In
Louisa's case, it appears clear that Louisa does not have a contract based on
consideration with Mr. Rich. Nevertheless, she did change her position in reliance on Rich's promise. Most courts would not enforce the promise unless they
believe that Louisa was reasonable in changing her position based on the prom-

ise. The test for consideration adopted by most courts does not state the need for reasonable reliance explicitly, but it does seem to be a universal requirement for actions in reliance. In other words, a court will not enforce a promise if it believes that the party seeking performance was not reasonable in the action that it took.

Restatement 90 (First) of Contracts

The *First Restatement of Contracts* enunciated the doctrine this way, at Section 90:

> A promise which the promisor should reasonably expect to induce action or forbearance of a definite and substantial character on the part of the promisee and which does induce such action or forbearance is binding if injustice can be avoided only by enforcement of the promise.

The linchpin concept of Promissory Estoppel is foreseeable reliance on a promise that induces injury and requires a remedy to prevent injustice. Parsing the doctrine into separate elements, we see that the party seeking a remedy under the doctrine (the plaintiff) must prove:

1. There was a promise by the defendant;
2. The promissory should have expected his promise would induce plaintiff's change of position in reliance on defendant's promise;
3. Plaintiff changed his position in reliance in a definite and substantial way;
4. Plaintiff's reliance was both reasonable and foreseeable to the promissory;
5. As a consequence plaintiff suffered substantial harm;
6. Enforcement of the promise is necessary to prevent injustice.

Let's take a closer look at each element

Element #1: Promise

It is essential that the defendant made a promise, giving a commitment of some kind. The statement must have substantial definiteness. Whether a statement is a promise is a question of fact to be resolved by the finder of fact.

Element #2: Type of Promise

Plaintiff must also show that promisor should have expected that his statement would induce an act or forbearance by the promisee. Additionally, promisor should reasonably expect that the promise would change his position by relying on the promise.

Element #3: Reliance

The plaintiff must, in fact, change her position, by either acting or fore-bearing to act as a result of the promise. A court will find a plaintiff acted by forebearing if the plaintiff refrained from taking an action (such as bringing a lawsuit) as a direct response to the promise. This action or forbearance must be in reliance upon the promise. Under the approach articulated in *Restatement (First) of Contracts*, the change of position must be substantial, definite, and bear a causal relationship to the promise.

> ▶ In response to a promise by her Uncle to give her a motorcycle to help with her business, Bernice starts a pizza company. On the other hand, if Bernice bought a new washer-dryer for her home in response to her uncle's promise to help with her business, the connection between the promise and the change of position is more tenuous.

Starting the company is an act in reliance. Buying a new washer-dryer bears no relation to the promise and, thus, presents a harder case.

Element #4: Reasonable and Foreseeable

Under *Restatement (First) of Contracts* the plaintiff's reliance must be sub-stantial. It also must be definite and motivated by the promise. Finally, the court will only enforce the promise if it sees it as reasonable and foreseeable that the plaintiff would rely. The question for the court is whether a reasonable third party in the promisor's position would foresee that the plaintiff would change his position in reliance upon the promise.

Element #5: Injustice

The approach of the *First Restatement* requires a showing that enforcement of the promise is necessary to avoid injustice. This last element is a question of law for the court to decide. The standard is more demanding than a test that requires a showing that enforcement would further justice. This test requires injustice exists if the court does not enforce the promise. We have seen that contract law is public law enforcing the private law (the bargain) of the parties. Public law reserves for itself the authority to decide when the interests of public policy or notions of equity and justice might be interposed to preempt the rules of ordi-nary contract law. Here is an instance of that dynamic. Even when the alleged agreement between the parties does not amount to a contract under the rules of contract law, courts will enforce the promise as if there were a valid enforceable contract and plaintiff will receive the remedy she would have received if this were so, pursuant to the *First Restatement*'s version of Promissory Reliance.

The purpose of the Doctrine is to avoid injustice. To that end, the ordinary rules on formation of a contract and its enforcement are softened.

Restatement 90 (Second) of Contracts

The *Restatement (Second) of Contracts* retains the basic concept of Promissory Reliance enunciated in the *First Restatement* but its Section 90 modifies the elements, somewhat. It states:

(1) A promise which the promisor should reasonably expect to induce action or forbearance on the part of the promisee or a third party and which does induce such action or forbearance is binding if injustice can be avoided only by enforcement of the promise. The remedy granted for breach may be limited as justice requires.

(2) A charitable subscription or a marriage settlement is binding under Subsection (1) without proof that the promise induced action or forbearance.

The *Second Restatement* modifies the first Section 90 in the following ways:

a. It eliminates the requirement that the reliance of the plaintiff be "definite and substantial." This change broadens the scope of the coverage of the doctrine, helping the plaintiff who seeks damages under the doctrine.

b. It adds protection for the reasonably foreseeable reliance by a third party. In other words, the party who changes he position will not need to be one who received the promise. This change also broadens the scope of the coverage of the doctrine and allows a better chance of recovery by the plaintiff asserting the claim.

c. It allows flexibility for the court in fashioning a remedy. Thus, a court may grant a reliance measure of damages rather than awarding the full expectation interest remedy. That is, the court may decide that compensating plaintiff for his actual out-of-pocket reliance interest damages is all that "justice requires." This change does not necessarily favor the plaintiff.

d. It expressly allows courts to enforce promises to give money to a charity without compelling the charity to prove any act or forbearance in reliance on the promise. Similarly, promises to marry do not require proof of reliance. In both cases the liberalization of proof rests on public policy grounds. Public policy favors both charitable gifts and marriage settlements. Moreover, in both contexts evidence of reliance is often elusive. Thus, the law relieves the plaintiff of that proof problem in these contexts.

Application of the Doctrine

Courts apply the Doctrine of Promissory Estoppel or Promissory Reliance in situations where plaintiff cannot prove that a contract has been formed.

Formation, of course, requires the manifestation of a mutual intent to be bound, evidenced by an offer, an acceptance and consideration. The absence of consideration and absence of a clear offer and acceptance do not defeat a claim of Promissory Estoppel or Promissory Reliance.

The most common application of Promissory Estoppel and the context in which it first arose was a case in which the plaintiff relied on a promise that lacked reciprocal consideration. Recall that consideration requires a "quid pro quo": 1) either a benefit to the promisor 2) or a detriment to the promisee 3) and something given in exchange for the other. The critical element here is the reciprocal inducement: each side's consideration must induce the other. Thus, under the rules of contract law, if a promisor's promise is not induced by consideration offered by plaintiff, the promise is gratuitous and unenforceable.

Contracts fail the test for consideration in a variety of situations, including illusory promises, indefiniteness, preliminary negotiations, and past consideration. In such cases, the plaintiff may be able to enforce a promise based on Reliance or Promissory Estoppel. Consider the following case.

> ▶ Employer's promise to pay Employee a pension for life after she retires because of her "many years of loyal service to the Company" is unenforceable because, as you know, past consideration is not effective consideration. Reciprocal exchange or inducement is lacking in this case. Employee's service was not induced by the promise of a pension. The promise of a pension lacks consideration.

In this case of past consideration, a court may grant enforcement if it determines that the Employee changed her position in reliance on the promise. For example, if the Employee quit her job as a result of the promise, she may have a claim based on reliance. She will need to convince the court that the promisor should have expected its promise of a pension to induce her action of retiring. The difficult question is often the element relating to whether "injustice can be avoided only by enforcement of the promise." In one case included in many case books, the court held for the plaintiff Employee because she had developed cancer and could not get a replacement job as a result. The court found that her inability to work after retiring justified enforcement.

Preliminary Negotiations
and the Intent to Be Bound

> ▶ Suppose A and B are negotiating a contract of employment whereby B would act as Chief Financial Officer for A's Company. It is inevitable

that B will need to quit his current job in order to relocate to A's corporate offices to take the employment offered. Though not all of the terms have been agreed upon, A suggests that B make the move anyway to help A's Company negotiate a merger with another company. That way, says A, we can learn how to work together. A assures B that B's employment is "virtually a done deal."

At this point there is no employment contract manifesting an intent to be bound and no consideration that binds either party. If A later decides not to hire B, after B has moved to Connecticut to work on the merger contract, B has no remedy under the bargain rule of consideration. In such cases, courts have entered awards for the prospective employee (B in the case above) when the promisor should have expected its promise to induce the action of moving to come to the promisor's location. Courts often limit damages to the out of pocket expense of the move unless additional facts require a different remedy.

Even if a contract is found to be valid, plaintiff may not receive a remedy for its breach if the contract fails to comply with one of the enforcement rules. For example, if the contract fails to comply with the provisions of the Statute of Frauds, it will be unenforceable. Nonetheless, a court may grant a plaintiff a remedy if the plaintiff can show reliance on promisor's promise induced his change of position and loss.

Restatement (Second) of Contracts includes a special provision for the Construction contract situation at Section 89. But in fact, most courts rely on Section 90 for all Formation problems that trigger Reliance analysis—including construction contracts—because courts are more familiar with its terms and interpretation.

Checkpoints

- There are exceptions to the rule that a contract is unenforceable unless supported by consideration.
- Courts may enforce an obligation to prevent injustice on the additional basis of restitution.
- Actions based on restitution are called actions in "Quasi-contract."
- Actions based on restitution are related to contract law but they also have an independent legal basis of restitution.
- Modifications of Sales Contracts require no consideration under the UCC.
- Promissory Reliance may help a party secure a remedy when he cannot prove a valid contract.
- The party invoking the doctrine must prove that promisor should have foreseen his reliance on a promise.
- Actions based on Reliance provide the most common exception to the requirement that a enforcement will be provided only when a promise is supported by consideration.
- Prevailing in an action in reliance on a promise is not an easy task.
- Courts require the plaintiff to establish Plaintiff's reasonable reliance to his detriment on a promise by the defendant and that an injustice will exist if the court does not enforce the promise to some extent.
- Promissory Estoppel may provide a basis for enforcing promises that are unenforceable because of the Statute of Frauds and the Parol Evidence Rule.
- Equitable Estoppel is a similar doctrine but it is triggered by a misstatement of facts rather than by a promise.

Chapter 9

Special Issues of Enforceability

Roadmap

- Introduction
- Statute of Limitations and the Doctrine of Laches
- Statute of Limitations under the UCC
- Statute of Frauds
- Parol Evidence Rule

Introduction

Recall that the Five Sequential Questions of Contract Law have a particular order because each question can result in dismissal of a suit in contract. While the actual arguments in a case may vary, in analyzing a contracts case, it is helpful to proceed through the sequential questions and to analyze the case and assess the legitimacy of the parties' claims. After determining first (in question #1) that the parties did enter an agreement that the law would consider a contract, we next need to determine whether the contract is enforceable. Special issues relating to enforceability are presented by the three areas covered in this chapter: (1) Statute of Limitations and the Doctrine of Laches, (2) Statute of Frauds, and (3) The Parol Evidence Rule. The issues dealt with here do not depend on whether the parties formed a contract. They arise from other interests in the law. For example, arguments relating to the Statute of Limitations and the Doctrine of Laches have to do with whether the contract claim has been brought to court within the time allowed. Thus, the questions raised in this area do not turn on whether there is a valid contract claim. The Statute of Frauds presents a legal judgment that some claims should not be enforced unless the parties created evidence of the contract. The idea here is that some bargains are of such significance that the parties should write them down. If the parties do not create a document indicating that the promise exists, the court will deny enforcement of the promises. Generally this evidence is presented in a written document of the contract. The Parol Evidence Rule does not require that the parties write down their promises. Rather, when the agreement is written down, it bars non-written terms (such as oral ones) that undermine the written terms.

The Statute of Limitations
and the Doctrine of Laches

No matter how meritorious a claim, at some point in time the plaintiff loses the right to use the judicial system to pursue the claim. Issues of when a party loses his right to enforce a contract claim are determined under the law of Statute of Limitations and laches. The rules found in Statute of Limitations and the Doctrine of Laches are sometimes referred to as rules of "repose," meaning they determine when the claim has died. These rules relate to all areas of civil law. The question of when a claim has lapsed or is barred by the Statute of Limitations is fairly straightforward. The question is handled in the same way in a tort case as in a contracts case. The question of when a claim is barred by Statute of Limitations does not involve the merits of the underlying cause of action. Rather, the issue and purpose of the Statute of Limitations relating to contract law is the same as the purpose of statutes of limitations generally: to provide an end point for claims.

Many states have a six-year Statute of Limitations applicable to contract actions. Courts hold that the Statute of Limitations applies to quasi or implied contracts as well as express and bargained for contracts. Thus, courts have applied state statutes of limitation actions to indemnify, to recover money received by defendant, to obtain the restitution, and settlements based on tort claims. Because the Statute of Limitations for a contract claim is generally a longer period of time than the Statute of Limitations for a tort claim, a plaintiff's lawyer will sometimes cast the claim based on a contract as well as on the tort.

The question of whether parties can change the applicable statute by agreement is clear under the UCC and less clear in the case of common law claims. Parties may include in the contract the period of limitations, seeking to override the period stated by the statute. This practice is recognized and given deference in the UCC. Section 2-725 allows the parties to a contract to reduce the period of limitation in their original contract. It extends this right of the parties to change the period under the principle of freedom of contract. Nevertheless, the freedom of parties to negotiate a different Statute of Limitations period by agreement is not absolute. This right is limited in that an agreement to limit the period to less than one year is ineffective. Moreover, parties in a consumer contract do not have the power to reduce the Statute of Limitations under the UCC. This is a good example of a protective statute, which is intended to prevent a merchant from taking advantage of a consumer by extinguishing the right to bring a claim.

Laches is a separate claim that a plaintiff's delay in bringing a claim should mean that the court dismisses the action. This defense is made independently of the Statute of Limitations. The idea here is that a delay can be inequitable to the defendant and, thus, the delay should create an estoppel against the claim. The operation is the same as estoppel in other areas we have discussed. In the case of laches, the defendant is arguing that the court should exercise its equitable discretion to dismiss the claim and, thus, leave the parties where it finds them. To succeed in a claim of laches, the defendant argues that plaintiff's delay has lead to such detriment to defendant that it would be a miscarriage of justice to enforce the contract — even if it would have been a valid claim if brought in a timely fashion. Thus, laches is a doctrine of discretion of the court to prevent injustice. Generally the defendant makes two showings to establish laches: first that the plaintiff caused an unreasonable delay in failing to assert its claim in a timely manner, and second, defendant needs to show that this delay prejudiced the defendant in some serious way.

The Statute of Limitations under the UCC

Under the UCC, § 2-725 provides that "an action for breach of any contract for sale must be commenced within the later of four years after the right of action has accrued." Accrual under the UCC is generally when the breach occurs. Thus a contract right can accrue (and the Statute of Limitations clock begins to run) even though the aggrieved party does not know the breach has occurred. The rule under the UCC is different for a breach of a warranty. A claim for a breach of warranty accrues when the seller has tendered delivery to the buyer. The UCC leaves questions of the law relating to tolling of the Statute of Limitations to state law. The four-year limitation period 2-725 is not an absolute. The provision creates some flexibility by allowing a plaintiff additional time by a discovery rule that allows an action within one year after the breach should have been discovered. This flexibility is limited in that it cannot extend the statutory period longer than five years.

Statute of Frauds

Introduction

As we have seen, the general rule of contract law is that oral contracts are ordinarily enforceable. This principle is contrary to the beliefs of many people beginning in the law. Most of us have a feeling that contracts should be put in writing and signed. This is a good practice, quite apart from the Statute of Frauds. It is a good idea to write down agreements so that both parties can see what they actually agreed to do. Probably the principal reason that people believe they contracts should write and sign their contracts is the Statute of Frauds. It is an exception to the general rule noted above: contracts are enforceable without regard to whether they are evidenced by a writing. The important effect of the Statute of Frauds is that some promises (those that falls within the Statute) must be evidenced by a writing to be enforceable. A promise outside the Statute need not be in writing to be enforced. "Satisfying" the statute means that a sufficient writing was made.

The Statute of Frauds requires that particular types of contracts be written down or otherwise memorialized to allow enforcement of the contract. The rationale often given for the Statute of Frauds is generally that some types of promises are more susceptible to fraud. Having a written document that states the contract has many advantages. It serves to caution people of the significance of their promise and the enforceability of their promise. It also serves an evidentiary function, giving clear evidence that the promise exists. A writing also helps the parties to a contract as they go forward in performing their deal, by making them more confident about their obligations and the details of performance.

The Statute of Frauds is a defense to contract liability. Generally it is raised by the defendant or the party resisting enforcement of a promise. Sometimes the focus on the Statute of Frauds makes students feel that if the plaintiff wins the argument on the Statute of Frauds he wins the case. This is not accurate. When the plaintiff wins the argument on the Statute of Frauds he wins the try to go forward to make the case that a contract does exist and the defendant breached the contract. On the other hand, if the defendant successfully establishes a defense on the Statute of Frauds, the case is over and the defendant wins the case in the sense of being able to resist enforcement.

In reality there are many different statutes that require that contracts be written down or memorialized. For example, some states require that the sale of intangibles such as stocks and bonds be in writing. Others require that waivers of conflicts of interest of a lawyer be in writing. When we cover the Statute of Frauds in contracts class, we focus on several traditional statutory provisions that have been adopted in virtually all the states in the U.S. These statutes were modeled on the English Statute of Frauds, which was enacted in 1677 (29 Chas. 2 c. 3).

The British Parliament passed the Statute of Frauds based on a belief that some people might falsely assert that a contract exists. In other words, the Statute is intended to prevent enforcement of a claim when it is a lie. This is the type of fraud the Statute is designed to prevent. Thus, the Parliament passed legislation that mandated that courts could not enforce certain types of contracts unless the party seeking enforcement had a written document that set forth the obligation and bore the signature of the defendant. The British statute stated it was intended to combat "fraude and perjurie." The fraud of alleging a contract falsely was the single fraud that the legislation addressed. After the Revolutionary war, the colonies all adopted the statute, either as part of statutory law or common law. Most states have retained the rule although England abolished it in 1954.

Courts limit the effect of the statute in various ways, creating exceptions to the rule. They recognize that just as people might lie to assert the existence of a contract, so they might also lie (and defraud the other party) by denying the existence of the contract. This central problem creates the off-again on-again atmosphere of opinions dealing with the statute. The terminology of the cases focuses on whether the contract "falls within" the statute, meaning a writing is required, or whether it "falls outside" the statute, meaning a writing is not required. In our discussion and in court opinions, you will see analysis that follows the following path: (1) plaintiff asserts a contract, (2) defendant asserts the Statute of Frauds prevents enforcement of the contract, even if it does exist, (3) plaintiff asserts that either the statute does not apply or the case comes within an exception to the statute and thus the contract is enforceable, or the defendant did sign a writing that satisfies the statute.

Most people know that signing a contract is a significant step. Nevertheless, the general rule of contract law is that contracts can be enforced although they are entered based on the spoken word. Thus, courts generally enforce contracts that are not written down or recorded anywhere. It is more accurate to say that courts are not barred from enforcing oral contracts. Issues of credibility can also mean that an oral promise may not be enforced. In other words, the trier of facts may not believe that Defendant's claim is true. Statutes of frauds set forth the exception to this general rule, establishing that some contracts cannot be enforced against a person who has not signed a written commitment. You can see the Statute of Frauds itself as an exception to the general rule of enforceability of oral contracts. Additionally, there are exceptions to the prohibition of enforcement in contracts that do fall within the Statute of Frauds. This section considers both the bar to enforcement in particular cases and the exceptions to that bar.

Terminology

In dealing with Statute of Frauds cases, courts address three issues. First, is the contract *within* the scope of the statute? Only certain classes of contracts are subject to the writing requirement. Second, is the document being offered as evidence of the contract *sufficient* under the statute? Third, assuming that a contract is unenforceable under the statute, does some exception apply that would nevertheless make it enforceable? The statute provides that a contract that is within its scope is not enforceable unless it is evidenced by a writing that is (a) sufficient to show the existence of the contract, and (b) is signed by the "party to be charged."

A note on language usage is helpful. Sometimes people refer to a "verbal" contract or a "verbal" promise. They usually mean an "oral" contract. Both oral contracts and written contracts are "verbal" because they use words. While it is possible to have a non-verbal contract—one based on conduct rather than words—this is not usually the distinction being made by use of the term "verbal." Since language is important in the law, remember to refer to "oral" contracts when you mean ones that are spoken rather than written.

A One-way Street

You may have heard the old saying "what's good for the goose is good for the gander." In various legal cases, lawyers call on this old saying to argue for equal treatment of both parties under the law. In other words, generally speaking, if one party gets a certain benefit or right, the other party gets a corollary benefit or right. The Statute of Frauds is an exception to this general rule. One party can enforce even in a case in which the other party has no right to enforce if one party signed and the other did not. This point is captured in the phase "signed by the party to be charged." In other words, if you sign a contract and the other party does not sign it, he can enforce it and you cannot. This fact emphasizes the good practice of only signing a contract when the other party has signed. Of course this is not always possible, especially when the parties are remote geographically from each other while they are bargaining. In such a case some trust is involved at the time of signing.

If only one party has signed the written memorandum, the writing can only be used against that party. This point is true in essentially all statutes of frauds.

In other words it is true under the UCC and also under state statutes dealing with the traditional categories of land sales and long-term contracts (longer than a year).

Principal Classes of Contracts

We have noted the UCC provisions governing some points of contract law. The differences between the UCC Statute of Frauds and others are significant, both as matter of understanding the different categories that apply and also the different rules and exceptions. You should remember the dividing line that we often see between the sale of goods (which is governed by the state version of the UCC) and other contracts, which are governed by state statutory law and common law. In the case of the Statute of Frauds, both areas are statutory.

The state statutes of frauds cover a variety of topics, most of which are drawn from the English statute of 1677. The wording of these state statutes is remarkably similar on the central categories. The five basic topics are covered in virtually every state. Some states have add-on provisions. Below is an excerpt from Tennessee Code § 29-2-101 (2006):

a) No action shall be brought:
   1) To charge any executor or administrator upon any special promise to answer any debt or damages out of such person's own estate;
   2) To charge the defendant upon any special promise to answer for the debt, default, or miscarriage of another person;
   3) To charge any person upon any agreement made upon consideration of marriage;
   4) Upon any contract for the sale of lands, tenements, or hereditaments, or the making of any lease thereof for a longer term than one (1) year; or
   5) Upon any agreement or contract which is not to be performed within the space of one (1) year from the making of the agreement or contract;
   unless the promise or agreement, upon which such action shall be brought, or some memorandum or note thereof, shall be in writing, and signed by the party to be charged therewith, or some other person lawfully authorized by such party.

The example demonstrates the categories that exist in virtually all state statutes of fraud, which are: surety contracts, contracts to answer for the duty of another, contracts not to be performed within a year (i.e. long term contracts), contracts in consideration of marriage, and contracts for the sale of an interest in land. Additionally, the UCC creates a statute of frauds in the sale on goods context.

State statutes present variations in the Statute of Frauds categories. For example, the Tennessee statute contains the five traditional categories included in most states and dealt with in most contracts courses: (1) a promise to answer for the debt of another, (2) surety contracts, (3) promises in consideration of marriage, (4) sale of land, (5) promises not to be performed within a year (aimed at long-term contracts). Because some of these types of contracts are of little significance today, we treat the less important categories briefly.

1. The Executor or Administrator Promise to Answer for the Debt of Another

The English Statute of Frauds took special care to protect one who tried to help another person by promising to answer for his debts. This general category is similar to the surety arrangement, the next category.

2. Surety Contracts

A surety contract creates an obligation on a party who agrees to be responsible for the debts of another. This is a particular context of the "duty of another" situation discussed above. The surety is often a contingent obligation. It is contingent on the first party failing to pay a debt. Some of you may have had the benefit of a surety when you purchased your first car. If your parents wanted to support your desire to buy a car, they may have signed the financing agreement on the car as a surety, meaning that if you failed to pay the debt as agreed they would be responsible. They may also have signed as a non-contingent co-signer with an equal obligation. In either case, they are agreeing to answer for the debt you incurred on the car. Commercial surety arrangements are similar to insurance. The surety on a construction bond agrees to complete the construction in the event the original contractor fails to complete the construction.

A promise by an executor or administer of a decedent's estate to pay the decedent's debts out of the executors own money is is a particular type of surety agreement. It is mentioned specifically in the original English Statute of Frauds and is often discussed separately. We take it up here as a type of surety agreement because it falls within the general category of a surety. Like the general Surety Rule, this particular example is intended to protect persons who act as executors and administrators.

Several situations have a similarity to the surety contract but do not meet the requirements and, thus do not receive protection under the rule. Parties sometimes refer to a surety as an "accommodation party." When the surety on a contract signs the contract, any Statute of Frauds issue is normally obviated because the signed writing satisfies the statute. Sometimes courts face difficult issues relating to whether a party is a primary obligor or a surety and, further, if the party is shown to be a surety, whether his primary purpose was to protect his own interests. This situation is an exception to the protection of the surety provision of the statute referred to as the "Main Purpose Rule." Some courts refer to the situation as the "leading object" rule. The issue courts decide in cases about this exception is whether the promissor claiming to be a surety is a surety entitled to protection of the Statute of Frauds. If the surety is held to be within the Main Purpose exception, he loses the protection of the Statute. If the court finds the Main Purpose Rule does not apply, plaintiff will need to satisfy the Statute of Frauds by showing that the surety signed a written document promising to serve as surety.

This rule holds that a plaintiff may enforce the obligation against a surety without a writing if the primary purpose of the surety was to benefit himself. If the surety agreed to serve as a surety to protect his own financial or business interests, the reason for the protection of the Statute of Frauds is not justified and the surety loses that protection. The *Restatement* makes this point succinctly. Section 116 states:

> A contract that all or part of a duty of a third person to the promisee shall be satisfied is not within the Statute of Frauds as a promise to answer for the duty of another if the consideration for the promise is in fact or apparently desired by the promisor mainly for his own economic advantage, rather than in order to benefit the third person. If, however, the consideration is merely a premium for insurance, the contract is within the Statute.

The traditional example of the Main Purpose exception is provided in Illustration 2 to Section 116:

> D [debtor] owes C [creditor] $1,000. C is about to levy an attachment on D's factory. S [surety], who is also a creditor of D's, fearing that the attachment will ruin D's business and thereby destroy his own chance of collecting his claim, orally promises C that if C will forbear to take legal proceedings against D for three months, S will pay D's debt if D fails to do so. S's promise is enforceable.

Similarly, if a court finds that the promise sued on is a novation or if the promise made by the person claiming to be a surety is actually an indemnification of the primary debtor, the Statute of Frauds does not provide protection. Some courts refer to the novation as an exception to the statute. Others consider the novation not a surety arrangement at all. The *Restatement* makes this point succinctly. Section 115 takes the later approach, stating that a contract that is "itself accepted in satisfaction of a previously existing duty of a third person to the promisee is not within the Statute of Frauds as a contract to answer for the duty of another." A novation is a substituted contract that includes a new party to the agreement. This new party can be either the obligee or the obligor. Courts sometimes refer to a novation as a rescission followed by a new contract between the parties.

3. Contracts in Consideration of Marriage

A promise made in consideration of marriage comes within the Statute of Frauds and, thus, requires a signed writing to be enforceable. This category is not often brought up in modern contract litigation. It should be noted that this category of a "promise made in consideration of marriage" is not the same as a promise to marry. If you promise to marry someone, the promise does not need to be in writing to be enforceable. On the other hand, few people bring claims on promises to marry in modern times.

4. Transfers of an Interest in Land

Virtually all state statutes of frauds include requirements that contracts for the sale of an interest in land be in writing to be enforceable. Some states include leases of a year or longer in the statute relating to the sale of an interest in land. Additionally, some states include within the Statute transfers of land even when the transfer is not a sale. Thus gift transfers must be in writing to be enforceable in these states. Many states construe an "interest in land" broadly to include in their Statute of Frauds leases of one year or longer, a promise to will an interest in land, or a promise to assign an interest in land. Some states refer to "transfers" of real estate. Thus, they include gifts of land as well as sales of land within the statutory requirement of a writing. Many states construe the term "interest" to include any right, privilege, power, or immunity.

> ▸ Lucy and Zehmer are sitting in a restaurant drinking. Zehmer offers to sell the Ferguson place for $50,000. After some negotiation, the two shake hands on the deal. Lucy subsequently tries to enforce the contract but Zehmer refuses.

If this contract is oral and has no writing, it is unenforceable. If, however, the seller writes out a short statement of the sale with his signature, as happened in the famous case involving these parties, a court could find the contract enforceable. In that case, the seller merely jotted down the statement of the sale on a café check. Some courts require more detail about the contract when it involves land rather than goods or services. This is probably because of the great value our legal system places on land. Generally, courts enforce such contracts as long as the description of the land in the writing is sufficiently specific regarding the plot of land to be sold.

Most states recognize an exception to the statutes of frauds for sellers of land who have conveyed the land to the buyer. Thus, the seller who has transferred land can recover from the purchaser without a writing. This situation is sometimes referred to as the exception for full performance.

5. Contracts Not to Be Performed within a Year

A good way to remember the category of "Contracts not to be performed within a year" is to recognize that the drafters of the statute sought to mandate writings on important contracts and ones that deserve special protection. Long term contracts fall within these purposes for two reasons. First, long-term contracts have more significance because of the amount of time committed to the contract. Second, some courts have reasoned that it is likely that "slippery memory" make contracts entered a long time ago harder to remember accurately. Some contracts teachers believe that the Statute of Frauds' one-year provision came into being to provide a limit on the sympathies of the jury in cases where an employee (called a "servant" in many older cases) claimed his employer (called a "master") had orally promised to hire for a long period of time. Fearing a sympathetic jury would allow enforcement of the alleged promise, the legislature drafters added the provision to require significant contracts (i.e., long term contracts of over a year) to fall within the requirement to have the promise in writing to be able to enforce it.

Probably because of the tension between concerns about the statute working injustice or a fraud when it is used to defeat meritorious claims, courts often apply this provision literally. In other words, the provision only defeats enforcement when the parties clearly intended that the contract could not be performed in a year or less. This interpretation removes from the statute performances that are expected to take a long time when it is conceivable to perform the contract in less than a year. Thus, building a building that is expected to be constructed over two years could be held to fall outside the statute because it did not set a time frame or limit that would make it impossible to perform in one year. In other words, the issue is not one of likelihood of performance but rather did the parties specify that the contract was "not to be performed within one year." The fact that it is extremely unlikely that a contract will be performed within the year does not cause it to fall within the Statute of Frauds. In fact there are cases in which a plaintiff brings suit more than a year after the contract was made but the court holds that the contract does not fall within the Statute of Frauds provision because the parties did not make clear that the contract was not to be performed in a year.

> ▶ Contractor orally agrees to build a multimillion dollar building with a time table that estimates work will last two years. Owner later repudiates the contract and ejects Contractor from the building site. If Contractor sues, the court may enforce the contract, finding that the agreement does not fall within the statute because the parties did not agree that the contract could not be performed in one year. The fact that more than a year has passed at the time of the action does not alter this result since the contract is to be judged by the intent of the parties at the time of contracting.

Here, the parties estimate that the contract will take two years to perform. The estimated time is not the test, however. The question is whether, by its terms, the contract is not to be performed within one year. While it seems literally impossible to perform the contract within a year, a court may hold it is not within the Statute of Frauds provision relating to contracts not to be performed within a year because by its terms it does not require a performance over a period longer than a year.

With enough money and labor, it is theoretically possible to do the work within a year and therefore the contract does not fall within the scope of the Statute of Frauds and is enforceable.

> ▶ Borrower and Lender agree that Borrower will borrow $100,000, with an obligation to pay the money back in 18 months.

In the case of a debt, which debtor can repay over 18 months, the court may hold that the contract could be performed within a year if the debtor could pay off the debt early under the contract. This would be full performance and would occur within a year on the terms of the agreement. This interpretation seems justified by the literal language of the statute. It narrows the scope of the certain operation of the statute to contracts that specify a term of years.

> ▶ Employee and employer agree to a term of employment of two years. This is an example of a contract that is within the Statute of Frauds provision of a contract "not to be performed within one year." Of course employer could terminate employee for cause and employee

could quit for cause. The fact that the parties could terminate a contract prior to the one year anniversary does not take the contract outside the Statute of Frauds since this is termination rather than performance. The statute deals with performance.

A few additional examples will make the one-year provision clear:

(1) A orally agrees to work for B for five (5) years.

This promise cannot be performed within one year and therefore is *within* the statute and can only be enforced if some writing evidencing the promise exists.

(2) A orally agrees to work for B for a one-day period 13 months from now.

This promise cannot be performed within one year and therefore is *within* the statute and can only be enforced if some writing evidencing the promise exists.

(3) A orally agrees on January 1, to work for B for one year beginning on January 1.

If A starts on January 1, A will finish performance on December 31. It can be performed within one year. Therefore, this promise is not within the statute.

Lifetime Contracts

Contracts that specify employment for life are rare. They provide a good example of how courts interpret statutes such as the Statute of Frauds. Generally courts hold that a lifetime contract does not fall within the Statute of Frauds' one-year provision since death will be full performance of the contract and death could occur within one year.

▶ Employer hires Employee to work for him "for the life of Employee." A few months later, Employer fires Employee. Employee sues, seeking to enforce a lifetime contract. Most courts would hold this contract is not encompassed in the Statute of Frauds' one-year provision of a contract. Thus, no writing is required to enforce.

The result will not be altered if the employment contract is "for the life of Employer."

▶ Elderly Employer needs an assistant because he is infirm. He hires Employee to work for him "for the life of Employer." A few months later,

Employer fires Employee. Employee sues, seeking to enforce a life-time contract. Most courts would hold this contract is not encom-passed in the Statute of Frauds' one-year provision of a contract. Thus, no writing is required to enforce.

While it might seem that this contract, which runs for the term of Em-ployee's life, is intended to be a long term contract, it does not fall within the literal test set by the statute. Even though both parties expect the contract to last a long time, if we take the statute literally, the measurement of the term of the contract does not state a contract "not to be performed within one year." Employee might be run over by a bus tomorrow, in which case the lifetime contract would have been performed within a year. Again, the question is not whether it is *likely* that the contract be performed within a year, the questions is whether the contract sets a promise "not to be performed within one year."

> ▶ Elderly Employer needs an assistant because he is infirm. He hires Employee to work for him "for ten years or for the life of Employer." A few months later, Employer fires Employee. Employee sues, seek-ing to enforce a lifetime contract. Most courts would hold this con-tract does not need a writing. It is not literally within the statutory provision since the death of the employer will mean the contract is fully performed. This could occur within a year.

Such cases can turn on terminology and the facts of the case. There may be a dispute regarding what the offer and acceptance entailed. Did the employer say he would hire Employee to work for him "for ten years or for the life of Employer"? Or did he say the employment would be "for ten years but would terminate in the event Employer died"? This would make a difference since the statute speaks in terms of performance, not termination. You can see the fac-tual disputes can be intense, especially since the debate on the facts relates to oral statements rather than to a writing. The problem of debating the oral statements of the past is of course the very problem that the Statute of Frauds was intended to correct. Nevertheless, there is a good argument for reading statutes literally and this statute deals in terms of contracts "not to be per-formed within one year."

Other Provisions

Many state statutes add other types of promises to their Statute of Frauds beyond the traditional categories. Because of the problem with lifetime contracts at least one state (California) passed a Statute of Frauds provision that requires contracts to be performed within a measuring lifetime to be in writing. From this fact you can see that legal authorities are not uniformly critical of the Statute of Frauds. Some states expressly include long-term leases of land within the land provision. Others include gifts of real estate within the statute. The Tennessee statute provides a good example of the diversity of provisions found in statutes of frauds. In addition to the traditional categories noted above, it includes language making the promise of a lender or creditor to lend money unenforceable without a writing. Tennessee Code § (b)(1) 29-2-101 provides:

> No action shall be brought against a lender or creditor upon any promise or commitment to lend money or to extend credit, or upon any promise or commitment to alter, amend, renew, extend or otherwise modify or supplement any written promise, agreement or commitment to lend money or extend credit, unless the promise or agreement, upon which such action shall be brought, or some memorandum or note thereof, shall be in writing and signed by the lender or creditor, or some other person lawfully authorized by such lender or creditor.

Exceptions to the Statute

We have dealt with some of the exceptions to the Statute of Frauds in the foregoing discussion. Additional exceptions exist. For example, The *Restatement (Second) of Contracts* recognizes an exception to the statute based on full performance. Section 145 states: "Where the promises in a contract have been fully performed by all parties, the Statute of Frauds does not affect the legal relations of the parties." This result is justified by the fact that the Statute relates to judicial enforcement, not to prohibiting performance of contracts made without a writing. Additionally, the Statute of Frauds in the UCC presents new exceptions, which we will discuss in our treatment of the UCC Statute of Frauds.

Satisfying the Statute

Satisfying the statutes in most states occurs when the memorandum contains: (1) a signature (2) on behalf of the party to be charged, (3) reasonable identification of the subject matter of the contract, (4) sufficient indication that a contract has been made between the parties, or offered by the signor; and (5) the essential terms stated with reasonable certainty.

Requirements of the Writing

When a court determines that a promise is within the Statute of Frauds, this does not mean that the defendant automatically wins and the action is thrown out of court. It is possible that the party charged (the defendant) may have created evidence that is sufficient to satisfy the statute. Courts often refer to a sufficient "memorandum" or a sufficient "writing," although most modern courts that have faced the question accept an electronic document as well as a physical document to satisfy the statute. To satisfy the statute the writing or memo or electronic documents must provide evidence that the parties entered a contract and reasonably identify the subject matter and the "essential terms" of the contract. What counts as reasonable identification of the subject matter and as "essential terms" varies significantly among different types of contracts. Clearly the least demanding standard for the plaintiff seeking to satisfy the statute occurs in the sale of goods area. We will save the discussion of how little is required for our separate treatment of the Statute of Frauds under the UCC later in this section. Courts seem to require the most detail and convincing evidence in a writing in the context of a sale of land. This is probably because of the special regard held for real property in our legal system. There is considerable flexibility and discretion for the trial court's decision regarding what evidence is sufficient to satisfy the standard. Additionally the court's philosophy regarding the statute itself can come into play in these decisions. In some cases, courts allow parties to combine documents to satisfy the statute, meaning that separate documents can be read together to give evidence of the subject matter and the essential terms. In one famous case included in many casebooks involving the Elizabeth Arden cosmetic company, the court allowed the plaintiff to provide several items with the signature on one of these items to satisfy the requirement of a writing. In *Crabtree v. Elizabeth Arden*, a sales manager who had been fired asserted he was hired under a two-year contract. In response to defendant's Statute of Frauds defense, plaintiff convinced the court to combine several documents, including a schedule noting the plaintiff's initial salary, promised raises, and Crabtree's expense account and a payroll card, which a company executive initialed. The court allowed the combined documents to be combined to show the terms of the contract and to establish the signature by the executive's initials.

The writings that parties produce in entering a contract can be lengthy, detailed, and exhaustive documents, prepared by teams of lawyers. Much less detailed and less formal documents can satisfy the Statute of Frauds. One of the famous cases included in most casebooks (*Lucy v. Zehmer*), involved a hand-written note on a restaurant check. Some casebooks include a picture of the contract on the Ye Ole Virginie Inn bill. The requirement of the Statute of Frauds is simple: does the writing provide evidence that the asserted promise occurred and does the writing give enough information to know what the important terms are and how to enforce the promise? The point of the statute, after all, is to avoid fraud and therefore the writing should be sufficient to show that it is unlikely that the claim is fraudulent. Because this is inherently a subjective determination by a fact-finder, and because situations tend to be highly contextual, the cases vary widely. It is easy to find cases in which relatively detailed memoranda have been found insufficient and cases where the briefest and sketchiest of writings have been deemed sufficient.

As we noted above, the Statute of Frauds requires that the memorandum be signed by the party to be charged (or his or her agent). The law of agency is a subject you will probably take up later in law school in your business organizations course. For now, you need simply recognize that the law sometimes permits one person to legally bind another by signing his or her name. The person who authorizes the other to act is known as the "principal." The person who acts on behalf of the other is known as the "agent." Where a principal gives an agent authority, the agent's acts are fully binding on the principal. The most common example of agency is the employment relationship. An employee acting within the scope of his or her duties can bind the principal.

While the best signature is the full name of the party in ink on the document, courts accept much less formal signatures. Modern courts hold that a signature can be any symbol used to authenticate the writing as that of the party. Initials, an "X," thumb prints, type-written names, printed forms, embossed seals, and impressions from a rubber stamp, electronic signatures, and marks on faxes have been found to constitute a signature for purposes of the Statute of Frauds. If the court is convinced that the party is using a symbol to authenticate the writing, this is generally sufficient for a signature.

Disappearing Memorandum

In some cases parties lost or destroyed the memo of the agreement. Some courts hold that if the parties have reduced their agreement to writing, the statute is satisfied, even though a copy of the agreement cannot be produced in court.

Sales of Goods for $500 or More

The Statute of Frauds for Sales of Goods is widely adopted in this country. While the amended UCC 2 provides a higher amount to trigger the requirement of a writing for sales of goods, the version of the UCC Statute currently adopted in most states has a triggering price of $500. The usual provision provides as follows:

§ 2-201. Formal Requirements; Statute of Frauds.

(1) Except as otherwise provided in this section a contract for the sale of goods for the price of $500 or more is not enforceable by way of action or defense unless there is some writing sufficient to indicate that a contract for sale has been made between the parties and signed by the party against whom enforcement is sought or by his authorized agent or broker. A writing is not insufficient because it omits or incorrectly states a term agreed upon but the contract is not enforceable under this paragraph beyond the quantity of goods shown in such writing.

(2) Between merchants if within a reasonable time a writing in confirmation of the contract and sufficient against the sender is received and the party receiving it has reason to know its contents, it satisfies the requirements of subsection (1) against such party unless written notice of objection to its contents is given within 10 days after it is received.

(3) A contract which does not satisfy the requirements of subsection (1) but which is valid in other respects is enforceable
a) if the goods are to be specially manufactured for the buyer and are not suitable for sale to others in the ordinary course of the seller's business and the seller, before notice of repudiation is received and under circumstances which reasonably indicate that the goods are for the buyer, has made either a substantial beginning of their manufacture or commitments for their procurement; or
b) if the party against whom enforcement is sought admits in his pleading, testimony or otherwise in court that a contract for sale was made, but the contract is not enforceable under this provision beyond the quantity of goods admitted; or
c) with respect to goods for which payment has been made and accepted or which have been received and accepted (Sec. 2-606).

There are several key elements of 2-201(1) worth noting. The $500 limitation operates as a bar, not a lid. In other words, if the statute applies, the promise is not enforceable at all. Enforcement is barred by the Statute of Frauds. Plaintiff cannot enforce up to $499. If the statute applies and he does not satisfy the statute he cannot enforce for any amount. The essential terms requirement from other statutes is relaxed in the UCC context. Terms that are usually considered "dickered terms" can be omitted without impairing a memorandum's ability to satisfy the statute. However, the quantity term must be included. Significant exceptions to the writing requirement exist in Subsections (2) and (3) of 2-201. Whether Subsection (1)'s prefatory language prevents reliance from creating an exception to the writing requirement (see 1-103) is disputed. As mentioned earlier, the amended UCC Article 2, which has not yet been adopted in many states, presents a narrower Statute of Frauds than in the past since it increases the amount of the statute of frauds bar in a contract for the sale of goods to $5,000 or more.

Under the UCC, a record is not insufficient because it omits or incorrectly states a term agreed upon, but the contract is not enforceable under this subsection beyond the quantity of goods shown in the record. Between merchants, if within a reasonable time a record in confirmation of the contract and sufficient against the sender is received and the party receiving it has reason to know its contents, it satisfies the requirements of Subsection (1) against the recipient unless notice of objection to its contents is given in a record within 10 days after it is received.

The Uniform Commercial Code creates additional exceptions to the Statute of Frauds in this context in three situations: (1) specially manufactured goods, which are not suitable for sale to others when seller has begun production of the goods before notice of repudiation is received, (2) when a party admits the contract in court pleadings or under oath, and (3) when payment has been made and accepted for goods or goods have been received and accepted.

A claim of Promissory Reliance (or Promissory Estoppel) may provide a bar to be used by the party arguing against the defense of the Statute of Frauds when the elements summarized in *Restatement 139* are met. This Rule is a more specialized rule of the action in reliance generally.

What Does the Statute Require for a Writing?

Generally, the different statutes of frauds do not require a lot of formality in the writing offered to defeat the bar of the Statute of Frauds. Most states allow an agent to legally bind another (the principal) by signing on behalf of the principal. Context does matter here. Courts generally require more detail in a contract for the sale of land than a contract for the sale of goods.

Most jurisdictions do not require that the signature be at the end of the document. Those that have such a requirement call for a "subscription" of the signature. While it is not necessary for the party to be charged to have signed each of the writings that are cumulated or incorporated together to meet the Statute of Frauds requirement, Plaintiff must have the signature of that party on some document that is clearly related to the other documents necessary to show the essential elements and identify the land. Courts determine whether the documents are sufficiently related to read them together for purposes of satisfying the Statute of Frauds. Many courts regard this issue not as one of intent of the parties, rather, but as an issue of whether or not the statute requires a signature at the bottom of the document or allows a signature at any point on the document to serve to satisfy the statute. Thus, a court applying a Statute of Frauds that simply using the term "signed" will likely view the statute as satisfied if there is a signature from the party to be charged (defendant) almost anywhere on the writing. The test is whether the signature (any symbol) is used to authenticate the writing. In this sense, "authenticate" means that it comes from a particular party and the party is indicating that it comes from him by the signature. Only in cases where a statute calls for a subscription will the court necessarily require a signature of the bottom of the document.

The writing required by the UCC is generally regarded as the least demanding of the different statutes. A very simple document will do. It need not have any of the trappings of a formal contract. It does not need to be the full contract or even anything you would call a contract. This is because the statute merely calls for evidence of the contract. The official comment to the UCC makes the non-demanding nature of the writing clear. It notes that the writing "need not contain all the material terms of the contract. Moreover, it states that the material terms stated "need not be precisely stated." Both courts and the comment are clear that in the sale-of-goods context the writing could be created without intent by the parties that it serve as a contract or even that it serve as writing for purposes of the Statute of Frauds. It is easy to see that the writing called for by Statute of Frauds is a much less formal or full-blown writing than the type of writing needed to trigger the Parol Evidence Rule. The very low level requirement is clear from the comment to the UCC: "All that is required is that the writing afford a basis for believing that the offered oral evidence rests on a real transaction." In other words, the Statute of Frauds simply gives the court some recorded document to indicate that the parties really did enter into a contract. The writing could even be incorrect and still be sufficient for purposes of the Statute of Frauds. This means that once the plaintiff survives the statutes of frauds defense, plaintiff could put on evidence to show that the writing was inaccurate. There is a limit to this point, however. The plaintiff cannot enforce the contract for a quantity of goods greater than the quantity referenced in the writing. Thus, a plaintiff could reform the contract to show that it required a smaller volume of goods but could not increase the volume beyond that shown in the writing.

The writing necessary to satisfy the Statute of Frauds is a much less formal or full-blown writing than the type of writing needed to trigger the Parol Evidence Rule. On the other hand, the Parol Evidence Rule does not specifically call for a signature. Be sure to compare the Statute of Frauds and the Parol Evidence Rule, two very different rules that deal with writings relating to contracts.

Parol Evidence Rule

The Parol Evidence Rule is often dealt with in conjunction with the issue of interpretation of contracts. We discussed the rule briefly in Chapter 3 on interpretation because of the inter-relationship of the two topics. In a sense the rule is not about interpretation. Rather it is a decision by the court of what is part of the agreement that can then be interpreted.

The Role of Writings in Contract Law

Parties often reduce agreements to writing. Sometimes parties do so in order to satisfy the writing requirement of the Statute of Frauds. More often, however, parties reduce contracts to writing to avoid the inherent risk of ambiguity and misunderstanding that accompanies oral agreements. By reducing an agreement to writing, the parties expect to achieve greater certainty about the obligations under the agreement. The Parol Evidence Rule (PER) is intended to effect these goals. A party may assert the Parol Evidence Rule in court to oppose the introduction of evidence about a written contract on the ground that the writing precludes presentation of the proffered evidence. The concept of the PER can be expressed both as a rule at trial and as an effect in the process of agreement. The effect of the PER at trial is that it bars evidence from being introduced when that evidence conflicts with a writing that expresses the final agreement or part of the agreement. The effect of the PER in the process of agreement is that it merges (and destroys) earlier or contemporaneous terms that conflict with the writing that the parties created.

Title of the Rule

You will see two different spellings on the rule: "parol" and "parole." The term "parol" comes from a French term meaning "word" or "spoken word." The title is misleading. The rule is not restricted to "parol" evidence in the sense of "oral" or "spoken word" evidence. It relates to extrinsic evidence (meaning evidence outside the document that expresses all or part of the contract). Second, but still looking at the first word (parol), the title is overstated. It does not exclude all parol (extrinsic) evidence. It only excludes evidence that came into being before the written agreement or at the time the written agreement was agreed to by the parties. Thus, the use of "parol" in the title of the rule is something of a misnomer. The third reason the title is misleading relates to the second word of the title (evidence). The rule is not really an *evidence* rule. Courts treat the rule as a matter of substantive law rather than as a matter of evidentiary law. You will learn more about the effect of this classification in your class on Civil Procedure. Having said that, the term "rule" in the title is accurate. It is a rule. Even though two of the three terms in the title can be attacked as misleading, you will see that the title does serve as a legitimate description of the rule. Along the same lines, we should note that the Parol Evidence Rule is not a rule of interpretation. Rather than aiding in interpretation, the rule defines the subject matter that is to be interpreted. It renders prior agreements within the scope of the rule without effect, whether these are oral or written agreements.

Effect of the Rule

The Parol Evidence Rule is a rule that encourages parties to write down their agreement. Under the Rule, when the parties express their agreement or part of the agreement in writing, the court will not allow evidence that is inconsistent with the written expression agreed to by the parties. The effect of the rule is to keep assertions out of a trial when they would undermine the written agreement. A plaintiff will wish to prevent another from bringing evidence that undermines his assertion of a contract and a breach. The Parol Evidence Rule provides a basis for plaintiff to prevent the introduction of such evidence if the court finds that the parties expressed the contract or some part of the contract in a writing. For the rule to bar the introduction of evidence, the court will also need to find that the parties agreed that the writing was the final expression of either their entire agreement or some part of the agreement. Once the court makes this finding about a writing, it will not allow evidence in the trial that contradicts the writing.

The effect of this rule at trial is exclusionary. That is, when the rule applies the court will disallow a statement or a writing, denying the party's right to bring the information into evidence in a trial. This is the effect when a court is convinced that the statement or writing contradicts a writing that the parties intended to be a final expression of their agreement. An illustration from the *Restatement* is helpful:

> ▶ C Corporation regularly borrows money from B Bank. S, the principal stockholder in C, offers to guarantee payment if B will increase the

amounts lent. There is a bank custom to make such loans only on adequate collateral supplied by the borrower and B promises S that B will follow the custom. S then executes a written agreement with B guaranteeing payment of future loans to C "with or without security." If the written agreement is a binding integrated agreement, C's prior promise is discharged.

If the court finds that the parties intended the writing to be the final expression of the entire agreement or even only the final expression of the agreement relating to security, it will not allow evidence of the custom of the bank or the promise to provide security. Even if B promised to follow the custom of giving security, in court he may successfully argue that the parties dropped that promise from their final agreement. Certainly when S executed a written agreement with B it should have read and challenged or rejected the wording that stated the guarantee would be "with or without security." If the written agreement is a binding integrated agreement, B's prior promise is discharged. It is possible but not likely that the court will find that the written agreement is not integrated in relation to this term.

Purposes of the Rule

The Parol Evidence Rule builds on the natural inclination to place more faith in the writings of the parties than in asserted oral statements. Assertions of oral statements are susceptible to a failure of memory. Additionally, parties sometimes remember things in a way that serves their own interests. Courts and scholars sometimes refer to the temptation of "myth making." Some people might even be wary that parties could lie to serve their own self interest, asserting falsehoods to bolster their side of a case or to escape liability.

The rule also serves the purpose of avoiding misunderstandings. When parties discuss the contract orally they may be saying and meaning different things. When speaker and hearer disagree on the obligations they undertake in their agreement, they could often avoid misunderstandings and prevent future disagreements if they would write the contract down—reducing their oral agreement to writing. The Parol Evidence Rule encourages parties to write down their contracts. Thus, it could be said to have some of the same effects as the Statute of Frauds of encouraging written contracts. Lawyers like to have things written down because the writing helps the parties understand their obligations as the days, weeks, and months pass between the time of entering a contract and time of fully performing a contract. The writing serves as evidence that the parties actually did enter a contract together. Additionally, it is evidence of the terms of the contract obligations each party accepted.

Exceptions to the Rule

The statement of the rule makes it seem a bit more straightforward than it is. As with many contract rules, this rule has exceptions. Although the court will not allow into evidence an oral or written statement that contradicts the writing agreed to by the parties, it will allow such statements to explain or supplement the writing and for other purposes. Evidence introduced by a party to interpret the contract is not excluded by the rule. Similarly, the rule does not bar evidence that relates to whether the document is integrated.

Restatement Section 214 sets forth a list of exceptions to the rule. When any of the following purposes are the reason that the evidence is presented to the court, the Parol Evidence Rule will not bar the evidence:

a) that the writing is or is not an integrated agreement;
b) that the integrated agreement, if any, is completely or partially integrated;
c) the meaning of the writing, whether or not integrated;
d) illegality, fraud, duress, mistake, lack of consideration, or other invalidating cause;
e) ground for granting or denying rescission, reformation, specific performance, or other remedy.

What the Parol Evidence Rule Does Not Do

As you can tell from the list above, the Parol Evidence Rule does not prevent the admission of evidence in all cases. Even when a complete integration is involved the court may allow evidence to come into the trial. A party can present evidence to oppose the contention that the writing was intended to be final, for example. Drafts do not fall into the category of protection, no matter how detailed and well crafted they are. This issue often comes down to a question of credibility. In addition to the issues noted above, the rule will not prevent a party from introducing evidence of a modified writing in a trial. It also will not prevent a party from establishing that the writing had no force (was not an expression of an agreement) unless and until a condition was met.

> ▶ For example, in one case a court found that although the parties agreed to a detailed agreement to set up a company and to transfer stocks from an existing company to form the new company, the agreement was subject to a condition of raising a certain amount of capital to finance the new company.

Section 241 to the *Restatement* makes the point that parties can orally agree that a writing will not have effect unless some future condition occurs. The illustration to this section makes the limitation on the Parol Evidence Rule clear. It follows:

> ▸ A and B make and sign a writing in which A promises to sell and B promises to buy goods of a certain description at a stated price. The parties at the same time orally agree that the writing shall not take effect unless within ten days their local railroad has cars available for shipping the goods. The oral agreement is operative according to its terms. If, however, the writing provides "delivery shall be made within thirty days" from the date of the writing, the oral agreement is inoperative.

Purpose of the Evidence Presented

From the discussion above, you can see that it is important to know the purpose evidence is presented to serve. The exceptions to the rule come into play, for example, when a party seeks to present evidence to interpret the contract. When a court faces the question of whether a document is integrated, it should look at all the evidence relevant to the question of integration. That is, whether the parties intended the writing to serve as a final (binding) expression of the deal. If the language of the writing is reasonably susceptible to more than one interpretation, courts will allow evidence of what the language means. Thus, the purpose of interpreting the meaning of the contract is an important exception to the exclusionary effect of the rule.

You may be skeptical about the point just made because it may seem an easy end-run around the rule. It seems that a lawyer could overcome the rule by simply saying: "Your honor, I'm not presenting evidence to contradict the writing but rather to supplement it or interpret it." While a party may try such an end-run tactic, it is not likely to be successful. If the court is convinced of the meaning of the language of the writing, it will not allow a contradiction to that language to come into court by masquerading as a supplement or interpretation. For example, let's return to the illustration from the *Restatement* noted above and try out the arguments of supplementation and interpretation.

> ▸ D Corporation regularly borrows money from C Bank. S, the principal stockholder in D, offers to guarantee payment if C will increase the amounts lent. There is a bank custom to make such loans only on adequate collateral supplied by the borrower and C promises S to follow the custom. S then executes a written agreement with C guaran-

teeing payment of future loans to D "with or without security." If the written agreement is a binding integrated agreement, C's prior promise is discharged.

Would a court allow evidence in despite the Parol Evidence Rule simply because the lawyer for the bank argues he needs to interpret or supplement the agreement? If the evidence is the predicable statement that C actually promised S to follow the bank's custom of giving collateral, the court is likely to see this statement as directly contradicting the writing. If it so finds, the court will disallow the evidence. On the other hand, if the bank argues that the borrower engaged in fraud or some other basis for rescinding the contract, the court will not allow the Parol Evidence Rule to bar credible evidence that there was an invalidating cause or that there is a ground for rescission, such as fraud.

A mistake can be a basis for allowing evidence to come into court despite an integrated writing. For example, if parties enter an integrated agreement for the purchase and sale of land but enter the contract under a mutual mistake about the land to be purchased and sold, the court will allow prior evidence that is relevant to establishing the mistake and, thus, the right to reformation of the contract.

Interpretation: Plain Meaning or Reasonably Susceptible

The discussion above about the right of a litigant to present evidence of the interpretation will make you realize how important and difficult this issue of interpretation can be. An important point we noted earlier in Chapter 3 on Interpretation is that the Parol Evidence Rule is not a rule of interpretation. Rather, the Parol Evidence Rule determines the terms included in a contract. While this is true, interpretation is necessary to determine this threshold question of what terms are in the contract. This may seem odd, but in this sense, interpretation of the circumstances and expectations of the parties plays a role in most questions of contract law. For example, it is necessary to interpret the words of the parties in determining whether there was an offer to enter a contract. We need to interpret the words and circumstances to understand whether a communication served as an acceptance. In this way, courts are interpreting the communications between parties and the reasonable expectations created by their communications at nearly every stage of the process of arguing about contract claims.

The argument that something is presented to help the fact finder interpret the agreement, while not always a winning argument, is a powerful one. Because of the importance of the argument, different judicial views have developed on how receptive (or skeptical) courts should be about allowing evidence on the ground that it serves the purpose of interpreting the contract. Some courts are reluctant to admit evidence. This judicial reluctance is the basis for the Plain Meaning Rule.

The Plain Meaning Rule

The Plain Meaning Rule appears both in the area of interpretation in its own right and, also, in the area of interpretation for purposes of applying the exception to the Parol Evidence Rule. This view of interpretive evidence essentially holds that no such evidence should come into the trial unless the language used in the writing is ambiguous. Courts that follow the Plain Meaning Rule look to the document's structure and content and do not admit evidence outside the contract unless they find the contract itself to be unclear. This task of restricting the inquiry to the contract document unless it appears unclear is sometimes referred to as the "four corners" test. An example of a decision that reflects the restrictive approach is found in the Gianni case discussed above. The court refused to allow the evidence that Mr. Gianni sought to introduce. Gianni's evidence would show that the parties intended the right to sell soft drinks included the right to sell soft drinks without competition from other vendors in the building. Of course courts are likely to vary on whether they regard a term of a contract as "plain" and clear or as ambiguous. In fact, sometimes both parties argue that a term is plain. They disagree on the plain meaning of the contract.

The Reasonably Susceptible Approach

We discussed this approach to interpretation above in our principal discussion of interpretation. The same sort of reasoning used in the interpretation area generally has application to the question of whether to exclude evidence, keeping it from the trier of fact when the parties have adopted a written contract. The *Restatement* clearly suggests that a court should not put on blinders when considering the issue of whether the written document is integrated, meaning the parties agreed it was the final expression of that part of the contract.

Comparing the Parol Evidence Rule with the Rule on Modification

The Parol Evidence Rule does not apply to modifications. This is because modifications are not prior or contemporaneous to the formation of the contract. They occur after the formation of the contract. The Parol Evidence Rule dispense with earlier variations. It does not apply to modifications because modifications occur after the time of the contract. The parties can modify the written contract either in writing or orally subject to the Statute of Frauds.

The Parol Evidence Rule applies when the parties to a contract put their agreement (or a portion of the agreement) in writing, intending the writing to be the final expression of their agreement (or portion of the agreement). The terms of the writing may not be contradicted by evidence of any prior or contemporaneous agreement or negotiations. (In the case of complete integrations the terms may not even supplemented by additional terms.)

By contrast, when parties reach an agreement to change their earlier agreement, intending that the second agreement should trump the first, their second agreement controls their obligations. It takes precedence over the first agreement. It may even destroy the first entirely. This point relates to the power of parties to contract generally. The Parol Evidence Rule does not apply. We could call this rule the "Last in Time Rule," or "Subsequent Agreement Rule." It is the rule about modifications to contracts. We discuss it in detail in Chapter 7 on modifications. The Parol Evidence Rule applies only when the subsequent agreement is in writing. It discharges prior agreements. Additionally, the parties sometimes seek to limit their power to change a contract by a No-Oral Modification Clause ("NOM clause").

Visualizing the Parol Evidence Rule

Pre-agreement	Contemporaneous with Agreement	Modification (Post-agreement)
PER APPLIES		PER does not apply
←————————— —————————→		
Oral or Written	Oral or Written	(but think about effect of NOM clauses)

Applying the Parol Evidence Rule

The Parol Evidence Rule applies only to a writing that the parties intended to be a final expression of one or more terms of their agreement. Application of the rule depends upon a party first alleging that it applies. The issue usually arises in trial. If a party alleges that the rule applies, then the court must decide whether the parties intended the writing to be their final expression of agreement or part of the agreement. That is a fact question upon which any relevant evidence can be admitted. If the writing includes a merger clause, courts often answer the question in the affirmative and declare the analysis at an end.

For purposes of the Parol Evidence Rule, there are three categories of agreements: (1) completely integrated writings; (2) partially integrated writings; and (3) unintegrated writings. The legal effect of the Parol Evidence Rule in any particular case depends upon which of the three categories is involved, and determining the category a writing falls into depends on the answer to one (and maybe two) questions:

Question 1:
Is the agreement integrated? See *Restatement 209(1)*.
If the answer to this question is "No," the agreement is unintegrated.
If the answer to this question is "Yes," ask Question 2.

Question 2:
Is the agreement completely or partially integrated? See *Restatements* 210 and 216(2).

Unintegrated Agreements

Unintegrated agreements have no special legal effect. Unintegrated agreements receive no special legal protection from the Parol Evidence Rule.

Integrated Agreements

Integrated agreements (both complete and partial) cannot be contradicted by evidence of prior or contemporaneous agreements or negotiations. *Restatement 215*. Also, integrated agreements (both complete and partial) discharge prior inconsistent agreements (to the extent of the inconsistency or contradiction). Res. 213(1).

Completely Integrated Agreements

Completely integrated agreements cannot be contradicted or even supplemented by evidence of prior or contemporaneous agreements or negotiations. *Restatement 216(1)*. (Partially integrated agreements can be supplemented with consistent additional terms. *Restatement 216(1)*.) Also, completely integrated agreements discharge prior agreements to the extent they are within the scope of the completely integrated agreement. *Restatement 213(2)*. (Partially integrated agreements do not discharge prior, consistent agreements within the scope of the integration.)

Signatures Not Required

You can see the Parol Evidence Rule is a powerful litigation tool. Because of the power of the rule, you might think that parties would need to have a signed writing to convince a court that it presents an integrated or completely integrated agreement. This is not the case, however. While having signatures will be evidence that the writing is a final expression of the deal or part of the deal (i.e., that it is an integrated agreement), a signature is not required.

The Parol Evidence Rule of the UCC

In one precisely drafted section, the UCC contains a formulation of the Parol Evidence Rule and rules in aid of interpretation. This statement is fairly similar to the *Restatement* formulation of the rule. The Parol Evidence Rule articulated in UCC 2-202. The provision states:

> Terms with respect to which the confirmatory memoranda of the parties agree or which are otherwise set forth in a writing intended by the parties as a final expression of their agreement with respect to such terms as are included therein may not be contradicted by evidence of any prior agreement or of a contemporaneous oral agreement but may be explained or supplemented
> (a) by course of dealing or usage of trade (Section 1-205) or by course of performance (Section 2-208); and
> (b) by evidence of consistent additional terms unless the court finds the writing to have been intended also as a complete and exclusive statement of the terms of the agreement.

The comment to this provision makes clear that the section rejects some approaches to the rule. For example, it is not necessary that the parties worked out all aspects of the deal. A writing can be final only on some matters relating to the contract and still have the force of the rule. Thus, even an incomplete statement of the contract can trigger the exclusionary effect of the rule. To have this effect, the court must be satisfied that the parties intended the written terms to be "a final expression of their agreement" with respect to those final terms. In other words, the contract does not need to be fully stated in the writing to have the effect of excluding evidence that is outside the writing.

"Consistent additional terms" are not excluded by the Parol Evidence Rule. When terms are consistent with the writing, the court will allow those terms to be asserted in court. However, if the court finds that the parties intended to set down their entire contract in the writing, then it will find that even terms that may appear to be consistent with the writing are in fact contradictory and must be excluded. The idea here is that the assertion that there are more terms in the contract is a contradiction of the parties' intent to set forth their entire agreement in the writing. In declaring a contract completely integrated, the parties are asserting (or even bargaining) for a message to the court that there are no additional terms. In such a case, the assertion that the parties provided additional terms is a contradiction to the assertion that the writing is complete. If the court finds that the parties intended the writing to be a "complete and exclusive statement of the terms of the agreement," then no additional terms can come into the trial.

Favorable Admission Rule on Course of Transactions under the UCC

When the UCC applies to a transaction, special attention should be paid to evidence of course of dealing, usage of trade, or course of performance. The UCC approach is even more receptive to admission of extrinsic evidence than the common law rule when the evidence is in one of these categories. Under the UCC even when a writing is completely integrated it may be explained or supplemented by evidence of course of dealing, usage of trade course of performance.

Merger or Integration Clauses

The following discussion of some sample clauses illustrates the way a party might plan for use of the Parol Evidence Rule. As you review the following three clauses, consider which clause you would prefer if you were a party to a dispute who wished to exclude evidence based on the Parol Evidence Rule.

Many contracts contain a "merger" clause. The purpose of the merger clause is to exclude any other terms from coming into the contract. The idea is that all of the terms have "merged" into the writing. Courts refer to a contract that is entirely written down as a "total integration." Thus, some courts and some contracts refer to the merger clause as a "total integration clause" or as an "integration clause." When integration clauses are included in written contracts, they are usually found near the end of the writing. Below are three samples of a clause that seeks to avoid any additions or changes to the contract.

Sample #1

Merger Clause. This document contains the entire agreement of the parties. There are no promises, terms, conditions, or obligations other than those contained in this document. This written contract supersedes all previous communications, representations, or agreements, either oral or written, between the parties.

Sample #2

Entire Agreement. This Agreement constitutes the entire understanding between Client and Seller with respect to the terms expressed herein. It may be modified only by a written instrument duly executed on behalf of both parties.

Sample #3

Integrated Agreement. This Agreement (i) constitutes the entire contract between the parties with respect to the subject matter hereof; (ii) supersedes all prior oral or written understandings and agreements which are merged herein, and (iii) may be amended only by a written instrument duly signed by both parties.

Notice the different headings on the clauses. Also notice that each of these clauses seeks to prevent the parties from having other agreements or terms that are not included in writing. All of the headings point to the conclusion that the contract document is the only evidence of the contract that should be admitted in a dispute. Although the headings are different, they all suggest that the writing "merges" or "integrates" all the terms and is the entire understanding. Despite the heading of Sample #2, the language of that provision may create a problem. By its literal terms, it states that the writing is "the entire understanding" between the parties "with respect to the terms expressed herein." This phrase raises a question of whether the agreement is merely a partial integration rather than a complete integration. Thus, a party (often the consumer or the less knowledgeable party) will assert that he received assurances relating to some aspect of the contract that is not spoken to in the contract.

Criticisms of the Rule

The last point noted above ties in with the issue of criticisms of the rule. Some scholars argue that the rule protects the dominant party from genuine efforts to enforce promises that were made during negotiations. The answer to this is generally that each party can protect himself by reading the writing before agreeing that it is a final statement of the contract or part of the contract. For example, in one case that appears in many casebooks, a man who ran a concession store in an office building asserted that he was told that he would have the exclusive right to sell soft drinks. In other words, Mr. Gianni, the lessee, said that no other vendor in the building could sell soft drinks. The contract signed by the parties clearly gave Mr. Gianni the right to sell soft drinks. It did not, however, state the right as an exclusive right. Students (and professors) reading this case are often sympathetic to Mr. Gianni. He is the economic underdog and there is language in the opinion that seems to suggest that he might be a blind vendor. Although the result does seem harsh, keep in mind that Mr. Gianni could bring in evidence to show fraud or even mistake if this is his basis for seeking to establish that the deal included an exclusive right to sell soft drinks.

Checkpoints

- A contract that can be barred by the statute is said to "fall within" the Statute of Frauds.

- A spoken contract is "oral", while both spoken and written contracts are "verbal."

- When a contract is signed by only one party, ONLY the party who did not sign may seek protection through the Statute of Frauds.

- Via the Main Purpose Rule, if a surety's main purpose in promising to pay someone else's debt is a benefit to himself, then the promise may be enforced against him, even in the absence of a writing.

- Most transfers of land are required to be evidenced by a writing to be enforceable.

- Contracts that cannot, by the terms of the contract, be performed within one year of the date of the contract fall within the statute.

- Sales of goods of over $500 in value must be evidenced by a writing to be enforceable.

- The purpose of the rule is to determine the terms to be interpreted as part of the agreement of the parties.

- The rule encourages parties to put contracts in writing.

- The rule dispenses with prior and contemporaneous terms not included in the writing.

- The rule does not apply to interpretation of terms.

- The rule does not apply to modifications.

- The rule does not bar evidence relating to the issue of whether a writing is completely or partially integrated.

- The rule does not bar evidence relating to fraud or other reasons for invalidating a contract.

- Once the statute of limitations has expired for a given case, a claimant can no longer bring the claim, regardless of the merits of the claim.

- A contract that can be barred by the statute is said to "fall within" the Statute of Frauds.

- A spoken contract is "oral", while both spoken and written contracts are "verbal."

- When a contract is signed by only one party, ONLY the party who did not sign may seek protection through the Statute of Frauds.

- Via the Main Purpose Rule, if a surety's main purpose in promising to pay someone else's debt is a benefit to himself, then the promise may be enforced against him, even in the absence of a writing.

Chapter 10

Performance and Breach

- Immaterial Breach
- Substantial Performance
- Comparison with Contract Formation
- Perfect Tender Rule
- Contract Condition Function
- Condition of Satisfaction
- The Choice of Subjective or Objective Standard
- Requirement of Good Faith
- Claims of Conditions Rendering a Contract Illusory
- Forfeiture
- Distinguishing Conditions from Timing Devices
- An Exercise to Identify Conditions
- Promises Implied in Conditions
- Promissory Conditions
- Anticipatory Repudiation
- Assurances of Performance
- Warranties as Conditions

Introduction

Now we are ready to explore the dimensions of the Third Sequential Question. We now assume that the parties have a valid, enforceable contract. The next question is whether one party breached the contract. For example, did one party refuse to perform or did a party perform in a defective way that gives the other party the right to damages for the defective performance? A decision not to perform is not always a breach. In some instances, the party refusing to perform may have a legitimate excuse. For example, a condition of his performance may not have occurred. The difference between a breach and other causes of the non-performance of a contract is critical: if the cause was a breach then remedies are available to the non-breaching party. If the cause is not a breach, remedies are unavailable.

For purposes of this chapter, we assume that the parties formed a contract. The issue of whether the parties formed a contract is taken up in the discussion of Formation. The good news for contracting parties is that the vast majority of contracts are successfully performed without dispute, or at least without dispute at a level that requires legal assistance. Nevertheless, the focus of this chapter is breach rather than performance because that is the focus of law practice and, thus, of contracts classes. From the lawyer's perspective, these issues generally arise because one party is unhappy with contract performance and objects or brings a claim against the other for breach. Sometimes both parties are unhappy and bring counter claims against each other. Thus, the focus of this area of law is whether a party has broken an enforceable promise. Like it or not, the legal perspective is all about disputes: problems that have developed or are likely to develop. People say "what could go wrong?" often meaning that everything looks good. When lawyers ask "what could go wrong," they are seriously considering all the ways things could turn out badly for either or both parties in a particular transaction. This point of view is part of the lawyer's job. It is part of the lawyer's role in advising the client and protecting the client's interest.

Tolstoy said that all happy families are the same, but unhappy families each have their own unique story. In a sense his point applies to contract performance as well. All performed contracts are the same from the point of view of the law. Fully performed contracts are unremarkable: Party A has provided performance and Party B has performed paying for A's performance or providing another exchange performance. The parties fulfilled their promises and no one has a dispute. Everyone is happy. More accurately, no one is unhappy enough to take action against the other. Lawyers and legal doctrine are not needed. Contract breaches, on the other hand, present unique (and sometimes fascinating) stories. Many times, the promise was incompletely or imperfectly performed. Perfection is unlikely in human endeavors, and thus performance is rarely perfect. Only when the unhappiness of a party to the contract is so significant that it is presented to a lawyer does a formal legal dispute ensue.

The performance stage raises an infinite variety of questions relating to what the parties intend by their contract. These are issues of interpretation regarding the meaning of the agreement and the intent of the parties. A lawsuit for breach of contract presents at least two significantly different stories about the same events as seen through the eyes of the opposing parties. For guidelines on interpretation of Contract terms, see Chapter 3.

Contract Enforcement

Contract law protects individual rights in promises. In doing so, it protects society's interest in encouraging contracts. Society's desire for certainty of obligation comes from the need of a commercial society to encourage contracts for future performance as opposed to instantaneous transfers. Enforcement of private contracts produces a belief by the public in the power of contracts and, thus, ensures more reliable promises. A society in which contracts are secure is one in which markets flourish. To make parties secure in contracting, the law enforces promises by respecting the benefit of the bargain (the deal). Accordingly, individuals can reasonably rely on contractual commitments. Each party values the exchanged performance he receives more than the exchanged performance he renders or he would not agree to the contract. The payoff, or benefit, to the contracting parties is the surplus of value in the deal. The payoff for society is the surplus of value created by the transaction and in the market at large by increased economic activity that results from giving individuals security to make contracts for future performance. In this way, contract law furthers the public good.

Two different types of breach should be noted: (1) breach by nonperformance; and (2) breach by defective performance. One response to the first type of claim is that the parties did not in fact enter a contract. Our earlier discussion on contract formation deals with this argument. The argument that there was no contract is unlikely in the second category since the party allegedly in default has begun performance. The fact that he has begun performance undercuts the claim that no contract exists. If there is no contract, why is this party going forward by performing?

People who enter a contract with each other know (or should know) that the broken promise brings more than disappointment or a change of the relationship. When the broken promise is recognized by the law as a contract, the party injured by the broken promise has recourse. The promise is enforceable through the machinery of government. Thus, the expectations of parties making commercial promises or others that meet the test for enforceability know that exchanged promises are an exchange of power, a mutual empowerment of the other to hold the other liable for the promise. These promises are not mere social interactions; they have credible weight. Parties who enter contracts recognize that this important subset of promises we call contracts can bring them significant benefit or significant losses.

The law has not always enforced promises as it does today. The history of the common law shows that courts rejected claims for enforcement, saying that the "mere expectation" of the injured party did not entitle it to damages. The attitude of the law at this point in history was that parties lacked legal recourse for broken promises. Courts did not recognize a contract since it did not accomplish a transfer of property but merely an obligation to transfer property or services at some later point in time. The result of this approach was a smaller universe of commerce; the trust given to a promise was a personal and risky matter, and, thus, few parties exchanged promises with people beyond their immediate peer group.

Each lawsuit or threat of a suit reminds contracting parties of their commitments. If Seller refuses to deliver the goods contracted for, Buyer, the injured party, has the right to obtain the goods from another source. This action of purchasing a substitute performance is referred to as "cover." If Buyer covers, he can sue under UCC 2-712 for damages based on the difference between the cover price and the contract price.

> ▶ So, for example, if Buyer entered a contract to purchase corn from Seller at $1.00 per bushel and Seller failed to deliver the corn, the Buyer could cover by purchasing from a different seller. If Buyer paid $2.00 per bushel, he would sue Seller for the difference between the two purchase prices: ($2.00 cover minus the $1.00 contract price). The point is discussed in detail in Chapter 11 on Remedies. The injured party has the right to bring a suit to recover the benefit of the bargain. If the injured party sues on the breach, it is unlikely that the breaching party will profit from the breach. At the time Seller assesses his interests in performing or breaching, he cannot fully know the extent of damages to the injured party. The breaching party also bears the risk that the injured party's rights under the contract may include specific performance. Thus, the breaching party runs the risk that the market conditions that influenced the rise in the market price (creating the opportunity to sell at a higher price) will also affect the injured party's cover costs.

The injured party has a right to damages for any breach, regardless of how serious. If the breach is a minor one, then the injured party is only entitled to damages. If the court finds the breach is serious or "material," then the injured party may have an additional right. In addition to damages, she may also be entitled to withhold her own performance that would otherwise have been due under the contract.

The Temptation to Breach Promises

A short exchange from the movie *Treasure Island* makes the point that the incentive to break promises is not unusual:

Long John Silver: "Treaties are only good till you find time to break 'um."
Jim Hawkins: "Not very honorable."
Long John Silver: "Aye, but very smart."

Whether a breach is "smart," as Long John Silver asserts, is subject to debate both as a general matter and in specific cases. Some economists argue that a breach may be a good thing from the point of view of society as well as from the point of view of the breaching party. They refer to this concept of a socially beneficial breach as an "efficient breach." The issue of the efficiency of a breach is the subject of significant scholarly debate. In large part, the courts ignore the debate and continue to treat contract liability as a form of strict liability.

The Theory of Efficient Breach of Promises

The law and economics focus of some scholars and professors suggests that some breaches of contract are efficient, meaning that these breaches are actually a good thing for society. The idea has been explained with the following story: suppose A enters a contract with B (buyer) to sell a certain quantity of widgets for $10 each. If C is willing to pay more for the widgets, the theory says that it may be efficient for A to breach the first contract (with B) and sell to C at the higher price. Other scholars point out that the obligation to sell to B means that B (not A) should get the benefit of selling to C for a higher price. This theory has provoked a lot of scholarship.

The theory of efficient breach has appeal, because it presents the issue of breaching in a simple analysis from the point of view of how much value the parties place on the item for which they are contracting. When you are practicing law, however, keep in mind that courts are not applying economic principles to breaches. Rather, they focus on the obligation accepted by each party. Thus, the efficiency of obligation (rather than that of breach) is central to damages. To apply damage rules, it is not necessary to know the values parties place on the performance. Rather, to apply damage principles, the court needs to know what the promise is (how much buyer promised to pay) and how much buyer must pay for a substitute performance. In other words, the court will not compare the value placed on the widgets by parties B and C. Instead, it will look at how much extra B (the first buyer) needs to pay to get the widgets promised under the contract. The efficient breach theory takes this point into consideration by saying that if A can pay damages to B and still make a profit on the resale to C, then the breach is efficient. It will be very difficult to calculate the damages prior to breach, however, making it unlikely the analysis will help the party trying to decide whether he will be better off by performing or breaching. This is because the law looks at the situation through the perspective of the injured party, the party the law seeks to put in a position promised under the contract. Injured party may cover at the time of breach or within a reasonable time. If C wants to pay more for the widgets, it is likely that the market price for widgets has gone up after the parties contracted for the sale. Thus, it is likely that when B looks for a substitute deal he will find the widgets at the higher rate ($20.00 here). If that is the case, the breach will not be efficient; it will not net more money for seller.

The damages principles set forth by the UCC make clear that the law seeks to put the injured party in the position he would have been in had the contract been performed. It is worth noting that this does not mean that damages should secure for injured party the benefit he "expected" or even what he "reasonably expected." Rather, it figures damages based on giving the injured party the ability of obtaining a substitute performance at the time set for performance. The market model of damages protects the original buyer by figuring damages as a matter of the market to make the injured party whole.

Through the use of market price of cover, contract captures the value of the contract at the time set for performance. Thus, contract law recognizes that a party who does not get the promised performance is worse off if he loses his allocated benefit from the contract. The damage formula subtracts contract price from the cover price, securing the goods to B in the example above (injured party) at the original price by requiring breaching party to pay the differential to current market.

If we think of efficiency of *obligation* rather than efficiency of breach, contract law makes more sense. Between the time of contracting and the time for performance, a party has the power though not the right to reallocate resources (goods or money) even though he has allocated those same resources by contract. When a party exercises this power in violation of his promise, he seeks to retain the right to reallocate resources in ways he deems efficient at that point in time. The central reason the parties enter a contract, however, is to limit such reallocation of resources. After all, if a party wishes to retain the right to reallocate his resources, the clear-cut way to accomplish this is to refrain from entering a contract relating to those resources.

Promises and Conditions

It is often important to distinguish between promises and conditions to determine whether a party has breached his obligation under a contract. A condition is an event that is not certain to occur, which the parties agree must occur in order for a contractual obligation to come due. If the condition does not occur, the duty that it modifies does not come due. A promise is a commitment that may cause an event to occur. (In rare cases it is a promise that an event will not occur. For example, in a covenant not to compete the promise is to refrain from doing something, i.e., competing for a specified amount of time in a certain job or profession in a certain geographic area.)

Relation of Condition and Performance

When a condition exists in a contract, the party seeking to enforce the contract needs to show that the condition has occurred. Generally conditions are closely linked to contract performance.

> ▸ For example, a common condition in a contract to purchase a house or a building is the condition that the buyer is able to obtain a loan. This condition is closely linked to performance. In fact, it often makes the purchase possible. Contract law does not require this kind of linkage between the condition and the contract performance, however. Thus, parties could make virtually any event a condition to the obligation so long as the event is "not certain to occur."

To offer a frivolous example, I could agree to paint your house and you could agree to pay me a certain sum of money—say $10,000—on the express condition that the Chicago White Sox win the World Series. Obviously this condition has nothing to do with the contract performance. Unlike the example of obtaining a loan, the condition is unrelated to the contract. In fact, this seems almost like a wager or a gamble. Nevertheless, for purposes of contract law, this stated condition is an operative condition. Keep in mind that contract law does not trump statutory law. Thus, a contract containing a condition unrelated to performance could violate gambling laws. If the jurisdiction in which the contract is made prohibits gambling, the contract may violate such a statutory prohibition. In this circumstance, the contract would be unenforceable as a violation of public policy. Criminal sanctions may also be applicable.

Conditions

Parties often set conditions that limit the scope or existence of a contractual obligation. When parties to a contract make their obligations under the contract contingent on the occurrence of some event, the duties of the contract do not come due unless the conditioning event occurs. Once the time for performance has passed and is no longer worthwhile, Plaintiff's performance under the contract is discharged. She no longer has any obligation to perform if the breaching party never made good on its performance. Often the existence of a contract condition is expressed by language such as: "provided that," or "subject to."

▶ For example, party A will pay party B $10,000 for painting a house (or a portrait, for that matter) subject to the condition that party A is able to obtain a loan at a certain interest rate or even on condition that the purchaser is satisfied with the painting.

Contract law does not treat passage of time as a condition. The passage of time does fail the test of being "not certain to occur." Thus, if you buy boots from a custom boot designer and promise to pay the purchase price for the boots within 21 days, the passage of the 21 days is not regarded as a condition. The time period has the same effect on you as a condition. You do not need to pay until the agreed time for payment has come. But it does not fall into the legal definition of a condition. You might say that the passage of time is not certain. The world may end someday. If that happens, the definitions of contract law just don't matter.

Terminology Relating to Conditions

Like many legal terms, the term "condition" is used in several different ways. Many times parties speak of the "terms and conditions" of the contract, meaning all of the provisions of the contract. These are often printed in small print on the reverse of a form that sets forth essential information such as quantity and delivery. Such "terms and conditions" can be a few pages or potentially hundreds of pages for a major business contract. These may or may not be true conditions. By "true conditions," we mean the condition spoken to in *Restatement Section 24*: "an event not certain to occur which must occur before performance under the contract to come due."

Parties also often refer to "business conditions" to indicate a way of setting a price or value of performance in the future. Again, this term may or may not refer to a true condition. Parties also speak of conditions that "trigger" some change in the contract.

▶ For example, suppose a tenant's payment obligation under a lease is set by using a flat rate and then an additional amount that is part of the profits of the tenant. The percentage to be paid as an add-on to the flat rate may increase as the profit of the tenant goes up. Suppose that at profit of $10,000 per year, the flat rate for rental might be $10,000. If the tenant makes a profit of $200,000 for the year the rent provision might indicate that the rent would be the base amount of $10,000 plus one percent (or one-half percent—the numbers don't matter for our conceptual point) for profits of $200,000 to $250,000 and two percent for profits above $250,000. This is a legitimate way to set the rental price, benefiting the landlord for the success of the tenant in the building. We might say that the "trigger" of hitting $250,000 is a condition of the higher rent. If the event of hitting $250,000 never occurs, the condition of paying the higher rent never occurs and the obligation to pay the higher rent never arises. It does not mean, of course, that the contract obligations go away. It simply means that the specified additional rent is not due.

Condition Precedent

Courts sometimes refer to a condition by the term "condition precedent." (It is pronounced with a long "e" and emphasis on the **second** syllable.) This term points to the relationship between the conditional event and the obligation to perform the contract. The condition precedes and thus is "precedent" to the obligation to perform under the contract. Often, the duty that is subject to a condition is the duty to pay the contract amount. Although the *Restatement (Second) of Contracts* does not use the term "condition precedent," it is synonymous with the term "condition" used in both judicial opinions and in the *Restatement*.

Conditions Subsequent

Courts use the terms "condition subsequent" to refer to an event that cuts off a duty. It is sometimes difficult to distinguish between the two types of conditions. The condition subsequent is rare. Sometimes the parties state a condition in terms that make it seem to fit the definition of a condition subsequent. In other words, the statement of the event seems to cut off a duty. In such cases, courts sometimes find that despite the form of the expression of the contract language the substance of the event is, nevertheless, a condition precedent. The term "condition subsequent" has fallen out of use by most courts, and the *Restatement* abandoned the use of "condition" for events that extinguish obligations. Nevertheless, you will see this usage in old opinions and occasionally in modern ones. A condition subsequent is a condition that relieves a party of the requirement to perform. For example, an insurance policy may provide for payment of a claim within a certain timeframe and also extinguish the right to payment at the end of that time. Similarly, a statute of limitations operates like a condition subsequent since it cuts off the right of a party to bring an action. Of course, how a statute of limitations operates differs from a condition subsequent in that it is created by law rather than by the parties. In some cases, parties may alter the applicable statute of limitations. For example, UCC 2-725 provides the statute of limitations applicable in contracts for sale. It expressly allows parties to a contract to change the applicable time period of set by the statute in some situations, allowing parties to make this change of time period for filing a claim in the original agreement that they entered to make the purchase and sale of goods. When parties enter such an agreement with a stated period of limitation that is different from the statute of limitations that would otherwise apply, the parties have set a condition subsequent, barring by private agreement a right under the contract. Since we are talking about this provision in the UCC, we should note that how it limits the right of the parties is limited. Even if bargained for in the original agreement, the parties do not have the power to reduce the period below one year. Also, the statute denies the right to alter the period of limitations in consumer contracts.

The importance of the distinction between a condition subsequent and a condition precedent relates to pleading and proof. When a condition exists in a contract, the party seeking to enforce the contract needs to show that the condition has occurred. By contrast, the party resisting enforcement (generally the defendant) is the one who would need to prove that a condition that cut off a duty occurred.

Types of Conditions

Courts use three categories to analyze issues in this area: (1) Express conditions, (2) Implied conditions, and (3) Constructive conditions. Whether a condition is express is a judgment for the court. Thus, it is often a subject debated by the parties. In clear cases the parties label the condition an "express condition" in the language or heading of the contract. Of course, a court may still consider and decide the issue of the nature of the condition. The fact that parties designate an event a condition is evidence that the court may find relevant in determining whether to deem the event a condition. Thus, the category of a condition turns on the interpretation of the contract by the court. The classifications of conditions precedent and conditions subsequent are discussed in the terminology section. The maxims of contract interpretation are found in Chapter 3.

Express Conditions

An express condition is a condition on the duty of one of the parties to a contract that is expressly created by the terms of the contract. Courts respect and generally give effect to the conditions that parties expressly set forth in their contract. This fact is consistent with the approach in many areas of contract law, such as allocations of risk and other judgments left to the parties. The general rule relating to express conditions is that courts give them full effect, strictly enforcing the will of the parties expressed in the contract. This discussion uses the example of obtaining a loan in order to purchase a house because it is included in most contracts for purchase of a house as an express condition of the duty to buy.

Example of an Express Condition

An example of a common express condition is found in a contract to buy a house, which is conditioned on the buyer obtaining a loan at a specified interest rate. The condition of obtaining the loan modifies Buyer's obligation to purchase the house. The event that parties identify as a condition is often related to some performance under the contract. The home loan is a good example because most people are not able to purchase a house without getting a loan. Although conditions are often closely related to the performance of the contract, such a relationship is not a requirement of contract law. The condition can be an event unrelated to payment of the purchase price and unrelated to any performance of the contract. For example, the condition could be subject to party A sitting for the portrait for 20 hours between the dates of January 1and April 1, 2008. The parties may specify essentially anything as a condition, subject to other law and their powers of imagination.

A house may be a desirable purchase for a party at a certain price and a certain interest rate but not a desirable deal at some higher price or higher interest rate. It is likely that the purchasing party will not have the full purchase price at the time of the contract. Few people pay the full price of the house at the time of purchase. Even people who could pay the full price will generally finance the purchase with a loan to take advantage of the income tax deduction for mortgage interest payments. In such cases, the purchaser will arrange for a loan. The total purchase price is affected by the interest rate. Over the term of a 15-year loan, the total purchase price for a house is much higher using a higher interest rate.

If the purchaser is not able to obtain the loan at the specified interest rate, the condition does not mature and, thus, his contract obligation never matures. Thus, a purchaser can commit himself to the purchase of a house without committing himself to that purchase at an undesirable interest rate. Thirty years ago, when one author purchased her first house, the interest rate was around 12 percent. Currently, interest rates on loans run around 5 to 7 percent. These numbers could change quickly, given the volatility of the housing market lately. What a purchaser is willing to accept as a realistic or reasonable interest rate will vary based on the market. While contracts for sale and purchase of homes typically reflect the interest rate for the time and the market area, parties have the right to set the price and interest rate independent of the market price.

Strict Enforcement of Express Condition

The legal rule is that express conditions are "strictly enforced." This means that if the condition does not occur by the express terms of the contract, then the purchaser's obligation to purchase does not come due. He will not be in breach of contract if he declines to close on the sale when he cannot obtain the loan at that specified interest rate.

▶ Assume that Buyer agrees to a contract to purchase a house for $200,000, subject to the condition of finding a loan at 6% interest rate. Assume also that Buyer found a loan at an interest rate of 6.2% — or even 6.1% — but could not find a loan with a 6% interest rate. Buyer may decline to purchase the house. In refusing to go through with the purchase, Buyer is not breaching the contract because her obligation to purchase was subject to the express condition of finding a loan at the 6% rate. In *Luttinger v. Rosen*, 316 A.2d 757 (Conn. 1972), a case included in many casebooks, purchaser indicated he was unable to obtain a loan at the specified interest rate. On behalf of Seller, Seller's lawyer offered "to make up the difference" between the rates, presumably by reducing the price. The idea here is that the seller would make the deal equal to the total price buyer would have paid with the specified rate. The buyer declined to go through with the deal. The court found in favor of the buyer, holding that the condition of the financing rate was an express condition and buyer's refusal to buy was not a breach of contract. It may seem that this holding elevates form over substance. After all, the seller was willing to reduce the price. On the other hand, it is often difficult to know all of the reasons behind a condition. Thus, enforcing express conditions strictly seems to promote the intent of the parties. In the *Rosen* case, for example, perhaps the buyer's intent in requiring a specified loan rate was to confirm the value of the house.

Obligation of Good Faith

It may seem that the rule of strict enforcement of conditions gives a party a "free card" or a convenient "escape hatch," allowing him to get out of the contract. He may have found another house that he likes better, for example. Thus, you may wonder if this gives Buyer an "out" if he wishes to escape from a contract. Perhaps he could escape the burden of the contract by simply not seeking a loan. This is not the case, however. If the buyer refuses to go through with deal, claiming that he did not find a loan at the 6% rate when he did not try to get the loan, the seller may recover against the buyer on the basis that the buyer failed to live up to the good faith obligation of trying to find a loan at the agreed interest rate.

The law places an obligation on the party with the power to make a condition occur to act in good faith. The *Restatement of Contracts* notes the requirement of good faith in numerous sections. This rule results in difficult burdens of proof. Seller will need to show that the interest rate was available in the market at the time of the contract. In this situation, the court will find that the failure to obtain the loan was a breach by the purchaser. If it dealt with the issue of the condition of obtaining a loan, it would excuse the condition because of the buyer's failure to act in good faith.

Waiver of a Condition

The party benefited or protected by a condition can waive that condition, choosing to go forward with performance although the condition did not occur. In the example given above of a loan to buy a house at a certain percentage rate, Buyer's obligation to purchase is conditional on obtaining a loan at a certain interest rate. If Buyer has been unable to find a loan at 6%, he could waive the condition and take a loan at a higher interest rate and go forward on the purchase. He might find a loan at 6.2% or 6.5% and go through with the purchase. The step of waiving the condition would be within Buyer's right under the contract. In such a case, Buyer may be said to have "waived" or "excused" the condition.

In situations like the above example, Seller cannot waive or excuse this condition because it is not a condition on seller's obligation to sell the house. This is because the condition is not a condition on seller's promise to sell. It is included in the contract to protect Buyer from an obligation to purchase when the interest rate is not available. It would not make sense to make this condition of getting a loan a condition of Seller's duty to sell since he has no interest in the issue. His only legitimate interest is in receiving payment for the house. If he receives payment, how Buyer manages his financial obligations is between Buyer and his creditors.

> ▸ Seller may require inclusion of a condition to protect her interest. For example, a seller who is lending money to the buyer of her house would be wise to require as a condition of the sale that the buyer provide a credit check and employment information. If the buyer failed to provide this information, Seller would be justified in refusing to perform by going forward with the sale since the condition on his duty to perform would not be met.

A condition can be waived or excused by the party whose duty is subject to the condition. Additionally, a court can waive or excuse the condition when justice so requires. The term "waiver" is used in a variety of contexts in contract law. Courts can find a waiver by virtue of an express or implied promise. There are cases in which the Seller would like to cancel the deal and might seize upon the nonoccurrence of a condition as a way of escaping the deal.

> ▸ For example, Seller may have located a purchaser who would pay more for the house and, thus, he would like to be free of this original contract of purchase. In the case described in the last paragraph in which Buyer was unable to find a loan at 6% but did find one at 6.2%, Seller might argue that the condition of the interest rate was not met. Thus, he might assert that because Buyer found only a loan at the higher interest rate the express condition is not met and he, the seller, is free of the deal. This argument is unlikely to succeed. The condition of a certain interest rate relates to Buyer's duty to buy, but not to

the Seller's duty to sell. In Chapter 12, the concept of waiver under UCC 2-209 is discussed.

Failure of Express Condition

When an event does not occur and one party refuses to perform on the basis the event conditioned his duty to perform, the court must determine whether the parties intended the event to be a condition. *Restatement (Second) Section 227* summarizes the factors courts consider in making the determination of intent. These factors include the language of the contract, the course of the performance by the parties under the contract, established maxims of interpretation, and the anti-forfeiture maxim.

Implied Conditions

Contracts include two different types of implied conditions: (1) implied-in-fact conditions, and (2) implied-in-law conditions. An implied-in-fact condition is one that the court finds the parties intended although they did not state it expressly. For example, duties performed under the contract are often conditioned on actions that are necessary in order to allow the promised performance. If party A promises to paint B's portrait, then the parties must intend that B will sit for the portrait, or provide a photograph, to allow A to be able to perform. Thus, the contract includes a condition that it did not state expressly. An implied-in-law condition is a condition created by the court to facilitate justice. The *Restatement* discusses this point in Sections 226 and 204. The *Restatement* also provides a helpful example in Illustration 7 to Section 226. it states as follows:

> ▶ A promises to make necessary interior repairs on a building that he has leased to B, but reserves no privilege of entering the building. B's giving reasonable notice to A of any necessary interior repairs of which A would otherwise be unaware is a condition of A's duty to make those repairs, although B is under no duty to give notice.

Illustration 7 makes clear that when the parties do not state a condition that is needed to make the rights and duties of the contract workable, the courts will imply the condition. In this case, A would not be able to perform his duty to make repairs on the inside of B's building unless B informs him of the need for repairs. Thus, courts will imply a promise to perform when the parties go forward with a contract even though they did not spell out all the conditions necessary to performance.

There is some confusion in the use of these terms. In fact, Black's Law Dictionary references "constructive conditions" for the entry on "implied-in-law conditions." The *Restatement* notes that it is wise to reserve the term "constructive" condition for "construction" of the contract rather than "interpretation" of the contract. Thus, in this book and in most contracts courses, we save the term "constructive condition" for the constructive conditions of exchange discussed below.

Constructive Conditions of Exchange

Courts use the term "constructive conditions of exchange" to refer to the notion that obligations under the contract are linked to each other and depend on each other. If one party does not perform his obligation, the other party is free from his corresponding obligation under the contract. There is potential here for a standoff where neither party wants to perform. Courts generally regard the promises by one party collectively as the performance to be exchanged under an exchange of promises. This has not always been the approach under the law. The traditional common law treated performances of a contract as independent covenants. This meant that if Party A entered a contract to sell a goat to Party B each party had the right to enforce the contract against the other without regard to whether the plaintiff had rendered performance. If Party A failed to deliver the goat, Party B would sue Party A for the goat. Party B would still need to pay the price since it was an independent obligation. If Party A delivered the goat and Party B failed to pay, Party A would need to sue for the purchase price. This seems like a lawyer's paradise in the sense that parties needed to perform and seek enforcement in court rather than using the self-help mechanism of withholding performance.

Terminology

The terms "constructive," and "implied" both signal use of a legal fiction. Courts create fictions to configure the law to promote justice. For example, a professor might say that a student has "constructive" absence from class, meaning that the student is present physically but not mentally—or at least not mentally prepared for class. The terms have different meanings, however. The term "constructive conditions" refers to the default of dependency of promises under an exchange of promises. The term "implied condition" is used for other types of conditions that the court either finds or creates.

Modern Approach

The modern doctrine of constructive conditions is directly contrary to the old traditional rule. In fact, the modern rule simply flips the presumption. Rather than assuming that performances in a contract are independent of each other, courts regard performances promised in the contract as dependent on the performance of each unless it is clear the parties have chosen to make them independent. The case credited with introducing the modern rule of constructive conditions is *Kingston v. Preston,* 99 Eng. Rep. 437 (K. B. 1773), in which the English court held that the performances under a contract of a sale of a business were dependent.

▶ In the *Kingston* case, a silk merchant sold his business to his apprentice. The apprentice buyer promised to provide "good and sufficient security," a promise of particular importance since the apprentice was "worth nothing," meaning he had no credit or property of his own. When the buyer failed to provide security, the seller refused to convey the business. In other words, the seller used the self-help device of withholding his performance. The court ruled in favor of the seller. Bringing an action against buyer would offer no protection for seller because the buyer had neither property nor credit. The effect of treating the promises as independent in this case would have been to delete the buyer's promise to provide security.

Order of Performance

You can tell from the discussion above that the system's choice of constructive conditions means that parties may find themselves in a stand-off situation in which neither party is performing nor in breach. The order of performance is particularly important because of the rule of constructive conditions of exchange. Under this, a party (Party A) can be in breach despite the lack of performance by the other party if Party A has an obligation to perform first. If you have hired someone to paint your house and your contract does not specify whether the painting goes first or the payment goes first, the rule is that the painting must precede the payment. This is sometimes called the "Work First Rule." The default rules discussed below indicate the reason for this result.

Two Situations and Two Defaults

When the parties do not specify the order of performance, contract law provides a default, or, in this case, two different defaults. First, if the performances bargained for can occur simultaneously, the default rule is that they are both due at the same time and neither party has the obligation to go first unless the parties agree to that in the contract. For example if we contract to buy and sell goods with each other and do not mention the order of performance, the default is that the performances are due simultaneously. Simultaneous performance is the default when simultaneous performance is possible. In the sale of goods situation this is possible if there is only one delivery date. The second part of this default involves the situation in which one performance takes a significant amount of time. This is not an unusual situation. This is the case in construction contracts and service contracts, for example. In this case, the performance that takes some time is the first performance, followed by the payment after completion. This is the "Work First" Rule referred to above.

Freedom of contract allows parties to adjust the defaults to fit their needs and their bargain. The order in which parties are expected to perform becomes very important. If you are to perform second, you do not risk as much on the deal. You get to await performance by the other party. As with other matters in contract law, the parties can designate the order of performance. They can change the default so that payment comes before delivery or payment is over a long period of time.

This stand-off is the result of more than mere inertia. The act of beginning performance is an act of reliance on the contract. It involves some trust as well as an expenditure of resources. Perhaps each party is apprehensive about the other and waiting for the other to take the first step by beginning performance. Whatever the reason for the stand-off, it is wise for the parties to recognize the natural reluctance to "go first" and take the issue out of play. This is easy to do. The parties can indicate in the contract which party will perform first.

Independent Obligations

Parties to the contract can change the default rule of constructive conditions. By their agreement, the parties may make the obligations independent. The views of courts on independent clauses in leases have changed significantly over the years. The modern default is that exchanged promises are dependent, under the doctrine of constructive conditions. Nevertheless a court may find that the circumstances justify seeing a covenant or promise as independent and thus enforceable even when the other party did not perform. For example, parties often include a covenant not to compete in the sale of a business. Courts have held that a covenant not to compete by the seller that is held unenforceable will not necessarily relieve the seller of the duty to convey the business. Nor will it necessarily relieve the buyer of the duty to purchase the business. Courts enforce covenants not to compete by specific performance when they find the covenant to be reasonable in scope and duration. Section 232 of the *Restatement* provides a good example in Illustration 3:

> ▶ A employs B under a five-year employment contract, which contains a valid covenant under which B promises not to engage in the same business in a designated area for two years after the termination of the employment. It expressly provides that "this covenant is independent of any other provision in this agreement." After B has begun work, A unjustifiably discharges him, and B thereupon engages in business in violation of the covenant. A's employing B and B's working for A are to be exchanged under the exchange of promises. The quoted words indicate an intention that A's employing B is not to be exchanged for B's refraining from engaging in the same business. If the court concludes that this intention is clearly manifested, A has a claim against B for damages for breach of his promise not to compete.

Unilateral Promises and Conditions

A unilateral contract is one in which only one party has undertaken a commitment. In a "unilateral" contract, parties often expressly indicate they intend a performance in exchange for a promise. The arrangement need not be set forth expressly in these terms, however. The example often used in explaining this concept is a walk across the Brooklyn Bridge.

> ▶ If A says to B: "If you will walk across the Brooklyn Bridge, I will pay you $1,000," A has undertaken a unilateral obligation for himself. He is obligated to pay B if B walks across the Brooklyn Bridge within any timeframe set. B, on the other hand, has no commitment. Instead, B has an option to walk across the Bridge. If he does perform by walking across the bridge, he is entitled to collect the money. You might see this doctrine as suspect since it provides for unequal treatment of the parties. Only one party is bound. Keep in mind, however, that

the party who is bound is the one who created the obligation. Party A unilaterally and voluntarily set up the arrangement, creating an obligation for himself, conditioned on B's performance, and leaving B without an obligation. B has a right to the money if he performs.

The doctrine of unilateral contracts has practical application when one party wants to create an incentive for people to perform an act without entering contracts with all the potential parties on the other side. For example, a party who has lost a diamond ring might set up a reward based on the unilateral contract. He could post a notice giving a general offer to pay any person who finds and delivers the diamond ring to him. See Chapter 4 on the mechanics of offer and acceptance for treatment of this point. For purposes of this chapter, the important connection is that the unilateral contract creates a condition on the promisor's duty to perform.

Types of Remedies

Before discussing material breach, it is helpful to note some of the types of remedies available under contract law. Depending on the context, the injured party may have a right to one or more of the following remedies: (1) damages, (2) withholding performance, (3) specific performance of the promise, and (4) rescission of the contract. Remedies are also discussed in Chapter 11.

Material Breach

When a party's breach deprives the other party of essentially the entire benefit of the contract, the court may find that the breach is "material." The significance of this category of breach is in the additional remedy available to an injured party. It is important to see this remedy in context. When a party breaches a contract to the extent that it is a *material breach*, the injured party has two remedies rather than one: (1) damages, and (2) withholding his performance. This additional remedy gives the injured party the right to withhold his own performance. If the injured party is the recipient (the payment side of the contract), his obligation to pay is discharged.

The argument that a breach is material breach often arises in disputes when a contract does not run its full course. The issue relating to material breach is whether the aggrieved or dissatisfied party has a right to withhold his own performance. In such cases, the recipient argues that the other party failed to perform or performed in such a defective fashion that he (the aggrieved party) should be released from his contractual obligations under the deal. The injured party's right to collect damages (remedy #1 above) is not affected by his ability to withhold performance (remedy #2 above).

The court usually deals with the issue after the time for performance has run and the parties are in a dispute, not in the heat of the moment when the parties are debating about the quality or timing of the performance due. The usual statement of the concept has a circular sound: A material breach occurs when the breach is so significant that the injured party should be excused by the court from rendering its own performance under the contract. The most straightforward example of a material breach is a failure to render any performance at all when performance is due. However, the concept of materiality is rarely discussed in the non-performance context because it is clear that the party who fails to perform at all has materially breached once the time for performance runs.

Restatement (Second) of Contracts § 241 summarizes the test for determining whether a breach is material. It states:

> In determining whether a failure to render or to offer performance is material, the following circumstances are significant:
>   (a) the extent to which the injured party will be deprived of the benefit which he reasonably expected;
>   (b) the extent to which the injured party can be adequately compensated for the part of that benefit of which he will be deprived;
>   (c) the extent to which the party failing to perform or to offer to perform will suffer forfeiture;
>   (d) the likelihood that the party failing to perform or to offer to perform will cure his failure, taking account of all the circumstances including any reasonable assurances;
>   (e) the extent to which the behavior of the party failing to perform or to offer to perform comports with standards of good faith and fair dealing.

This provision includes all the factors relevant to balancing the interests of the parties. The first two factors consider the legitimate interests of the injured party, both the extent to which he will lose the benefit he reasonably expected, and the extent to which damages can adequately compensate him. If the damage formula provides adequate compensation, there is no need to allow him to withhold performance as well since the remedy of damages gives sufficient protection. The final three factors consider the party failing to perform. They note that the court should consider whether he will suffer forfeiture, the likelihood of cure, and whether he has acted in accordance with good faith and fair dealing standards.

Courts generally encourage parties to go forward with contracts rather than breaching. The rule on material breach also operates to encourage parties to try to work out their differences rather than just "calling the whole thing off." Even when it is clear that a party is in breach of the contract and that injured party is entitled to sue for damages, the doctrine of material breach makes it hard for the injured party to withhold his own performance except when the other party either fails to perform at all or fails to perform the basic purpose of the contract. *Ellis v. Tower Health Club, Inc.*, 342 N.Y.S.2d 135 (N.Y. Civ. Ct. 1973) provides an interesting example. In this case, the plaintiff renewed her membership in health club on January 28, 1972 with a one-year membership. Like many of us, she did not maintain her exercise routine as well as she hoped. She returned to club in late March or early April and discovered that club had been transformed into a massage parlor. The court held that the club had materially breached the contract. It held for plaintiff, affirming her right to rescind and recover the full fee she paid for renewal of the membership.

Immaterial Breach

A party who suffers a less dramatic breach is entitled to the protection afforded by damages (remedy #1 above). When a party breaches a contract in a way that is not a material breach, the injured party still has a duty to perform. The injured party also has a right to prove damages. The fact that the breach does not seem significant from the perspective of the entire performance will not defeat the claim for damages.

For example, if a seller promised to deliver to buyer 1,000 blenders with six speeds, and delivers 1,000 blenders with five speeds, the buyer can sue for the difference in value between the blenders promised and those delivered. These blenders are not defective in the ordinary meaning of that word. They are "non-conforming goods," however, because they do not conform to the contract. Thus, this performance is a breach and plaintiff buyer can seek damages. Of course proof of the difference in value of the performance promised and the performance rendered can be difficult. This is probably a case of an immaterial rather than a material breach. The party is delivering the goods ordered (blenders) and the nonconforming nature of the blenders does not seem significant. Nevertheless, the default of the UCC is that buyer has a right to reject goods unless they are perfect. If buyer rejects goods then clearly he can also withhold his own performance of paying for the goods.

The following is an example of a claim by a party that he should be able to withhold his performance of payment.

> ▸ A dry cleaner enters a contract to purchase a sign to be installed at his place of business. As part of the purchase price the seller agrees to maintain the sign in "first class condition." Buyer becomes frustrated when seller fails to keep the sign clean. It is covered in cobwebs and has tomato splashed on one corner. The buyer gets increasingly frustrated when he has not heard from the seller. He sends a letter terminating the contract and stating he will make no further payments on the installment payment plan.

In this case, the court refused to find a material breach by the seller. The most important factor in the contract seemed to the court to be the sale of the sign, not the maintenance of the sign. The case is a good one for illustrating the fact that it can be frustrating not to receive full performance from the other party. Nevertheless, the decision to "call the whole thing off" is, as the court expressed it: "fraught with peril." The party who feels wronged is in fact the breaching party. He was the first to materially breech by terminating. The important lesson from this case is that it is better to try to work things out with the other party than to terminate the contract unilaterally. In fact, unless the situation is clear cut, such as non-performance by the other party, calling a contract off is clearly a material breach unless the court agrees that the other party breached the contract materially first.

Substantial Performance

The doctrine of substantial performance developed in the context of construction contracts. It makes clear that the party injured by a breach is not entitled to withhold performance (remedy #2 above) unless the breach is material.

> ▸ For example, a contractor who builds a house will virtually never be able to perform every detail in the building contract to perfection. When the performance side has breached by failure to meet some detail, the recipient has a right to damages to make him whole (remedy #1 above). The injured party does not have a right to withhold his performance (typically payment for the construction) if the breaching party has provided substantial performance. This concept dovetails with the concept of material breach. If a breach is material, it does not constitute substantial performance.

If a party has rendered substantial performance, he is not in material breach. This does not mean that the party has not breached. Rather it means only that any breach does not rise to the level of breach that justifies the other party withholding his performance. The injured party is entitled to damages when the other party has breached. The injured party is not entitled to withhold performance in response to a breach unless the breach is a material breach. This means the injured party will have to perform his side of the deal although he can get damages from the other party.

> ▸ The case of *Jacob & Youngs v. Kent* provides a good example of the doctrine of substantial performance and its rationale. The case involved construction of a house in 1914, which was really a mansion. The contract for construction of the mansion specified pipe "of Reading, Manufacturer." After the construction was complete, Mr. Kent, the purchaser, learned that some of the pipe installed in the building was not of "Reading Manufacturer" and, thus, did not comply with the contract terms. When he learned of the contractor's failure to use the designated pipe, Mr. Kent refused to pay the balance of the contract price and his architect refused to certify completion of the contract. Kent demanded that the contractor remove the pipe and replace it with pipe of Reading Manufacturer. The court held that the contractor's use of pipe that was not "Reading Manufacturer" was a breach of contract. It found the breach was not material, however, and refused to allow Mr. Kent to withhold payment. The contractor's performance was "substantial" and thus, the breach was not material. In such cases, the remedy of withholding the performance of payment is not available to the injured party, but the remedy of damages is available. In this case, Justice Cardozo held that there was no difference in value between the promised performance and the performance rendered with the other brand of pipe. For this reason, the court refused to award damages.

You may see this case as inconsistent with the concept that express conditions are strictly construed. It shows that the level of clarity required by a court to hold an express condition varies based on the contract. Even if a condition is held to be express, the court may excuse it to prevent injustice. In this case, the term relating to the origin of manufacture of the pipe was one item in a long list of specifications. You might wonder how parties could achieve the power of an express condition in this setting. If the use of the pipe is of importance, parties could single it out for liquidated damages or a clear statement of forfeiture. A court will consider all the circumstances of course in determining whether the parties really intended for the purchaser to secure a house without an obligation to pay when a specification is not met.

Comparison with Contract Formation

Express conditions that limit the enforceability of a contract are similar to conditions that may limit the formation of a contract itself. Parties can make acceptance of a contract occur only upon stated conditions. For example, the offer could require acceptance by the offeree meeting offeror on a particular corner at a certain time, wearing a clown suit. You may think that the offeror is ridiculous, and you may even question whether or not you want to enter a contract with such a ridiculous person. Nevertheless, contract law allows such conditions on acceptance. The offeror is master of his offer and can set such conditions. Although the usual mechanics of contract formation could be stated in terms of conditions, this is not the language or concept used by courts in contracts cases. An offeror offers to perform a promise in exchange for a promise from offeree. The statement "I will sell you this diamond necklace for $2,000," is an offer to sell. The creation of a contract depends on the offeree making a promise to pay the requested amount. We could say that the contract is conditioned, in an ordinary sense of the word, on the parties making an offer and an acceptance. Offer and acceptance are not, however, conditions in the sense we are talking about in this section. Even though you could think of the events of offer and acceptance as events "not certain to occur which must occur before the performance under a contract becomes due," this type of classification will cause confusion. To master contract law you should accept the terminology choices of courts.

When we discuss conditions in contracts, we are focusing on some event that has significance after the formation stage of contracting.

> ▸ For example, "I agree to pay you $2,000 for your diamond necklace, if it passes a test of authenticity by a certified diamond merchant." This statement offers to contract for a necklace with a condition in the contract. If you accept the offer we have a contract. This contract includes a condition. The condition is that a certified diamond merchant establishes the necklace is authentic. So a contract exists after the seller accepts the offer, but the duty to perform by paying for the necklace does not come due until the diamond merchant certifies the authenticity of the necklace. The condition survives the formation of the contract.

Perfect Tender Rule

In the sale of goods area you will hear of something called the "Perfect Tender Rule." The name is a bit overstated. Perfection is a rare commodity, even in the sale of goods area. The substance of this concept is that goods delivered must conform to the contract in all particulars. In fact, it is not only the goods that must live up to the agreement. Delivery also must conform to the contract. This means that the starting place for performance in the sale of goods area is complete performance, not merely substantial performance. It also means that the description of the goods in the contract and the terms of delivery are express obligations of the seller.

UCC 2-601 declares that the buyer who receives an improper delivery can reject the entire delivery, accept the entire delivery, or "accept any commercial unit or units and reject the rest." This is the current law that is sometimes referred to as the Perfect Tender Rule. Although it is powerful, it is not absolute. It does not apply when the contract is an installment contract. It is also subject to the right of the seller to cure the delivery, by sending a perfect one. It is also subject to the obligation of good faith. So if a buyer who simply wants to get out of a contract finds some small imperfection as a way of escaping the deal, he has violated the obligation of good faith. This can be difficult to show, of course. As we discussed in relation to the condition of satisfaction, a party's intent is difficult to show.

> ▸ Take as an example a contract for the purchase of cherries in one complete delivery. If the contract called for cherries that weighed a certain amount per bushel, failure to meet that weight requirement would be a breach. Buyer could reject the shipment as non-conforming so long as his rejection was in good faith and allowed seller an opportunity to cure. If, on the other hand, the parties did not have a standard for weight or quality and the buyer simply rejected by saying "these cherries are not perfect," a court will consider the quality of the cherries and also whether the rejection was made in good faith.

An "installment contract" is one allowing or requiring delivery in separate lots to be separately accepted. As UCC 2-612 states, when a contract allows or requires delivery in more than one lot, it is an installment contract even if it states that "each delivery is a separate contract." The UCC applies a less demanding test when the contract is an installment contract, perhaps because the deal is more of an on-going arrangement than a single transaction. In this case, a buyer may only reject the installment when its nonconformity "substantially impairs the value of that installment and cannot be cured."

▶ So, for example, in a contract that is not subject to the condition of satisfaction, a buyer might want to get out of a contract for cherries because the price for cherries has fallen. If he rejects the shipment of cherries, saying that the cherries are not perfect, a court may find this rejection to be a breach if the evidence indicates that buyer simply regrets the deal. This is especially true when the market price is lower than the contract price at the time of delivery. If buyer finds some insignificant term the court may reach the same result. For example, if the contract called for shipment in crates reinforced with plywood every 15 inches and seller shipped in crates reinforced every 12 inches, the court would be likely to refuse to allow buyer to reject the shipment based on this "imperfect" tender. The crates are actually better than the crates contracted for and, thus, the rejection is likely not a good faith rejection.

Contract Condition Function

▶ Of course, the buyer could have achieved essentially the same result by refusing to enter a contract until he received the certification he wanted. If he had done that, he would not need a condition to protect him. In such a case, the buyer would not have a contract for the necklace. During the time he is checking on the authenticity or waiting to hear from the diamond expert, some other buyer could come along and offer more for the necklace and buy it out from under him. It makes sense, then, for the buyer to prefer to enter the contract and protect himself against a bad result by requiring a condition of authenticity. This may be acceptable to seller because he has a deal at the time of the contract. This is something good for him even though it has a condition attached that could mean that the contract could be undone. If seller is confident of the authenticity of the diamond necklace, he may have no problem at all in entering the contract subject to the condition. This simple example is not the only kind, of course. The parties may agree to make a contract conditional on almost anything.

Condition of Satisfaction

A condition may even relate to the judgment of one of the parties. The judgment may be either objective or subjective, depending on the express terms of the agreement or the way the court interprets the intent of the parties. This type of condition is called a condition of satisfaction. This is a notable concept worth exploring, both because of its usefulness and also because it comes close to the line of an illusory contract. In fact, the early law of contract regarded condition of satisfaction as illusory. Since an illusory contract is not enforceable, looking at conditions of satisfaction helps understand the limits on what parties can bargain for under the law.

The condition of satisfaction will be a condition of an obligor's duty—generally the duty to pay. The condition is typically that the obligor will be satisfied with the performance of the other party, but the condition of satisfaction can relate to the satisfaction of someone other than a party such as a party's architect or lawyer. Ordinarily the party making a judgment on the performance is the party who receives the performance, or the "recipient." He is the party who will pay for performance from the other. (The other side is referred to as the performance side. Of course both parties are performing, but the party whose performance is simply paying is referred to as the recipient and the other party as the performing party.) If the party who receives performance is not satisfied, then he has no obligation to pay. This arrangement seems very risky for the party whose performance is subject to the judgment of the other party. You might question why anyone would enter a contract with a condition of satisfaction and accept the risk of nonpayment based on the satisfaction of the other party. Even though it carries risk for the performing party, this is the business model of many deals. For example, many consumer transactions are either explicitly or implicitly based on the satisfaction of the purchaser. This means, in many cases, when you are dissatisfied with a product you can return it for a full refund. Retailers have changed the rule by posting that it does not apply to certain purchases such as electronics, DVDs, CDs, and other products. They give notice of this limit to customers on sales receipts and on posted notices in the customer service area. In the sale of goods, the risk to the performing side of a condition of satisfaction is less pronounced than in personal services contracts.

Typically, a buyer would not be able to retain the benefits of the performance if he rejects the performance. In a sale of goods situation, when the original purchaser states that he is dissatisfied and rejects the goods, the seller is able to reclaim the goods and sell them to another purchaser. The dissatisfied purchaser does not pay for the goods but the seller does not experience forfeiture because he can reclaim the goods and sell them to someone else. In some cases, however, this is not the case. Consider situations where the manufacture or creation of custom goods may mean that there is no market for resale of the goods. The personal nature of the product may mean that no one else would have a need or desire for the goods.

▸ For example, the case of *Gibson v. Cranage*, 39 Mich. 49 (1878), involved production of a painting of the purchaser's deceased daughter. It is unlikely that any other buyer could be found for this painting. The condition of satisfaction provides an example of the fact that parties are free to contract for standards that are very difficult to judge. This circumstance reminds us that parties operate in a free market and can accept significant risk of forfeiture if they choose. The issue of forfeiture is dealt with in more detail below.

The Choice of a Subjective or Objective Standard

An additional difficulty exists in the area of conditions of satisfaction. Courts need to decide what standard they should apply in judging the defendant's assertion that he was not satisfied with the performance. The subjective standard is an honesty standard. This means that a party can be unreasonable in her dissatisfaction and still withstand enforcement if the parties contracted for a condition of honest (or subjective) satisfaction. So long as the party judging the performance is honestly dissatisfied, he does not need to pay. By contrast, the objective standard of satisfaction is a reasonableness standard. This means that if the trier of fact is convinced that the performance was satisfactory from a reasonableness point of view, then the defendant must pay for the performance. The fact that he is honestly dissatisfied is not enough to allow him to avoid the payment obligation. The proof in this case could be an expert who would testify that the performance was well done and that any reasonable person would be satisfied with the performance.

When the condition calls for subjective rather than objective judgment, it is more difficult to show a breach. You may wonder why anyone would enter a contract with a condition that is so hard to prove. It is important to keep in mind that the concept of freedom of contract means that parties are free to enter contracts that are difficult to prove. Thus, contract law does not limit the power of parties to contract for difficult standards of proof. Generally courts prefer to apply a reasonableness standard to satisfaction clauses. This is also called the objective test for satisfaction. The *Restatement (Second) of Contracts* makes clear that courts generally interpret a condition as setting an objective, rather than subjective, standard. Section 228 of the *Restatement* notes that if it "is practicable to determine whether a reasonable person in the position of the obligor would be satisfied, an interpretation is preferred under which the condition occurs if such a reasonable person in the position of the obligor would be satisfied." In other words, if it makes sense to apply a test of

reasonableness, then that is what the court should apply. Of course, this preference only applies if the parties did not choose a standard and state it clearly
in the contract. The preference of courts in this area is at play only when the
parties did not exercise their freedom to bargain over standards that apply to
their deal. Courts generally hold that it is practicable to apply a reasonableness standard in most cases except cases involving judgments of artistic merit.
Because such judgments are inherently subjective, courts apply a subjective
test.

> ▶ Let's look again at *Gibson v. Cranage*. The plaintiff promised to pro-
> duce a painting of the purchaser's deceased daughter and that the pur-
> chaser would pay only if he were "perfectly satisfied" with the painting.
> The purchaser indicated that he was not satisfied with the painting. He
> refused to take the painting and, more important to the seller, he re-
> fused to pay the purchase price. At first, Seller made some changes to
> the painting in response to the purchaser's dissatisfaction. Later the pur-
> chaser refused to look at the painting again. The opinion of the court
> does not reveal what the purchaser did not like about the painting.
> The court held that the circumstances and the communications of the
> parties made satisfaction of the purchaser a condition of the contract.
> It also held the parties agreed to a subjective standard of satisfaction.
> Thus, the plaintiff (the seller of portraits) had the burden of con-
> vincing the court the defendant was misrepresenting his mental state.
> Plaintiff could not meet his burden and the court held for the defen-
> dant-purchaser. Because this performance involved art and, addi-
> tionally, a very personal work since it depicted a deceased child, a
> modern court would be as likely as the 19th century court to apply a
> subjective standard.

You may think that no one would enter such contracts, but that would not
be correct. People enter contracts for performance to be judged by the recipient in many circumstances. As you stroll on a beach an artist may offer to do
a portrait of you. If she states clearly that you don't need to accept the portrait unless you like it, you are not required to take or pay for the portrait if you
actually do not like it. If you are satisfied with the portrait but you refuse to
take and pay for it, you would be in breach of contract. However, it would be
difficult for the painter to show that you are in breach because it is difficult to
prove your state of mind.

The *Gibson* case makes two important points: (1) a party can condition his
performance of paying on his own satisfaction, and (2) the test for satisfaction involved can be subjective rather than objective. The case also illustrates

the difficulty of proving a condition of satisfaction. The plaintiff needed to prove that the purchaser (defendant) was satisfied. Obviously it is difficult to show the mental state of the other party. Whether the purchaser is satisfied or is misrepresenting his state of mind is a question the trier of fact must decide. If the court finds that the party was indeed satisfied, however, it would enforce the payment obligation. A court will not simply accept the testimony of a party regarding his or her dissatisfaction. Rather, the court will take evidence on the issue. In making such a finding, the court is holding that the party is misrepresenting his own view.

To draw a hypothetical fact pattern from the *Gibson* case, suppose that testimony by the defendant established that he liked the painting but decided against taking it because of the cost. This evidence would establish a breach of the subjective (honesty) standard. For example, in one case, a defendant had entered a contract for the purchase of potatoes, subject to a condition of satisfaction. He was held liable when evidence showed he stated that at the time of delivery, he could buy potatoes at a price much lower than the contract price. A witness who had been talking with the defendant when he rejected the potatoes said the defendant had stated he could "buy potatoes all day long" at a lower price. This statement indicated to the jury that his dissatisfaction was not with the goods, but rather with the contract price. The market shifted after the time of contract and price of potatoes fell. This is not a legitimate reason for dissatisfaction since the risk of a drop in price is allocated to the buyer if the contract is silent about an allocation. While parties may be able to set conditions on price, if they give a party the ability to simply call the contract off based on his unfettered discretion, they have created an illusory contract.

Requirement of Good Faith

The condition of satisfaction includes the duty of good faith and fair dealing. If it did not, the contract would be held to be illusory and, thus, unenforceable. Parties do not need to mention the obligation of good faith in their contract for it to apply. Courts imply this obligation into all contracts, even contracts subject to a condition of subjective satisfaction. An illustration from the *Restatement* makes this point.

> ▸ A contracts to sell and B to buy 500 barrels of cherries in syrup "quality to be satisfactory in buyer's honest judgment," delivery to be in installments. After deliveries of and payments for a total of 100 barrels,

B states that he is not satisfied and refuses to take more. Since the agreement clearly provides a test of honest satisfaction, B's termination is effective if his judgment is in fact made honestly in accordance with his duty of good faith and fair dealing (§ 205). However, A may show that B's rejection was for other reasons by proving, for example, that B expressed satisfaction at the time of the first deliveries, that B's refusal was due to a drop in market price, and A's cherries were of the highest quality.

This story establishes the important role of good faith in this area. It also shows the type of evidence that could establish a breach of the subjective standard. A drop in price of the goods or performance contracted for is evidence that the party may be rejecting based on the economics of the deal rather than his true dissatisfaction.

Claims of Conditions Rendering a Contract Illusory

Early cases held the condition of satisfaction made a contract illusory. Later cases, such as the *Gibson* case discussed above, established that conditions of satisfaction, even subjective satisfaction, do not necessarily render a contract illusory. Although the condition may be difficult to establish, it may be a real limitation on the judgment of the party to be satisfied.

The plaintiff who establishes that the defendant's representation of her state of mind is false will prevail on defendant's obligation to pay. In such a circumstance, the refusal to pay is a breach of the contract. The showing could be made by evidence such as a deposition statement or implication by the party that he was satisfied but chose not to go through with the contract. Some plaintiffs have won on evidence that shows that a party who expresses dissatisfaction is misrepresenting his own judgment in order to escape from the contract. This is because dissatisfaction with the contract — as opposed to the performance — is not a basis for exercising a condition of satisfaction.

You might wonder whether it is possible for parties to set a condition that would allow the buyer to reject the contract if he is later dissatisfied with it. A contract that clearly states that a party had no obligation to attempt to fulfill a condition is likely to make the contract illusory.

▶ For example, take again the event of obtaining a loan at or below 6% in order to purchase a house. If the parties made it clear that Buyer has an obligation to try to find the loan, the Buyer clearly has that obligation. Thus, if 6% loans are available and the Buyer simply does not apply for one, then Buyer breached the duty to attempt to make condition occur. If the parties do not state this duty, the court will find it implicit in the contract. Finally, if the parties specify that Buyer has *no* obligation to seek a loan, the court may determine that the obligation is illusory and no contract existed between the parties. The fact that one party had complete discretion to go forward (by seeking a loan) or to decide not to go forward (by refraining from seeking a loan) means that the Buyer made no commitment at all. In such a case, one party had unfettered choice to perform the contract or to walk away from it and, thus, there is no contract.

Forfeiture

In some situations the seller may experience "forfeiture," meaning he cannot recover for the performance rendered. Forfeiture occurs in any case where the performing party cannot reclaim his performance. The law disfavors forfeiture. Section 227 of the *Restatement (Second) of Contracts* makes this point. Many contracts are subject to the risk of forfeiture. For example, a singer cannot "un-sing" the song. Realistically, the house painter cannot strip the house of paint if the owner refuses to pay. The golf teacher cannot pull back the information he has shared with the student. Cases that do not involve forfeiture are ones in which the party who has performed can recapture her performance and find a substitute buyer for the performance.

In many cases, a sale of goods holds little risk of forfeiture since the goods can be repossessed and resold. Of course, there is always a risk of damage or destruction of the goods. This point relates to property rather than to contracts. The issue when goods are destroyed is who bore the loss as owner of the goods. The issue of forfeiture specifically deals with the problem of losing the benefit of performance, not simply to the loss of property. Just as a supplier of goods often can repossess the goods, the seller of land can sue for return of the deed in response to a breach by the purchaser. These remedies are also time consuming and costly but they are not marked by complete forfeiture. In addition to applying a duty of good faith to avoid forfeiture, courts will also imply a duty on a party to make good faith efforts to attempt to make an event occur when it is within her control.

If it is clear that the parties intend one of them to bear a risk of forfeiture, courts will respect that allocation of risk. The *Gibson* case discussed above is

CHAPTER 10 · PERFORMANCE AND BREACH

a good example of such forfeiture. It is unlikely that the seller of the painting could sell it to another buyer because of the personal nature of the product. Nevertheless, the court allowed the forfeiture because the court held that the parties agreed to a subjective condition of satisfaction. In a free market the parties can accept risk of forfeiture if they choose.

Distinguishing Conditions from Timing Devices

Conditions of satisfaction are not the only difficult cases presented by interpretation of conditions. For example, sometimes courts must determine whether something that uses the language of condition may be intended by the parties as a timing device rather than a condition. The distinction makes a big difference because if an event is a condition, the failure of the condition will relieve a party of the duty to perform.

> ▸ The case of *Peacock Construction v. Modern Air Conditioning, Inc.*, 353 So. 2d 840 (Fl. 1977), provides an example. In this case between a general contractor and subcontractors, the court held that the contract created a timing device rather than a condition. The contract stated that the general contractor's duty to pay subcontractors would be due 30 days after 1) completion of the work, 2) approval of the work by the general contractor's architect, and 3) "full payment therefore by the owner." Such a clause is referred to as a "Pay-When-Paid Clause." When the owner defaulted on the deal, the general contractor refused to pay the subcontractors, asserting that his duty to pay was conditioned on receiving payment from the owner; i.e., if the owner did not pay then the subcontractors would suffer the loss. Focusing on the issue of risk, the court held the language was not clear enough to shift the risk of non-payment by the owner from the general contractor to the subcontractor. The subcontractor had no opportunity to meet the Owner or to assess the Owner's credit worthiness. He merely relied on the general contractor's credit worthiness in going forward with performance.

You might see the *Peacock Construction* court's determination that the contract clause was a timing device rather than a condition as an unimportant difference. After all, whatever it was (a condition or a timing device), it did not occur. The owner never paid. Thus, one might reason the subcontractor is out of luck either way. However, the court's ruling was significant. The issue of whether the provision was a condition or a timing device is determinative. Remember that a condition that never occurs relieves the party whose duty is conditioned free from the duty to perform his side of the deal. (In this case this would be the duty to pay the subcontractor.) By contrast, the fact that a timing provision fails does not destroy the payment obligation. When a timing provision fails to occur, a court will supply a reasonable time. Thus, if the provision is merely a timing provision the court will set a reasonable time for payment.

Many courts have held that a "Pay-When-Paid Clause" is not a condition precedent of the general contractor's payment obligation unless the parties have made this meaning completely clear. For example, assume the parties included the same language in their contract but also included language that noted the effect of the owner's failure to pay, such as "In the event Owner refuses to pay General Contractor, General Contractor has no duty to pay Subcontractor." Assume also that the subcontractor checked the credit of the owner before bidding on the contract. These facts suggested that the subcontractor intended to share the risk of non-payment by the owner.

An Exercise to Identify Conditions

Peacock Construction provides a good exercise for distinguishing between conditions and timing devices. You remember that the contract between a general contractor and subcontractors included a statement that general contractor would make final payment to subcontractors "within 30 days after the completion of the work included in this sub-contract, written acceptance by the Architect and full payment therefor by the Owner." This provision includes four separate events:

1) Event 1: 30 days after
2) Event 2: completion of subcontract work,
3) Event 3: written acceptance by architect and
4) Event 4: full payment by owner.

Which of these four events are conditions? Event 1 is not a condition since the law does not deal with the passage of time as a condition. Events 2 and Event 3 are conditions. Event 4 is not a condition in this case because the court held that the parties did not intend to shift the risk of non-payment by the owner from the general contractor to the subcontractors by this statement of an event.

Promises Implied in Conditions

The discussion so far indicates that a condition relieves a party of an obligation accepted under a contract when the condition does not occur. It is often important to determine whether an event is a condition, a promise, or both. The additional point here is that the same event may be both a condition and a promise.

> ▸ For example, my obligation to buy your house for $200,000 may be conditioned on obtaining a loan at 6% interest. The condition may also include my promise to try to obtain a loan at 6% interest. The promise may be express or implied. The contract could state: "Buyer hereby promises to make a good faith effort to obtain a loan at an interest rate at or below 6%." Even without this clause, a court is likely to see this condition as including an implicit promise by one party to attempt to make that condition occur. The implication is that the party whose obligation is conditioned promises to make a good faith effort to make the condition occur when it is within his power. This is true whether or not the parties state the obligation. If the parties do not state the obligation, the court will find such an implied promise. If the parties did not intend a good faith obligation, they are creating an illusory contract.

Promissory Conditions

An event that is both a condition and a promise is called a "Promissory Condition."

> ▸ In the example of building a house, the builder might promise to complete a house on a certain date. The contract will often state buyer's right to specify certain things, such as the color of the paint, the types of windows, and many other decorating choices. The contract is likely to state that Owner must provide the needed specifications to the contractor by a particular date. This makes sense because the contractor needs to finish the contract to perform within the time required. Obviously he cannot do so without knowing the color and other specifications he needs to meet. In such a case, the contractor's duty to perform is conditioned on the buyer providing the specifications. The buyer's specifications are a condition to the contractor's duty to per-

form. Giving these specifications is also a duty of the buyer. Thus, Owner explicitly or implicitly agrees to provide the information necessary to Buyer's performance. The buyer could not relieve himself of the obligation to purchase the property simply by never giving the specifications to the contractor.

▶ A good example of this situation is provided in the case of *Internatio-Rotterdam, Inc. v. River Brand Rice Mills, Inc.*, 259 F. 2d 137 (2d.Cir.1958), which appears in most Contracts casebooks. In this case an exporter contracted to purchase rice from defendant at a certain price "per pocket." The "pocket" was a packet containing a certain quantity of rice. The purchaser agreed to provide shipping instructions by a certain date and to a certain port. The court held that the purchaser's failure to give the instructions in time to ship to meet the provisions of the contract constituted a breach. Seller's duty to deliver the rice was conditioned on purchaser providing that information by that date. Because purchaser did not provide the information within the timeframe necessary, seller's refusal to deliver the rice was not a breach. The court noted that regarding the purchaser's obligation to provide shipping instructions as a simple condition would work an unfair and unjustified interpretation of the deal. Such an interpretation would allow buyer to speculate on the market and profit from market shifts. If the market price rose, he would go forward. If it fell, he could refuse to give the information necessary to finalize the transaction. Thus, the court saw the obligation to give delivery instructions and arrange for shipment as a promise as well as a condition. It was a promise by the buyer to provide the information, and it was a condition on the exporter's duty to provide the rice. By failing to give the shipping instructions, the purchaser prevented seller from delivering the rice. Buyer's failure entitled seller to declare the contract at an end. This case can be seen as a material breach, entitling the injured party to withhold his performance as well as seeking damages.

Anticipatory Repudiation

Anticipatory repudiation is a breach of contract. The term is a contraction of a longer, more descriptive term: "breach by anticipatory repudiation." When a party to a contract established that the other party committed an anticipatory repudiation, the injured party has the same rights he would have if the time for performance had arrived and the party had refused to perform. Proving that the other party has breached by anticipatory repudiation is a ground for cancellation if the same statement would be a ground for cancellation at the time for performance. A breach occurs when a party states or indicates to his contract partner that he will not or cannot perform. The *Restatement* refers to anticipatory repudiation simply as "repudiation." It notes that the party will repudiate either by words or by a "voluntary affirmative act that renders him unable or apparently unable to perform without a breach." Whether a party's repudiation entitles the other party to withhold his performance depends on whether the breach is material. The analysis of whether a breach is material is discussed in the section on "material breach." If the repudiation relates to the entire performance then it will be a material breach.

A court will treat a statement or act as a repudiation of the contract only if it finds a clear cut language or act. If a party merely states concern about his willingness or ability to perform he may not have repudiated. In other words, courts require a clear showing that the injured party was justified in believing that the other party was calling the whole thing off or stating he would not be able to go through with the deal.

The English case of *Hochster v. De La Tour* is included in virtually every first year contracts casebook both because it is the traditional statement of the rule and also because the case makes the operation and the purposes of the rule clear. The events occurred in 1852. The plaintiff was a courier who agreed to accompany the defendant to Europe from June 1 to September 1. Before the time for departure, on May 11th, the defendant stated positively that he would not take the plaintiff as his companion. Hochster brought suit for breach. He took another job before the case came to the court. The defendant acknowledged that he had terminated the contract without cause against Hochster. He argued that his repudiation on May 11th was not a breach, however, because performance was not due at the time the suit was filed. He argued that his statement was an offer to rescind and that the plaintiff could not reject his offer to rescind unless plaintiff stood ready to perform until the date set for full performance. In that case, this would have meant the plaintiff could not accept the second job offered to him. He would need to remain ready to perform until September 1. The court rejected the defendant's argument, noting that the rule benefited society and the parties because it allowed the plaintiff to take another job rather "remaining idle and laying out money in preparations which would be useless."

Comment 2 to Uniform Commercial Code § 2-610 makes the point that the repudiation must be clear. If the statement indicates an "intention not to perform except on conditions which go beyond the contract," it is a repudiation of the obligation. Of course a party considering not performing may not tell the other party. In such a case, the law of anticipatory repudiation does not apply and the injured party will not be able to act ahead of the time set for performance. If a party merely expresses concerns or doubts about being able to perform, the situation is not a repudiation and the law does not give the anxious party the right to treat the statement as a breach.

> ▶ The *Restatement* provides a clear-cut example in Illustration 1 to Section 250 in which A and B enter a contract on April 1. A contracts to sell land to B and B contracts to buy the land. Delivery of the deed and payment of the price to be on July 30. On May 1, A tells B that he will not perform. This is a repudiation by A.

You can see from this illustration that part of the importance of the doctrine of anticipatory repudiation is that the injured party does not need to wait until the date set for performance to act on the breach. The injured party could sue the repudiating party before the time set for performance. In the case in illustration 1, the injured party is the buyer. He can sue for specific performance after the repudiation on May 1. This may be important to his rights. If B could not sue until the time set for performance, A might have sold to a bona fide purchaser, making it impossible for B to obtain the land contracted for. Since B can act quickly after the repudiation, his chance of getting the land is greater. Additionally, the injured party can go ahead and seek a substitute transaction. For example, if it had been the buyer rather than the seller that breached the contract for the sale of the land in the illustration, seller could go ahead and find a substitute buyer. His remedy would be the difference in price between the first and second contract, in the event he had to sell the land for less on the second sale.

A party who has repudiated the contract can reinstate the contract by withdrawing or retracting his repudiation. If the other party has declared the contract at an end based on the repudiation, it is too late for the repudiating party to retract the repudiation. Also, if the other party has relied on the repudiation, say by entering another contract, it is too late to retract.

Assurances of Performance

The last section on repudiation discussed the situation when a party clearly indicates he will not perform. When the statement or act is not clear, the doctrine of anticipatory repudiation does not apply, but the party who has been made insecure by the other party's statements or actions has some measures he can take. Once someone says they may not be willing or able to perform, the party who expected the performance has been made insecure. The party who is reasonably insecure has the right to seek assurances that the other party will go through with the deal.

Courts often speak about the "obligee" and the "obligor" in this context. Of course each party is both an obligee and an obligor. But in this context, the obligor is the party who has done or said something that makes the other reasonably insecure; we are focusing on the obligation of the party who is likely to be unable or unwilling to perform. If he is the seller, it is the obligation to deliver that is at risk. The buyer then is the obligee of the seller's obligation to sell.

When a party has not clearly repudiated her obligation under the contract but has made the other party insecure about performance, the law gives a framework for negotiating. The concept of adequate assurance of performance is the legal framework for this situation. UCC § 2-609 provides a template for parties negotiating about going forward in circumstances of uncertainty and insecurity. It provides that when an obligee has "reasonable grounds for insecurity" he has the right to "demand adequate assurance of due performance." Until the obligee receives reasonable assurances he may have a right to suspend his own performance. Of course if he has already received compensation for the performance, he has no right to withhold the performance. So, if you are the buyer and you have received part of the performance (delivery of one installment of a delivery of goods for example), you will need to go ahead and pay for what you have received. The UCC also sets a maximum time for giving the assurances. This is thirty days unless a shorter period is reasonable.

To put it simply, when it is reasonable to believe that the other party is going to breach by not performing, the obligee has a right to demand assurances from the other party that he will in fact perform as he is obligated to do under the contract. This concept respects the fact that once parties enter a contract they are relying on each other to perform. The Uniform Commercial Code expresses this point by saying that a contract "imposes an obligation on each party that the other's expectation of receiving due performance will not be impaired." UCC § 2-609(1). This makes sense when you think of all the work that goes into entering a contract and how much the parties rely on the contract in the sense of changing their positions because they are depending on the other party to perform. Parties enter other contracts in reliance on the first contract.

▶ For example, if you make shirts for sale to retailers, you purchase cotton or other raw materials to make the shirts. You hire employees to sew the shirts. You rent or purchase a building or a plant to have a place for the employees to sew the shirts. You also enter contracts to sell the shirts to the retailers. If the cotton producer or the fabric maker breaches her contract to sell you the fabric to make the shirts, your contracts with others to make the shirts and to sell the shirts are at risk. You will be in breach of other contracts if you cannot get the fabric to make the shirts.

What does it mean to demand assurances? It generally means that the insecure party will write to the obligor and indicate that he is insecure and, also, what he needs to be made secure so he can await performance without doing anything more. What will it take to make him believe in the other party again? Ordinarily it will take more than mere words of assurance. It is not likely that simply telling the insecure party: "Don't worry, be happy" will satisfy him or the court that the problem is resolved.

In the case of a seller who has been made insecure, the assurances relate to the ability of the buyer to pay for the goods. A letter of credit from the buyer's bank might provide the necessary assurances. In the case of a buyer who has been made insecure, the assurances relate to the ability of the seller to manufacture or deliver the goods. Thus, if a seller's plant has burned down, the buyer who contracted with this seller may demand assurances that the seller has obtained goods from other sources so that he will be able to meet the contract requirements to deliver the fabric contracted for. It may be sufficient to share with the buyer the contract that the seller has entered to obtain the fabric from another manufacturer.

Warranties as Conditions

Warranties are a particular category of conditions that you will study in an advanced contracts class on the UCC. Warranties occur in areas outside the sale of goods as well. They may be express or implied. UCC sections relevant here are: 2-313 on express warranties, 2-314 on the implied warranty of merchantability (that a product is fit for its ordinary use), and 2-315 on the implied warranty of fitness for a particular purpose. Under UCC 2-315, an implied warranty of fitness for a particular purpose arises when a seller has reason to know that buyer is buying the good for a particular use. UCC 2-316 provides that warranties can be disclaimed by the parties.

Checkpoints

- Promises and Conditions are related.

- Conditions are events not certain to occur, which must occur before the duty promised comes due. If the condition does not occur, the duty never matures. Condition Precedent is a condition.

- Conditions Subsequent is an event that cuts off liability or duty.

- Express Conditions are strictly enforced.

- Implied Conditions are created by the court to preserve the parties' expectations or to prevent injustice.

- Constructive Conditions of Exchange are promises that are dependent on each other.

- Material Breach is such a total breach that the injured party is entitled to withhold his performance.

- Substantial Performance means that the injured party cannot withhold his performance but he may recover damages for a breach.

- Condition of Satisfaction is a type of condition that depends on the judgment of the party receiving performance or some other party's judgment about the quality of the performance.

- Forfeiture occurs when the performance is lost and cannot be recovered.

- When a Timing Devices does not occur the court may substitute a reasonable time. The court will not discharge the duty when a timing device fails.

- Promissory Conditions are conditions that a party has a duty to fulfill. Not fulfilling the duty means that the other party's duty is discharged and the party who must perform the Promissory Condition is in breach.

- Anticipatory Repudiation is a breach that occurs before the time set for performance. The full name for this doctrine is "breach by anticipatory repudiation." The repudiation must be clear for it to be effective.

Chapter 11

Remedies

Roadmap

- Introduction
- Specific Performance
  - Historical Background
  - Constitutional Dimensions
  - Necessary Showings
- Expectation Interest Damages
  - Purpose
  - Types
  - Limitations
    - The Foreseeability Limitation
    - The Degree of Proof Limitation
    - The Compensation Limitation/Punitive Damages Bar
    - The Disproportionality Limitation
    - The Measure of Damages Limitation
    - The Avoidable Consequences Limitation
  - The Lost Volume Seller Exception
    - The Emotional Harm Limitation
- Alternatives to Expectation Damages
  - Reliance Interest Damages
  - Restitution Interest Damages
  - Liquidated Damages
  - Nominal Damages
  - Attorney Fees and Court Costs
- The Issue of Election of Rremedies and the Problem of Double Recovery
- Remedies under the UCC
- Summary

Introduction

Clients want remedies. That is to say (as you will discover in the practice of law) that, when a party becomes embroiled in a contract dispute and seeks the professional assistance of a lawyer, his usual quest is one for a remedy. But, as we have seen, the lawyer's initial inquiry is not about the remedies that might be available to that client. Rather, the lawyer must first satisfy herself that the client is bound to a valid, enforceable contract which has been breached (these are the first three Sequential Questions of Contract Law). The lawyer understands that, with rare exceptions, a judge will not entertain the issue of remedies until those first three sequential questions of contract analysis have been proved.

In this chapter we assume that:

1. There is a *valid* contract
2. with *enforceable* provisions
3. that has been *breached*.

The issue before us is: What Remedies are available (Sequential Question Four)?

To frame this issue, analytically, we begin with the fundamental purpose of Contract Law: *To enforce the bargain of the parties.*

Contract remedies seek to achieve, in whole or in part, that fundamental purpose. They do so by compensating the non-breaching party for the damages he or she suffered as a consequence of the breaching party's failure to perform his or her duties under the contract.

Accordingly, contract law offers the non-breaching party several categories of damages to effect that purpose, by compensating the non-breaching party for some or all of his or her interests in the contractual relationship. Those categories are:

1. Specific Performance;
2. Expectation Interest Damages;
3. Reliance Interest Damages;
4. Restitutionary damages;
5. Rescission;
6. Liquidated Damages;
7. Nominal Damages;
8. Attorney Fees and Court Costs.

Specific Performance

Since the purpose of Contract Law is to *enforce the bargain of the parties*, and because the most obvious interest the non-breaching party has in the contract is that the breaching party perform his contractual duties, you might think that an order of the court mandating that the breaching party perform would be the most common remedy in contract law. However, that is not the case under our common law system. In fact, Specific Performance is an extraordinary remedy, which is available only when the plaintiff establishes that ordinary damages are inadequate to compensate the plaintiff.

While the civil law system of remedies, which evolved in Europe, prefers the remedy of Specific Performance, the common law system adopted in the United States prefers the substitutionary remedy of monetary damages. That is, it prefers a remedy based upon the monetary value of the performance. The basis for this preference is historical, but it also has constitutional and practical underpinnings.

Historical Background

The English Common Law system adopted in the United States developed around notions of property. English courts of law directed their orders *in rem*, or against the *property* of the defendant. If a plaintiff successfully pled and proved his case, the remedy would be directed against the defendant's property. English law developed a rigid system of writs through which a non-breaching party might plead his case. Indeed, until the sixteenth century, there was no special writ for breach of contract. Rather, the non-breaching party would need to plead his cause within a writ of debt. If he won his case, his remedy was monetary. The exclusive remedy in English courts of law was monetary damages. Contrast this to the remedy of Specific Performance, which was only available in the Chancellor's courts of equity. The equity courts directed their orders against the person (*in personam*) and could, therefore, order the breaching party specifically to perform his contractual duties. However, the Chancellor, as keeper of the King's conscience, only made this equitable remedy available if justice required it. In sum, Specific Performance developed as an extraordinary remedy which could be ordered only if the remedy at law (*in rem*) of monetary damages was inadequate and it would be inequitable to limit the non-breaching party to monetary damages. Specific Performance (*In personam*) damages under the English common law system were the exception, not the norm.

Constitutional Dimensions

In addition to the historical antecedents of the common law's preference for the substitutionary remedy of monetary damages, the remedy of Specific Performance has also been constrained in the United States by Thirteenth Amendment concerns about involuntary servitude. Thus, whenever the remedy seems to coerce the breaching party's personal performance (requiring an opera star to sing, for example) courts may refuse to order Specific Performance on constitutional grounds. In that context, the interest in personal liberty trumps the economic interest presented in the contract.

Necessary Showings

Courts also refuse to order Specific Performance when the remedy might require unreasonable court supervision to enforce the remedy effectively. Like the Thirteenth Amendment constraint, the pragmatic problems of this sort most often arise in service contracts which require a certain quality of personal performance on the part of the breaching party. Even if the court could successfully order Britney Spears to sing, could it realistically ensure that she would sing to the best of her abilities?

Consequently, and for the three reasons advanced above, Specific Performance—ostensibly the most obvious way to enforce the bargain of the parties by giving the non-breaching party complete redress for his damages—is not the preferred remedy under our common law system of Contract law.

Specific Performance is considered an equitable remedy, which is only available to the non-breaching party if she proves the following prerequisites:

1. Monetary damages are inadequate;
2. Justice requires an equitable remedy; and
3. She (the non-breaching party) has "clean hands."

  ▶ The requirement that plaintiff must show that damages are inadequate is often met by a showing that the promised performance is unique. If the thing sold is unique, it is not possible to obtain a replacement performance in the market. The typical example of a unique item is a work of art. If the seller of a Van Gogh painting refuses to deliver the painting to buyer after the two entered a contract for the painting it is not possible for the buyer to find the same item in the marketplace. The typical example of non-unique goods is something for which a replacement or substitute can be obtained on the market, like corn. Damages may be inadequate even with a non-unique performance, such as the sale of corn, when it is not possible for the injured party to obtain a substitute. One of the principles of the Chancellor's equity courts was that in order to receive equity, plaintiff had to act in an equitable manner. Suppose Shopkeeper contracted with Customer for the sale of an antique cameo, said to have been worn by Catherine of Valois, wife of King Henry I (1413–1422). But later, Shopkeeper changes his mind and refuses to sell the cameo. Certainly, the subject-matter of the contract is so unique that monetary damages would be inadequate. Arguably, justice requires Specific Performance of the contract. But before Customer can receive the remedy, she must show that she is "ready, willing, and able" to perform her end of the bargain/to pay the agreed upon price of the contract. In the Chancellor's courts, to *get* equity, plaintiff had to *give* equity.

▸ Similarly, imagine that Real Estate Mogul sells an office building to Businessman under a mortgage and promises to use his best efforts and influence to secure tenants for the building, and in exchange Businessman promises to later deliver a rare, extremely valuable piece of art. Real Estate Mogul fails to use best efforts to secure tenants for the office building. If Businessman defaults on his mortgage payments because he has only a few tenants in the building, Real Estate Mogul might demand Specific Performance (since the artwork is "unique") and demand delivery of the artwork. But because Real Estate Mogul failed to live up to his end of the bargain, his hands are not "clean" and Specific Performance will be unavailable to him.

Expectation Interest Damages

Purpose

Contracts are "all about" exchanges based on relative values. Each party exchanges a thing (e.g., widgets, land, money, or services) for a different thing which he values more (widgets, land, money, or services). Contract law seeks to enforce the manifestation of this agreed upon value exchange (*enforce the bargain of the parties*). Therefore, if the contract is not performed by one of the parties, the courts will try to put the parties in the position they would have been in had the contract been performed. As we have seen, the extraordinary remedy of Specific Performance is usually unavailable. The common law prefers the substitutionary remedy of expectation interest damages. Expectation interest damages are designed to give the non-breaching party the "benefit of his bargain" by awarding him the monetary equivalent of what the non-breaching party would have received had the contract been performed.

The interest protected by the principle of expectancy is the interest transferred by contract — the economic right to reallocate resources efficiently. This right is protected by securing to the injured party the performance allocated by the contract: the benefit of the bargain. Today, the expectation of the parties is that the breach of the type of promise we regard as contracts may support a lawsuit, and, if the plaintiff succeeds in establishing a contract, the court will provide compensation for a breach of the promise. The default measure of damages for a breach of contract seeks to put the party injured by the breach where he would have been had the contract been performed. In this sense, modern contract law allows the transfer of economic rights as well as products and services. Such transfers include rights that the parties would have otherwise under the law. An agreement to arbitrate disputes results in the sale or alienation of the right to a judicial resolution of disputes. A liquidated damages clause alienates the right to damages by a trial. Forum selection clauses alienate a party's right to jurisdiction based on the default set by the law. The default measure for breach of contract is replacement cost minus contract price. It aims to secure the benefit of the bargain for injured party. It does not aim to encourage breach. Expectancy is not what a party "expects" but rather a term to denote the substitute damage measure. Contract law thus functions to lock in future performance, allowing the parties to gain the security necessary for future planning. Contract law seeks to maximize wealth by encouraging contracting itself. Its incentive of efficient obligation protects the parties' allocated expectations.

Types

Expectation interest damages are measured by:

1. *General Damages:* The monetary value of the contract to the non-breaching party (*general damages*);
2. *Incidental Damages:* But because the breach may also have directly caused other harm to the non-breaching party, he would not be "made whole" (put in the situation he would have been in, absent the breach) without being compensated for them, expectation interest damages must also include these *direct or incidental damages*;

3. *Consequential Damages:* And, because the non-breaching party might also suffer other harm, tangentially related to the breach and as a consequence of it, the non-breaching party will not be "made whole" unless he is allowed to recover for these damages as well. However, because these tangential or *consequential damages* do not naturally arise either out of the contract or the context of its nonperformance, *consequential damages* will not be awarded to the non-breaching party unless he can show that the breaching party either knew or should have known of special circumstances that would create *consequential damages* if she breached the contract.

Let's take a closer look at these three kinds of Expectation Interest Damages.

> ▶ Suppose Lawyer just had a brand-new Michelin tire put on her Volvo. The contract for the Michelin provides warranties of quality and a guarantee of "no defects." On her way to the courthouse the next day, the Michelin suffered a "blow-out" because of a manufacturing defect in the tire. The "blow-out" caused the Volvo to swerve out of control and to broadside the Audi TT in the adjoining lane. The Audi TT lost control and hit the Chevy pick-up ahead of it and was almost simultaneously rear-ended by the Jeep Cherokee behind it. After the dust settled, and the damaged vehicles were towed to their respective dealerships or body shops, the police had recorded all necessary information and the drivers had exchanged insurance information, Lawyer called a cab to rush her to the courthouse where she was scheduled to begin a trial. Because the trial was scheduled for 9:00 a.m. and she didn't arrive until 11:30 a.m., the judge entered a default judgment against her client. She then took a cab to Rex's Rentals. She knew she would need to rent a car until her Volvo was repaired. Subsequently, she has received notice from the owners and insurance companies of each of the cars involved in the incident that they will sue her for the damages they incurred. Her client is also suing her for malpractice because of the default judgment and the body shop has sent her an estimate of what it will cost to repair the damage to her Volvo.

How should we categorize all the damages Lawyer suffered and for which of them should Michelin be liable? We said that expectation interest damages include *general, incidental,* and *consequential* damages. In the case of Lawyer:

1. *General damages* consist of the value of the non-defective tire for which
    she bargained. Can she recover monetary damages for the tire? Yes. *Gen-
    eral damages* are always recoverable as expectation interest damages be-
    cause they are the monetary equivalent of the duty promised by the
    breaching party. Michelin promised (warranted/guaranteed) a defect-
    free tire of a certain quality. It breached its duty to provide one to her.
2. *Direct or incidental damages* here include:
    a. Two cab fares (to the courthouse and to Rex's Rentals).
    b. Fee for rental car.
    c. Body Shop work on her Volvo.

Because each of them seems to arise naturally from the context or circumstance of the blow-out of a tire, she can recover for them.

    d. She can probably also recover for her liability for the damages suf-
       fered by the owners of the other cars involved in the incident. These
       damages could also be anticipated from a tire blow-out in traffic. Gen-
       erally, all of these *incidental* damages which appear to arise naturally
       from the context will be recoverable.
3. *Consequential damages* in Lawyer's case consist of her financial expo-
    sure (liability) in the lawsuit by the client, because of the default judg-
    ment the client received as a consequence of Lawyer's failure to appear
    in court at the appointed time for trial.

Unlike *general, direct, and incidental* damages, *consequential* damages are
"*special*," in the sense that although the damages were caused by Michelin's
breach, they could not ordinarily be anticipated by it. That is, at the time Michelin (by its dealer/agent) entered into the contract with Lawyer for the sale of
the tire, it could not ordinarily have anticipated that if it breached its contract
by selling her a tire that did not conform to its promises under the contract,
she would be sued by a client because Michelin's breach caused her to miss a trial
and, consequently, a default judgment would be entered against her client.
Michelin would only be liable for these *consequential* damages if it had actual
knowledge of the trial and Lawyer's probable exposure for failure to appear.

Hence, we see from this example that, although expectation interest damages may include all three kinds of damages (*general, direct or incidental; and
the special or consequential damages*), they are not automatically available.
Rather, they are subject to certain limitations. Lawyer's situation illustrates the
first limitation on expectation interest damages:

*Damages to be recoverable must be foreseeable to the breaching party at the
time of contract.*

Let's take a closer look at these limitations on expectation interest damages, beginning with the *foreseeability* limitation, illustrated above.

Limitations on Contract Damages

Contract law provides limitations on contract damages. These limiting doctrines mean that the damages an injured party can obtain in court are not as great as you might expect. The law is solicitous of economic activity; it does not want to discourage contracting. The interests protected under different types of legal principles are not all the same or entitled to the same weight. Legal norms are not uniform. The law gives different degrees of protection to different interests by various legal doctrines. Criminal law, tort law, and contract law all present different approaches to damages because they are based on the societal norms that protect different interests. It is not surprising that violations of criminal law carry stronger sanctions than violations of tort law or contract law. Likewise, damages for a violation of tort rules or norms are more generous than violation of the norms of contract law. The need for significant criminal sanctions is based on a judgment that the interests protected by criminal law deserve significant and serious legal incentives. The sanctions available for torts are not as severe as those of criminal law, but they are more severe than contract damages. Contract damages provide a more limited form of compensation. Contract damages are not intended to punish the breaching party unless the breach also constitutes a violation of a public norm, like the obligation of good faith. The principle against punishing a party for breach of the private contract norm presents a weaker norm than tort law. Tort law protects the safety and physical integrity of members of society. It provides incentives to encourage safe practices and discourage negligent conduct. Since negligent conduct is generally not a good thing, the law provides a strong incentive against it. The economic interest protected by contract law also deserves protection, but the scope of the protection is narrower and the sanctions for violation of the norm of contract law are not as great as criminal law or tort law.

1. The Foreseeability Limitation

To be recoverable, damages must be foreseeable at the time of contracting to the party who subsequently breached. In our Lawyer example, Michelin could have anticipated, at the time it sold the tire to Lawyer, that if it sold her a nonconforming tire it might suffer a blow-out, requiring her to buy a replacement tire (*general damages*). Moreover, Michelin should have foreseen that the blow-out might cause her car to careen out of control, causing damage to her Volvo and to other cars in traffic. Finally, Michelin would need to acknowledge that while the car was being repaired and the tire replaced, Lawyer would need to pay for alternate means of transportation (taxicabs; rental cars). And all of these damages, *incidental* to and directly arising out of the blowout of the flawed tire, were foreseeable at the time of contract. By contrast, the lawsuit filed by Lawyer's client was not foreseeable from the context itself. Thus, absent actual knowledge of the client's upcoming trial, Michelin could not be held liable for any *consequential* damages arising out of the client's malpractice suit.

This foreseeability limitation on Expectation Interest Damages was first enunciated in the case of *Hadley v. Baxendale*, 9 ex. 341, 156 Eng. Rep. 145(1854), the famous English case in which the shaft in a grist mill broke and the mill owner sent it off to a manufacturer as a model for a new shaft. Since the mill owner did not have a substitute shaft, he had to close down the mill until he received the new shaft. While the mill was shut down the owner suffered damages in the form of lost business. Because the delivery company inexcusably delayed the return of the new shaft for several days, the jury found that the delivery company should be liable for the mill owner's lost business damages during that delay. The appellate court reversed because the delivery company had no way of knowing that its delay would exacerbate the owner's loss. It didn't know the mill owner had no substitute shaft with which to carry on his business. The appellate court enunciated the foreseeability limitation: damages, to be recoverable must:

1) "[B]e such as may fairly and reasonably be considered either arising naturally ... according to the usual course of things, from such breach of contract itself" or

2) the damages must be "such as may reasonably be supposed to have been in the contemplation of both parties at the time they made the contract, as the probable result of the breach of it."

That limitation, in its modern form is stated in the *Restatement (Second) of Contracts § 351, Unforeseeability and Related Limitations on Damages*:

1. Damages are not recoverable for loss that the party in breach did not have reason to foresee as a probable result of a breach when the contract was made.

2. Loss may be foreseeable as a probable result of a breach because it flows from the breach:
   a. in the ordinary course of events or

b. as a result of special circumstances, beyond the ordinary cause of events, that the party in breach has reason to know.

In sum, the Foreseeability Limitation says it's not enough that the breach caused the harm. That it would do so must also be foreseeable at the time of the contract, either because the harm would flow naturally from that breach in that context, ordinarily, or because of special circumstances of which the breaching party is aware that make the harm the probable result of the breach. Since you are probably taking a course in tort law at the same time you are taking contracts, you may wonder why damages seem more generous in tort law than in contract law. You may see this difference as an example of inconsistency in the law. Before you criticize the law as inconsistent, however, you should think about whether there is a need for different standards for damages in different types of cases. One way to understand the difference in approach is to think about the strength of the norms of tort and contract law. Tort law deals with unreasonable risks of harm to other people. Contract law protects the economic interest. This economic interest is important but not as important as protection against physical harm. Thus damages are more limited.

The Foreseeability Limitation flows logically from the bedrock principle of Contract law itself. As we have seen, the purpose of Contract Law is to *enforce the bargain* of the parties and that bargain is evinced in the *manifestation of the parties' intent to be bound.* Thus, the law will only enforce those terms that the parties expressly manifest or that were impliedly manifest by their express terms and the context in which they are to be performed. It follows that a delivery company that had no reason to know that a mill would be shut down until a new shaft is delivered did not bargain for any liability for its tardy return. And it follows that, absent some special knowledge about Lawyer's circumstances, Michelin should not be liable for damage related to those special circumstances. Thus, the promise that Expectation Interest Damages should put the non-breaching party in the position she would have been in if the contract had not been breached leads to the rule that the breaching party should only be liable for the risks for which he bargained. The overarching limitation of contract law is to enforce only the bargain that the parties intended.

2. The Degree of Proof Limitation (The "Reasonable Certainty" Test)

As you know, in any lawsuit, the plaintiff must prove the elements of her claim. This requires probative facts and a certain degree of proof. This degree of proof is referred to as the burden of proof. The usual burden of proof is a preponderance of the evidence. This means that the plaintiff must prove each element of a legal claim is more likely than not. For contract law, one element must be proven at a higher level than the usual preponderance level. To prove Expectation Interest Damages, plaintiff must prove the amount of her damages by a "reasonable certainty." While there is no "bright line" definition of the term, this means something more than the usual standard of proof for issues in civil cases. That is to say the degree of proof of reasonable certainty is higher than the generally applicable "preponderance of the evidence" test. Because the evidence of Lawyer's damages will be in the form of bills, invoices, and judgments, her evidence will most likely meet the "reasonable certainty" standard. The "preponderance of the evidence" standard applies to most elements of any civil action, including the other elements that plaintiff must establish to prevail in a contract action such as the formation of the contract and the breach by defendant. This higher standard of reasonable certainty applies only to the proof of contract damages, not to other elements such as formation and breach.

Cases in which the standard causes plaintiffs the most problems involve "lost profits" damages, especially where the breach allegedly causes a "new business" to lose profits. Imagine, for example that Jake opens a new seafood restaurant.

> ▶ Imagine, further, that for opening night he plans a special Alaskan seafood menu with the fish to be flown in that afternoon by a specially chartered plane. The plane fails to deliver the goods. Jake is unable to produce his amazing opening night menu, and seeks to recover from the charter company the profits he thinks he could have made.

Jack's problem is that his claim seems to be conjecture. It does not seem possible to prove the claim with reasonable certainty. How can a new business prove to a "reasonable certainty" what profits it would have made from an unknown number of customers on a particular date? Some courts allow plaintiffs to submit evidence of the profits of similar businesses in similar circumstances. Nonetheless, you should be aware that the "reasonable certainty" standard can create a proof problem, especially for lost profits damages to a new business. Because of the view that lost profits are necessarily conjecture for a new business, courts traditionally treated such damages as categorically not recoverable. The plaintiff simply could not recover such damages. Today, courts retain the reasonable certainty standard and the difficulty of meeting that standard for lost profits for new business. Generally courts do not reject proof categorically. Thus, plaintiff can put on evidence sufficient to meet the required degree of proof for lost profits for a new business. Most modern courts will not bar the plaintiff from trying to show lost profits for a new business. For example, if the business was ultimately established, a court might allow proof of how much the business made per month after it was up and running. It might also allow proof of other comparable businesses in the area or a similar area.

3. The Compensation Limitation/Punitive Damages Bar

It is a fundamental rule of Contract Law that punitive damages cannot be recovered in a breach of contract lawsuit. This rule is logically deduced from the bedrock principle that the purpose of Contract law is to *enforce the bargain* of the parties. It is often said that, the goal of Contract Remedies is not to punish the breaching party but, rather, to compensate the non-breaching party for the loss occasioned by the breach. Nevertheless, there are cases in which courts have allowed punitive damages in connection with a breach of contract based on the culpability of the conduct. For example, some courts reason that if a party acted in bad faith, it breached a public nom and deserves a stronger sanction, such as punitive damages.

4. The Disproportionality Limitation

Courts also limit damages that are grossly disproportionate to the value of the contract to the breaching party. *Restatement (Second) § 351(3)* states that "A court may limit damages for foreseeable loss ... in order to avoid disproportionate compensation." Comment f to the Section explains:

> It is not always in the interest of Justice to require the party in breach to pay damages for all of the foreseeable loss that he has caused ... One such circumstance is an extreme disproportion between the loss and the price charged by the party whose liability for that loss is in question. The fact that the price is relatively small suggests that it was not intended to cover the risk of such liability. Another such circumstance is an informality of dealing, including the absence of a detailed written contract, which indicates that there was no careful attempt to allocate all of the risks.

Like other limitations, this one relates back to the fundamental purpose of enforcing the bargain of the parties and the terms under which they intended to be bound. Absent evidence to the contrary, courts usually refuse to infer that the breaching party intended to expose himself to liability in an amount that far exceeds the consideration due him under the terms of the contract. Another way to analyze the Disproportionality Limitation is to use the Foreseeability Limitation and to explain it in terms of assumption of risk.

▸ Assume, for purposes of illustration, a Michelin truck tire is put on a tanker carrying gas on an interstate highway in California. The tire is a replacement and it was put on the truck at a truck stop just out-side Oakland. The truck stop charged $25.00. There's nothing wrong with the tire but the mechanic failed to tighten bolts sufficiently to se-cure it. So, once the tanker regained its normal speed on the Inter-state, the tire came off, the tanker went out of control, collided with a retaining structure, flipped over, causing gas to spill and ignite and —in the conflagration that ensued—the heat of the fire melted the steel supports on the overpass above the Interstate causing the over-pass to collapse. The governor of California estimates billions of dol-lars in lost revenues for businesses while the highways are shut down for repairs. Should the truck stop be liable for this amount of dam-ages caused by its $25.00 tire replacement job?

It would be wise to assess this case from the perspective of tort law and statutory law. As a matter of contract law, a court would consider whether the loss was foreseeable. It is certainly arguable that some significant damage could be foreseen as a result of a tire coming off a gas tanker. On the other hand, this loss may seem disproportionate to a court applying contract principles. This would mean that the plaintiff would rely primarily on tort law for recov-ery. The illustration above presents a difficult case. The *Restatement* provides a clearer case for this limitation in Illustration 17:

> ► A, a private trucker, contracts with B to deliver to B's factory a ma-chine that has just been repaired and without which B's factory, as A knows, cannot reopen. Delivery is delayed because A's truck breaks down. In an action by B against A for breach of contract the court may, after taking into consideration such factors as the absence of an elaborate written contract and the extreme disproportion between B's loss of profits during the delay and the price of the trucker's services, exclude recovery for loss of profits.

The job of contract remedies is to compensate the non-breaching party to the extent that the injury suffered was foreseeable and the damage amount was reasonably contemplated as a risk assumed by the breaching party.

5. The Measure of Damages Limitation (Cost of Completion versus Diminution of Value and the Problem of Waste)

We begin, again, with the purpose of Expectation Interest Damages: to put the non-breaching party in the position she would have been in had the con-tract been performed, by giving her the substitutionary remedy of the con-tract's monetary value to her. This statement suggests that the non-breaching party has a right to receive "perfect tender" of the consideration for which she bargained. If she contracted to have her dream McMansion built and her contract calls for a particular type of imported Italian marble to be installed in the floor of the foyer, then she has a right to insist on that kind of marble. What if the builder substitutes a cheaper look-alike marble? Is her remedy the substitutionary value of the "real thing"? Under the old common law rule of perfect tender, the answer would be a resounding "yes." But commercial practices and considerations of efficiency have modified that rule somewhat by interjecting a limitation where perfect tender would result in unreasonable economic waste. The problem usually arises in construction contracts and it was, in fact, a home construction contract that established the modern rule. The case, *Jacob & Youngs v. Kent,* involved a contractor who built a house pursuant to the contract specifications except that he installed plumbing pipe of a different brand (but of equal quality) than the pipes called for by the contract. The Perfect Tender Rule would consider this a breach and require a substitutionary monetary remedy measured by what it would cost to complete the house with the proper brand of pipe. "Cost of Completion" is this traditional measure of substitutionary damages. But, in *Jacob & Youngs,* the remedy would require a measurement of what it would cost to tear out and then replace all the walls that covered the pipe, in addition to the cost to replace it with the brand of pipe (of equal value) called for by the contract.

In his opinion, Judge Cardozo declared that the Cost of Completion remedy would result in unreasonable economic waste and he applied a different measurement for damages, "Diminution of Value," equal to the value of the house with the brand of plumbing pipe required by the contract minus the value of the house with the existing pipe of the other brand (but the same value). Thus, Cardozo established the modern rule that the measurement of damages for breach continues to be derived from the Perfect Tender Rule: Cost of Completion. *But if,*

1) The contract has been substantially performed according to its terms;
2) The breach was inadvertent and in good faith; and
3) The remedy of Cost of Completion is great and would result in waste,

then the measurement for the remedy should be Diminution in Value, not Cost of Completion.

In *Jacob & Youngs,* the record showed the house was virtually completed; the difference in the two brands of pipe was inconsequential, both in appearance and in quality; the mistake was inadvertent; the breach did not affect the value of the house, and the replacement or Cost of Completion remedy was unreasonably costly and amounted to waste. Therefore, the appropriate measure of damages was Diminution of Value.

By contrast, in our McMansion example, the cost of replacing (the cost of completion) the marble may not be unreasonable; the difference in value between the two kinds of marble is significant, and the breach was intentionally designed to increase the builder's profit margin at the expense of the owner's bargained for terms. Here, the builder probably would not qualify for a Diminution in Value limitation. He is stuck with the traditional measure of Cost of Completion. Thus, while the Diminution in Value exception to the perfect-tender measurement of Cost of Completion is narrow, it can be important as a matter of damages awarded.

6. The Avoidable Consequences Limitation

Another limitation premised upon efficiency concerns has to do with the non-breaching party's opportunity to *mitigate* (reduce) his damages by finding a *cover* (substitute consideration) for the breach and then holding the breaching party liable only for any amount that the cover exceeds the contract price.

> ▶ For example, a building owner leases an office to a business (lessee) for a four-year term. After two years, the business abandons the space and breaks the lease. The business is in breach of its contractual obligation to make lease payments for the two years remaining on the lease, and the building owner is entitled to damages. But if the building owner can mitigate those damages by leasing the space to another business, the damages are reduced by the amount of the second lease. Thus, the breaching party's liability is the difference between the lease amount owed on the first lease and the lease amount by which the building owner "covered" in the second lease. If the building owner was able to lease the building to the second lessee for an amount greater than the first lease, the building owner arguably has not suffered a loss on the bargain. The building owner may have incidental damages if he incurred expenses in finding and negotiating the second lease.

Mitigation is the term used in common law cases to express the reduction in damages that courts apply when the injured party made a substitute transaction or could have made a substitute that would reduce damages. The Uniform Commercial Code refers to the substitute transaction as "cover." The substitute transaction helps the non-breaching party reduce his losses. This can also benefit the breaching party. If he can prove the total loss occasioned was avoidable because a substitute was available to mitigate the loss, and if the

non-breaching party did not avoid the consequences by cover, courts will reduce damages by the amount the injured party could have saved by making
the substitute transaction. The substitute must be sufficiently similar to the
original contract to make it a value to the injured party. In the lease example,
if the lease term was to run until May, 2008, and lessee breached in May 2007,
a lessee who offered to lease the space for five years beginning in May, 2008
would not mitigate the damages caused by the breach because the second lease
is not a substitute for the first lease. Its term does not fall within the term of
the first lease. However, a second lease covering the year remaining on the lease
would mitigate damages from the unexpired term of the first lease. Courts
often speak in terms of the injured party's "duty to mitigate" damages. This is
not literally true in the sense of a legal duty. The injured party does not have
a duty to mitigate; but the court will reduce damages by the amount he could
have mitigated by entering a substitute transaction. To put this point in terms
of the title of the doctrine explained here, the consequences of a breach may
be avoided by entering a new contract after a breach to take the place of the contract that was breached. Courts encourage parties to keep commerce moving
by making a new contract and avoiding running up damages—the natural
consequences of the breach. When a party has the opportunity to reduce damages that result from a breach, he should do that. This move saves costs to the
entire system. The injured party is not required to enter a substitute transaction, but his damages will be reduced by any consequent damages that he could
have avoided.

The Lost Volume Seller Exception

In some cases, there may be no savings to the injured party as a result of an
additional transaction after the breach. If the non-breaching party can prove
that he would have made the second contract if there had been no breach, he
may be able to withstand the argument that damages should be reduced by
the substitute transaction. In other words, the seller who makes a second sale
should not suffer a reduction in damages if the breach reduced the volume of
his sales. Where he could have made two sales, he made only one. In this case,
the non-breaching party is called a "lost volume seller." When the injured party
seller can show that he could have made both sales and profited from both
sales, his damages should include the profit on both sales. The breach caused
a loss in the volume of sales and thus, in plaintiff's profits. To successfully
make the case of a lost volume seller, the injured party needs to show that it
could have had both the original sale and the subsequent sale and that it had
the resources and production capacity to perform both the breached contract

and the next contract. In *Neri v. Retail Marine Corp.*, 285 N.E.2d 311 (1972), for example, a buyer contracted for a boat from defendant. Buyer breached the contract and sought return of its deposit. (Because the buyer was seeking the return of its deposit, it was the plaintiff in the case.) Seller was able to sell the boat to a second purchaser. In response to the buyer's claim, Seller made the claim of breach. It also successfully argued that if buyer had not breached, it could have made both sales (and the profit from both sales). Accordingly, the court awarded as damages the amount of seller's profit on the breached sale.

> ▸ Imagine a dealership parking lot filled with brand-new black F-150s (with a back-up supply available at Ford's manufacturing plant). Buyer enters a contract to purchase one of the F-150s (memorialized in a signed writing). Later Buyer defaults, and Dealer sells the truck to Buyer 2. Arguably, the second sale does not mitigate Dealer's damages and should not be regarded as mitigating his damages because the dealer could have made both sales.

The "lost volume seller" should receive his lost profits on a breached sale with no reduction for "mitigation" for the subsequent sale of the goods.

7. The Emotional Harm Limitation

Contract law, generally, does not provide a remedy for emotional harm. While parties may derive some emotional benefit from the performance of a contract, they cannot recover monetary damages for the loss of the emotional benefit or for the mental distress suffered as a result of a breach. Generally speaking, contract remedies are limited to compensation for economic injury. However, there are some exceptions where the subject matter of the contract itself is intensely personal and a breach would give rise to foreseeable emotional distress. Breach of a contract for funeral arrangements provides an example.

Alternatives to Expectation Damages

We began this section with the understanding that the purpose of Expectation Interest Damages was to put the non-breaching party monetarily in the position he would have been in had the contract been performed. But, as we have seen, the availability of that remedy is restricted by a number of limitations. Because of one or more of these limitations, the non-breaching party may not be able to prove his entitlement to Expectation Interest Damages. However, he might avail himself of other remedies: Reliance, Restitution, and Rescission, which we will now explore. It is important, at the outset, to be aware that while specific performance and Expectation Interest Damages are meant to compensate the non-breaching party for his entire loss, each of the following remedies may give the non-breaching party a different remedy for his loss, which may be less than the expectation measure would provide. A plaintiff will seek recovery based on one of these measures when there is a problem with proving expectation damages. Courts will not award double recovery or duplicative recovery. This principle means that generally expectation damages will be the measure of damages unless there is a problem with that measure as discussed above.

Reliance Interest Damages

A non-breaching party's reliance interest damages are his "out-of-pocket" expenses: expenditures he incurred in either preparing to or beginning to perform under the contract, prior to the other party's breach.

> ▶ Neighbor contracts with Painter to repaint her house on June 1 and, to prepare for the job, Painter buys the color, brand and type of paint called for under the contract (along with other requisite supplies) on May 29. Neighbor calls Painter on May 30 and cancels the job. She is in breach of her contract with Painter. If Painter is unable to prove his Expectation Interest Damages, he may be able to recoup his Reliance Interest Damages, measured by those out-of-pocket expenses incurred in preparing to perform the contract (paint and supplies). He should have no trouble proving that amount.

As you will see in other parts of this book, Reliance Interest Damages are flexible. Courts will not award damages that result from unreasonable reliance. Additionally, courts consider the entire context and circumstances in determining reliance damages. This point is discussed in the chapter on Estoppel and Reliance and the limitation announced in *Restatement 90* that Reliance Damages should be limited as justice requires. This very flexible test recognizes the wide range of judicial discretion in this area. Because the discretion of courts in Reliance damages is even larger than the ordinary ability of courts to exercise discretion, it is a good idea to think of the doctrines as arguments rather than clear categories.

Restatement (Second) of Contracts § 349 deals with the issue of Reliance Interest Damages. The section states that reliance damages provide "an alternative to the measure of damages stated in § 347," which is expectation damages. Section 349 affirms the right of an injured party "to damages based on his reliance interest, including expenditures made in preparation for performance or in performance." The section also notes that to the extent the breaching party can "prove with reasonable certainty the injured party would have suffered had the contract been performed" then the loss should be deducted from the reliance damages. The likely reason for a plaintiff to seek reliance damages is that proof of expectancy damages is difficult in the particular case. A comment to Section 349 notes that an injured party may choose to "ignore the element of profit and recover as damages his expenditures in reliance." It goes on to note the likely reason for this choice is that plaintiff "cannot prove his profit with reasonable certainty."

The comment also notes that the plaintiff may seek reliance damages in the case of a losing contract, when plaintiff "would have had a loss rather than a profit." It notes that such a case is vulnerable to the possible showing by the breaching party proving the amount of the loss. If the breaching party satisfies the burden of showing that plaintiff would have lost money on performance, the court should subtract this loss from the injured party's damages. For example, some courts have held that if the defendant successfully shows that the plaintiff would have lost money on the contract if defendant had fully performed, a court may decide to deduct from damages owed by the defendant the losses defendant shows the plaintiff would have suffered by full performance. Thus, some courts limit reliance damages because of a showing that the contract would have been a losing contract for plaintiff. It is important to note that it must be the plaintiff who would be losing money under the contract. This is an unusual case of breach since it means that the party who breached was likely to get more for the deal than anticipated. We can surmise this from the fact that he is getting performance that costs more (to the plaintiff) than the contract provides. Most parties will not breach when this is the case. If the contract is a losing deal for both parties, it is likely that they will agree to terminate the relationship or renegotiate it in some way.

> ▶ If Neighbor can prove that Painter had signed a "Losing Contract" (that, if both sides had performed the contract, Painter would have lost money under it because he failed to bargain for an amount of consideration that would cover his expenses and labor), then to that extent, the Painter may not be able to recover some (a partially "losing contract") or all (a totally "losing contract") of his out-of-pocket expenses. This is because the purpose of Reliance Interest Damages is to put the non-breaching party in the position he was in before he began to prepare to perform (his "status quo ante"), but only to the extent that it does not put him in a better position than he would have been in had the contract been performed by both parties.

Neither the breaching party nor the non-breaching party should benefit from the breach. The law's exclusive job is to compensate for loss caused by the breach. In a "losing contract," the non-breaching party may have, in fact, gained by the breach. If so, he will not be awarded any Reliance Interest Damages.

Restitution Interest Damages

Expectation Interest Damages and Reliance Interest Damages are considered "at law" remedies, originating in courts of law. Specific Performance originated in Courts of Equity, not in courts of law. Restitutionary Damages originated in a separate field of law: the law of Restitution. As a source of remedies in contract law, its purpose is similar to the Chancellor's concern that justice be done: restitution is strongly grounded in notions of equity.

How do Restitution Interest Damages differ from Reliance Interest Damages? Reliance Interest Damages focus on the non-breaching party and seek to *compensate* him for his out-of-pocket expenses. By contrast, Restitutionary Damages focus on the breaching party and seek to *take away* ("disgorge") from him any benefit he received from the non-breaching party prior to the breach (his "unjust enrichment").

> ▸ In our Reliance Interest Damages example, suppose that after the contract between Neighbor and Painter was signed, but before its performance date (June 1) began, Neighbor decided to take a vacation in Montego Bay. By the time she returned on June 15, Painter has painted approximately half of the house. Now, he has incurred not only Reliance Interest Damages in preparing and beginning to perform, he has also conferred a benefit on Neighbor in the form of his partial performance. But on June 15, upon her return, Neighbor says she changed her mind, doesn't want the house painted, and orders Painter off of her property.

We have seen how the law will protect Painter's Reliance Interest Damages. How will it protect his Restitution Interest Damages? It will "disgorge" the Neighbor's "unjust enrichment" under the concept of *quasi contract. Quasi contract* allows someone who confers a benefit upon another to recover the reasonable value of the benefit conferred on the unjustly enriched party even if there was no valid contract. That value can be measured either by the replacement value of the goods and services rendered (in our example, the market value of Painter's goods and services) or the amount by which the unjustly enriched party was benefited by the goods and services rendered (in our example, the amount by which the value of Neighbor's house was increased by Painter's work).

The remedy of Restitution is available when one party is unjustly enriched by the goods and services rendered by another. The remedy is, thus, available in a number of circumstances:

1) When the breaching party receives an uncompensated benefit from the non-breaching party under a valid, enforceable contract. That's our example of *Painter v. Neighbor.*

2) When a valid contract is unenforceable because of the applicability of the Statute of Frauds or of the Doctrine of Impracticability (or Frustration of Purpose) or due to the non-occurrence of a condition which results in a forfeiture;

3) When there is a valid enforceable contract that has been breached but the non-breaching party's principal damages consist of "lost profits" which he cannot prove under the expectation interest damage limitations;

4) When there is a valid enforceable contract that has been breached but the non-breaching party has no remedy either under Expectation Interest analysis or under Reliance Interest analysis, because it was a "losing contract;"

5) And, finally, even a breaching party might receive restitution for any uncompensated benefit she conferred on the non-breaching party.

Discharge and Rescission

Rescission terminates the parties' duty to perform. The parties to a contract have a right to rescind their obligations by mutual agreement. The agreement can be express or implied. Cancellation of a contract is similar to Rescission in that it terminates the agreement. Cancellation is a right of the party who is the victim of a material breach by the other party. Cancellation is a unilateral right of the injured party. A court may also grant Rescission based on fraud or proof that the contract is voidable and should be voided. This occurs, for example, when a protected party (for example, a minor) elects his power to void a contract by asking the court to rescind it.

Liquidated Damages

Rather than leaving it to the law to assess the amount of damages, the parties themselves might set a value in the contract itself for anticipated damages. That is, they might "liquidate," or establish a certain amount for anticipated damages from breach. Liquidated damages clauses in contracts will be enforced by courts as long as:

1) The contract manifests the parties' intent to agree upon (liquidate) the amount of damages before any breach has occurred;

2) Damages, in the event of breach, will be difficult to ascertain. That is, a breach will surely cause damage to the non-breaching party, but the measure of actual loss will be difficult, if not impossible, to assess. For example, if the contract relates to a new business, the lost profits that could result from a breach would be difficult to ascertain.

3) The amount of damages agreed upon is not a penalty. That is to say, the liquidated damage amount is not disproportionate to the loss that might reasonably result from a breach. This is the most important factor of the test and its justification is entirely consistent with the basic principle of contract remedies previously discussed: the purpose of contract remedies is to compensate the non-breaching party for his loss caused by the breach, not to punish the breaching party.

Nominal Damages

As the name implies, nominal damages are minimal and a mere formality. Their purpose is to indicate that a breach of the contract has been proven even if the non-breaching party suffered no damages from the breach or cannot prove any damages. For example, if a court finds a plaintiff was unable to prove damages but finds a breach occurred, it may order payment of nominal damages, such as $1.00.

Attorney Fees and Court Costs

No discussion of remedies would be complete without analyzing the problem of which party will pay the attorney. Attorney fees and court costs are two distinct items of damages, but we treat them here together because they often appear together. The analysis of the amount of remedy for breach is separate from the issue of who pays attorney fees and court costs. If a party retains a lawyer in a dispute, then attorney fees will accrue. If the dispute leads to the filing of a lawsuit, the court will assess court costs. Can the non-breaching party, as a part of her remedy, impose these expenses on the breaching party? Or must she expect that she will have to pay her costs, effectively reducing the amount she recovers?

Under the U.S. common law system, each party pays his own fees and expenses, no matter who is the breaching party and no matter who wins the lawsuit. This is called "the American Rule." Exceptions to the rule are found either in applicable statutes or (in lawsuits over contract disputes) clauses in contracts that preempt the American Rule and expressly state that the losing party in a lawsuit will pay both parties' fees and expenses. That is generally called the "prevailing party rule" or the "loser pays rule." It is also called the "British Rule" because it replicates the rule employed under the English common law system. A caveat of either system is that attorney's fee and court costs are two distinct types of fees, and a statute or contract clause that affects one generally doesn't affect the other. For example, if you sign a contract that says loser pays court costs in a dispute, but the contract doesn't mention attorney fees, then the attorney fees would be decided by whatever the rule (whether by statute or common law) is in your jurisdiction. Often rental contracts and consumer contracts now include a provision stating that attorney fees will be paid by the prevailing party. Some contracts provide one-sided attorney fees clauses, stating that if the landlord or dentist or vendor who provides the contract retains a lawyer to collect on the contract that the other side will pay "reasonable attorney fees."

The Issue of Election of Remedies and the Problem of Double Recovery

In this chapter we have identified an array of remedies which might be available to a party in a contract dispute. We have also seen that some of these remedies are designed to give the plaintiff (usually, the non-breaching party) complete relief for the economic loss caused by the breach (Specific Performance, Expectation Interest Damages and—perhaps—Liquidated Damages), other remedies may render only partial relief (Reliance Interest Damages, Restitution Interest Damages, and Rescission, to the extent that Rescission relieves the non-breaching party of the obligation to perform his obligations under the contract). The obvious question this palate of choices engenders is whether the plaintiff must choose (elect) only one of these remedies or whether there are situations where she might elect more than one.

The starting point for an analysis of the issue is the overarching concern of contract law that remedies should typically compensate the non-breaching party for losses occasioned by the breach but it should neither punish the breaching party for the breach nor reward either party for the breach in excess of the contract-related economic losses the non-breaching party sustained as a result of the breach. It follows that any remedy that seeks to compensate the non-breaching party for his total economic loss (Specific Performance; Ex-est Damages; Liquated Damages clauses) is an exclusive remedy and cannot be supplemented by any other remedy because that would result in "double recovery" or an amount in excess of the loss. But remedies that afford only partial relief (Reliance Interest Damages, Restitution Interest Damages and Rescission) may—in the proper case—permit election of all three remedies. What is the "proper case"? Recall that there are two contexts for Rescission: 1) voidable contracts and 2) breached contracts. If the plaintiff (a non-breaching party in the second context) asks for Rescission (to terminate her duty to perform) she may also seek Reliance (her out-of-pocket expenses) and Restitution (to disgorge the breaching party's unjust enrichment). In this situation, it is apparent that there is no double recovery. However, in the case of a voidable contract, the party who elects to invoke Rescission is asking the court to render the contract *void ab initio* (to obviate the contract entirely). The power to require the court to render the contract void is conferred because of the plaintiff's protected status, as a minor, for example. Once the contract is rendered void the minor is given his legal remedy—there is no longer a contract (it's as if it never existed) and, therefore, no *at law* remedies (like Reliance Interest Damages) are available to him. Nonetheless, because Restitution is a separate field of law, not a contract law remedy, the minor might also seek a restitutionary remedy for any uncompensated benefit conferred by him upon the other party.

> ▸ Suppose, in our case of Painter and Neighbor, that the Neighbor did not breach but the Painter was a thirteen-year-old boy. The youngster painted half the house and then decided he'd rather go fishing. His minority status means that the contract was voidable at his election. The minor's decision to disaffirm the contract may mean that Painter can neither recover his Reliance Interest Damages (out-of-pocket expenses) nor his Expectation Interest Damages. The Neighbor may be able to recover his *Restitution Interest Damages* in *quasi contract* if he compensated the minor Painter for the house painting before the minor abandoned the work. Minor might argue that he conferred a benefit on Neighbor because of the partial job of painting the Neighbor's house. Whether the half done job was a benefit is open to debate of course. It is likely the home owner would pay someone else to repaint the whole house. A half finished paint job might be worse than if the minor had never started the job at all. Indeed, the value of the Neighbor's house might actually go down due to the half finished job. Like many simplified hypothetical cases, there could be more to this case. Neighbor might have a tort claim against the minor.

Remedies under the UCC

Article 2 of the Uniform Commercial Code provides detailed provisions on remedies issues. Some first year Contracts classes include coverage of some of these provisions and others leave these points for later coverage in the second or third year of law school in a course covering sales of goods. Accordingly, we note only a general outline here. The UCC follows most of the principles laid out above on contract remedies, giving more specific coverage than the common law in many cases. Three types of damages are the focus of our discussion of Article 2 damages: (1) a substitute transaction, (2) difference money damages, and (3) specific performance. From the perspective of an injured party buyer, the specific remedies for these three types of damages are: (1) cover under 2-712, (2) difference money damages under 2-713, and (3) specific performance under 2-716. From the perspective of an injured party seller, the specific remedies for these three types of damages are: (1) resale under 2-706, (2) difference money damages under 2-708, and (3) the specific performance of obtaining the price promised under 2-709. In reality the Code has other types of remedies, such as incidental damages, circumstantial damages, liquidated damages, and other items of damages.

The Code provides for expectancy damages as the default remedy. Its provisions encourage cover as the primary expectancy measure. This default can be understood by focusing on the case of the injured party buyer. When Seller breaches by failing to deliver goods, Buyer can buy the same type of goods from another Seller and sue Seller for the difference between the price of the cover and the price of the contract.

UCC 2-716 expands the concept of specific performance beyond the original meaning of "unique" goods. Rather than limiting the remedy of specific performance to unique goods, the Code empowers the injured party buyer to obtain the remedy of specific performance when goods are unique or "in other proper circumstances." A comment to this section makes clear that the buyer's inability to cover by finding a substitute for the contract is strong evidence of "other proper circumstances," indicating that when the market does not provide a remedy the Code will protect the injured party. As a practical matter, it is often not possible for the injured party buyer to obtain the goods since seller has likely already sold the goods. If the market does not have substitute goods and the original goods have been sold to another, the injured party faces a difficult situation even though the UCC declares he has a right to the goods.

▶ Seller contracts with Buyer, promising to deliver a particular painting by Picasso. Of course this work of art is unique. If Seller refuses to deliver the Picasso, Buyer is entitled to specific performance of the painting.

This result would be the same under the common law and the UCC. Both the UCC and the common law regard money damages as inadequate to put the injured party buyer in the place he would have been had the contract been performed. Thus, specific performance is necessary to give the injured party the benefit of the bargain.

> ► Seller contracts with Buyer, promising to deliver 100,000 bushels of wheat. The wheat is not unique. If Seller refuses to deliver the wheat, Buyer's ordinary remedy is the right to cover and to receive the difference in price between the original contract (breached by Seller) and the second (substitute) contract. If a shortage makes it impossible for buyer to obtain the wheat on the market, buyer is entitled to specific performance of the wheat under 2-716.

This result would not be available under the common law approach because wheat is not unique. The UCC recognizes that the market remedy fails in the case where buyer cannot obtain a substitute on the market. Shortages can make it impossible for the injured party to obtain a substitute in the marketplace. Thus, the Code regards money damages as inadequate to put the injured party buyer in the place he would have been if the parties had performed the contract. Under this new approach, specific performance is necessary to give the injured party the benefit of the bargain. When the buyer breaches by failing to accept and pay for the goods contracted for without a justifiable cause, the seller has the right to resell the goods and obtain from the breaching buyer the difference in price between the original contract and the resale contract. This is a substitute transaction, just as the cover contract is a substitute for the injured party buyer. In each case, the injured party gets the goods contracted for and the breaching party is responsible for the difference in the price. If the buyer is able to get goods at a cost lower than the contract, he is not damaged, except for incidental and consequential damages.

The resale transaction must be made in good faith and in a commercially reasonable manner. The Code has specific provisions relating to the whether the resale may be at public or private sale and other details of the transaction. If the injured party seller chooses not to resell the goods, he can obtain damages under UCC 2-708. This measure is based on the price seller could have received if seller had sold the goods to another buyer at the time buyer should have accepted the goods. This measure is the difference between the contract price and the market price at the time and place set for tender by the contract. Seller can also obtain incidental or consequential damages.

In some cases, such as unique goods, no one else wants the goods. In such a case, the UCC protects the injured party seller, allowing him to recover price as it becomes due. The remedy of price is generally limited to cases in which resale is impracticable or have been destroyed after risk of loss has passed to the buyer. You can see the remedy of price is the equivalent of specific performance for buyer. It gives the injured party seller exactly what he would have received under full performance of the contract: the amount of money buyer owed for the goods.

Summary

To recapitulate the basics *of contract re*medies: always begin your analysis with the fundamental purpose of contract law, which is to "enforce the bargain of the parties" and its logical consequence that remedies are limited to compensating the loss suffered by the non-breaching party as a result of the breach. Remedies should not punish the non-breaching party nor should they reward either party for the breach.

When a party breaches a valid contract with enforceable terms, the non-breaching party is entitled to a remedy.

Contract remedies include Specific Performance, Expectation Interest Damages, Reliance Interest Damages, Restitution, Rescission, Liquidated Damages, Nominal Damages, Attorney Fees, and Court Costs. The typical remedy for a breach is an award of monetary damages based on the expectation interest of the non-breaching party.

Checkpoints

- Different kinds of remedies for breach of contract are available to serve different purposes.

- The purpose of the remedy of Specific Performance is to compel the breaching party to perform his obligations under the contract when any other remedy would be inadequate and justice demands actual performance.

- The purpose of Expectation Interest Damages is to compensate the non-breaching party with a money award that would be equivalent to the position he would have been in had the contract been adequately performed.

- The non-breaching party must show that the damages she suffered were both foreseeable and provable to a reasonable certainty.

- Generally, punitive damages are not recoverable for breach of contract.

- Generally, emotional damages are not recoverable for breach of contract.

- The purpose of Reliance Interest damages is to return the non-breaching party to his *status quo ante* by awarding him the out-of-pocket expenses he incurred by reasonably beginning or preparing to perform the contract before the breach occurred.

- The purpose of Restitution is to award the non-breaching party the value of the goods or services he rendered to the other party before the breach by disgorging the other party's unjust enrichment.

- The purpose of Rescission is to terminate the contract and the parties' obligations to perform it.

- The purpose of Liquidated Damages is to agree within the contract before the breach occurs to a sum that would reasonably reflect the probable damages caused by a breach when damages will be difficult to calculate.

- The purpose of Nominal Damages is to award the non-breaching party a token remedy when no actual damages have been proved.

- Each party's Attorney Fees and Costs are usually borne by that party (American Rule), but the Court may assess the payment of fees and costs against the losing party when either the contract itself or an applicable statute permits. This is called the Prevailing Party Rule.

- Parties may receive more than one kind of remedy unless they result in a double recovery.

- Punitive damage awards are not recoverable for breach of contract unless the breach is also a tort for which punitive damages are available.

- The purpose of contract damages is to compensate the non-breaching party, not to punish the breaching party.

Chapter 12

Third Parties' Interests

Introduction

The Fifth Sequential Question of contract law assumes a valid, enforceable contract which has been breached, giving rise to the availability of a remedy. It asks whether there are any third parties entitled to its benefits or bound by its obligations beyond the two parties to the contract. This chapter covers both the benefits to third parties under a contract (Part I) and their rights and duties created through assignment and delegation of contractual provisions (Part II).

Part I: Contractual Benefits for Third Parties

Privity and the Problem of Third Party Benefits

We reach, finally, the fifth and last of the Sequential Questions in Contract analysis: Assuming a *valid* contract (Sequential Question #1) with *enforceable* terms (Sequential Question #2) which have been *breached* (Sequential Questions #3) making *remedies* available to the non breaching party (Sequential Question #4), does any third party have standing to sue on the contract to enforce a right to benefits he or she could have anticipated receiving by its performance? (Sequential Question #5). Under the old common law, the answer to that question would have been "no!" This result flows logically from the most basic premise of contract law: that the role of the judiciary is to *enforce the bargain of the parties*. Contract law is, in a very real sense, public law (the judiciary) enforcing private law (the contract). As you know from the earlier discussions about Contract Formation (Sequential Questions 1 and 2), that principle plays into analysis of the bargain by which the parties to the contract *intended* to be *bound*.

This fundamental notion of contract law was captured effectively by the common law doctrine of privity: only the parties whose reciprocal consideration (promise or conduct) bound them to the contract could bring a lawsuit to enforce its terms. So the common law doctrine of privity is reasonable and remains consistent with the most fundamental principles of contract law. A logical consequence of that principle is that nonparties to the contract have no rights and duties as a result of the contract.

Similarly, in this chapter, as we discuss the rights and obligations of third parties under a contract, we will discover that, with regard to privity, the common law and the statutory law were modified to accommodate the real world of modern commercial transactions, but only to the extent that the accommodations are consistent with fundamental precepts of contract law. Privity, under traditional common law, said that only the parties to the bargain had standing to enforce the reciprocal rights and duties it created:

Quid

A → → → B

← ← ←

Quo

To restate the doctrine, privity said that:

Even if third parties may benefit by the performance of a contract or be harmed by its non-performance, third parties have no standing to sue on their own behalf for its breach.

Therefore under privity:

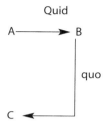

▶ Even if the contract between A and B called for B's consideration ("quo") to be delivered to C in exchange for A's consideration ("quid"), only A and B had standing to sue on (enforce the terms of) this contract.

The old common law only allowed enforcement by a third party when the third party was represented by an agent who was a party to the contract.

▶ If A was only acting on behalf of (and as an agent for) C, C was the principal (the actual party to the contract) who supplied the consideration ("quid") for B's performance ("quo"). C could enforce the contract.

The linchpin of the old doctrine of privity was that only those parties who negotiated the terms and reached mutual assent (which they made binding through their consideration) had standing to sue for enforcement. Thus, the corollary of the principle that contract law is public law enforcing the private law of the parties is that only the *parties* to that private law have standing to bring a lawsuit asking the public law to do so. That makes sense. It is entirely consistent with the premise of Contract Law: where two parties have a valid enforceable bargain, the law will enforce it if one party can demonstrate that the other party breached its terms. However, time marched on, and with it, commerce and new ways of forming contracts which put pressure on privity in its pristine form. Accordingly, courts found ways to modify privity, to find exceptions to it, but to do so in a way that retained its essential rationale.

The old rule emphasized the *parties* to the contract; the new version of privity emphasizes their *intent*. This modern rule divides third party beneficiaries into two categories:

1) those who were *incidentally* benefited by the contract ("incidental third party beneficiaries")
2) and those whom the parties *intended* to benefit by the contract ("intended third party beneficiaries").

It is important to remember that an incidental third party beneficiary has no right to enforce the contract.

> ▸ As an example of an incidental third party beneficiary, imagine a gated community neighborhood with a private road that has temporarily become impassable because heavy winds have uprooted a large tree which now traverses it. Imagine that homeowner Harry calls a tree removal service operated by Tom and contracts with Tom for the tree's removal. Dick, a neighbor, is delighted because once Tom clears the road (and Harry pays for Tom's services) Dick can drive his car down the road and get to work on time. Dick is clearly a third party beneficiary of this contract between Harry and Tom.

But does Dick have standing to enforce the contract if Tom tries to back out of the contract because he (Tom) got a more lucrative contract in another neighborhood with a similar problem? The answer is "No," according to the modern Privity Rule as well as the traditional rule. Dick is merely an incidental third party beneficiary of the contract and lacks standing to enforce the contract. Even though Dick clearly stands to benefit by the contract's performance, neither Harry nor Tom intended him to do so. The intent of the contract was to benefit Harry by Tom's performance and to benefit Tom by Harry's payment. Even under the emergent new rule, incidental beneficiaries of a contract have no standing to enforce the contract. As an example of an intended third party beneficiary, imagine the same gated neighborhood and a situation involving two separate contracts.

> ▸ In the first contract, Neighbor A says to Neighbor B, "If you will pick up my mail and forward it to me while I am on vacation, I will mow your yard every Saturday for a month when I return in July." So, in this contract between Harry and Tom, Harry's mail will be picked up and forwarded to him in exchange for Saturday lawn mowing services for a month.

B agrees to the terms of the bargain but when A returns he realizes he's committed himself to taking hang-gliding lessons every Saturday. So, instead of breaching his contract with B, he reaches an agreement with C. He tells C "If you will mow B's yard every Saturday during the month of July, I will give you that old college guitar of mine you have always liked." C agrees, but wants the guitar immediately. A delivers the guitar to C. In this second contract between A and C the promise of weekly lawn mowing service is exchanged for a guitar. By the time July rolls around, C decides to renege on his agreement to mow B's lawn. Does B have standing to sue C under this second contract? Yes. Here, B is an intended third party beneficiary of the Contract between A and C. In the second contract, the parties (A and C) have manifested their intent to benefit B. The consideration for A's performance (the guitar) is the benefit C agreed to confer on B (the lawn mowing).

While this approach can be said to modify the old Privity Rule, it is entirely consistent with it. If the contract itself provides for the benefit to flow to a third party, then part of the mutual assent to which the contractual parties bound themselves is this benefit to the third party. This benefit is an integral part of the contract. Therefore, it does no violence to basic contract concepts to give the third party standing to sue for enforcement of the benefit. Nonetheless, the old common law action required performance by the party suing to enforce the contract.

By way of analogy, let's return to the Statute of Frauds. In real estate contracts, the statute is a rule designed to protect, for example, a landowner from false allegations that she sold the land to someone on an oral contract (when, in fact, the landowner only intended to rent the property for 18 months). The basic rules of the Statute of Frauds would insist that evidence of the landowner's intent to sell the real estate be reduced to writing and signed by her or her agent. However, the law will recognize an exception to the rule requiring that the contract must be in writing to be enforceable, but only if there is part performance of the putative oral contract sufficient to show that the parties did indeed intend a sale of the land, not merely, for example, a lease. Thus, the part performance exception will require enough evidence (beyond the mere exchange of payment for possession that might merely indicate a lease was intended) to satisfy the court that the Statute of Frauds bar is not required because it is clear that the parties *intended* a sale. The purpose of the Statute of Frauds is preserved and satisfied by the part performance exception.

In the context of the modern Rule of Privity, where the mutual assent of the parties makes it clear that one party's consideration should be delivered to a third party, no basic concept of contract law is violated. It is clear that the agreement of the parties in privity (the parties to the contract) *intended* that one party's consideration would be delivered to a third party. Therefore, when the commercial practice of conferring benefits on parties not in privity with the parties to a contract put pressure on the law to change the Privity Rule, contract law was able to accommodate the practice. The modern rule first evolved through case law involving two particular classes of third party beneficiaries (donee beneficiaries and creditor beneficiaries). The *Restatement (First) of Contracts* characterization of modern privity retained those designations. It provided:

- § 133. Definition of Donee Beneficiary, Creditor Beneficiary. Incidental Beneficiary.
    1) Where performance of a promise in a contract will benefit a person other than the promisee, that person is …
        a) a donee beneficiary if it appears from the terms of the promise … that the purpose of the promise in obtaining the promise of all or part of the promise thereof is to make a gift to the beneficiary or to confer upon him a right against the promisor to some performance neither due nor supposed or asserted to be due from the promise to the beneficiary;
        b) a creditor beneficiary if no purpose to make a gift appears from the terms of the promise in view of the accompanying circumstances and performance of the promise will satisfy an actual or supposed or asserted duty of promise which has been barred by the Statute of Limitations or by discharge in bankruptcy, or which is unenforceable because of the Statute of Frauds;
        c) an incidental beneficiary if neither of the facts stated in Clause (a) nor those stated in Clause (b) exist.

Thus, the earlier rendition of the modern Privity Rule identified only two categories of intended third party beneficiary: donee and creditor. All other kinds of third party beneficiaries were excluded from this privileged category and had no standing to sue on the contract. By contrast, the *Second Restatement* states the fully realized modern rule and eliminates the labels of "creditor" and "donee" beneficiaries. The new section retains the distinction and legal consequences of intended beneficiaries, on the one hand, and incidental beneficiaries, on the other:

> *Restatement [Second] of Contracts § 302*
> § 302. Intended and Incidental Beneficiaries
>   1) Unless otherwise agreed between promisor and promisee, a beneficiary of a promise is an intended beneficiary if recognition of a right to performance in the beneficiary is appropriate to effectuate the intention of the parties and either
>   a) the performance of the promise will satisfy an obligation of the promisee to pay money to the beneficiary; or
>   b) the circumstances indicate that the promisee intends to give the beneficiary the benefit of the promised performance.

While the *Second Restatement* eliminates the labels "donee" and "creditor" and broadens the language describing an intended beneficiary to some extent, its text still suggests the presence of the two categories. Because case law occasionally references the donee and creditor categories, you should be aware of the gradual evolution of the modern Privity Rule.

▸ A graphic depiction of Third Party Beneficiaries may make the categories memorable and clarify when third party beneficiaries have standing to enforce the performance to their benefit. The basic graph of a bilateral contract is:

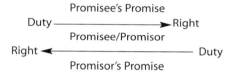

To give detail to this bilateral contract, assume that A Promisor/Promisee is a car dealership (A). B, the other Promisor/Promisee is a Father.

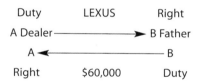

Example 1: To add the third party situation to this contract, assume B's promise is: I'll pay you $60,000 if you give my son, C, a Lexus." A's promise is "I'll give C a Lexus if you give me $60,000."

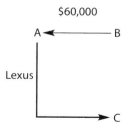

Example 2: B is the promisor on the promise to pay $60,000. A is the car dealer promisee and C is a bank/creditor of A. A's promise is: "I'll give you

a Lexus if you give C $60,000. B's promise is: I'll pay C $60,000 if you give me a Lexus.

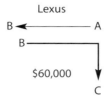

In examples 1 & 2: C is an *intended* beneficiary and, therefore, has standing to enforce the contract because:

1. Both parties to the contract intended that promisor's performance benefit the third party;
2. The intent was established at the time of contract;
3. Promisee's promise supplies the consideration for promisor's performance that benefits third party;
4. Both promisee and third party have standing to enforce promisor's performance; and
5. C in #3 is a *donee* beneficiary; in #4, C is a *creditor* beneficiary.

In the preceding examples, third party beneficiary rights seem simple and straightforward. There are, however, a few complications that should be addressed:

Changes by the Parties

What if the parties to the contract change their minds? Are their rights to modify their own contract foreclosed by the third party's right to enforce the beneficial term of their original contract? The answer is generally, "no." Under *Restatement [Second] of Contracts §311* the parties to a contract are free to modify or terminate the contract even though, in so doing, they extinguish the third party's benefit under the original contract. There are, however, exceptions. If the third party's rights have vested then the parties are not free to modify or eliminate those rights.

This vesting of rights in the contract occurs when the third party has (1) "materially" changed his position in reliance upon the contract or, 2) in some other way, has "manifested assent" to them.

▶ For example, what if Uncle sends an e-mail to Nephew, a happy ski instructor in Utah, and says, "Enroll in law school. I have just arranged to purchase a Lexus in your name! It's yours. All you have to do is quit your 'job' on the slopes, return home and attend law school." In exchange for Uncle's payment of $60,000, Lexus Development agrees to deliver a Lexus to Nephew.

Based upon the Uncle's e-mail, Nephew quits his job in Utah and returns home where (having miraculously been admitted to the local law school) he enrolls. Unbeknownst to Nephew, however, Uncle has second thoughts and convinces the Dealership to tear up the Contract. Can Nephew enforce the Contract anyway? The court is likely to say "Yes." Nephew has materially changed his position in reliance on it.

Difficulty of Intent

Here's another complication. How do courts know that a benefit for a third party was intended? The answer is: if the contract doesn't expressly specify that intent, courts generally consider whether the benefit claimed flows directly to the beneficiary. That is, does one party have a *direct* obligation to confer a benefit to the third party under the Contract?

> ▸ Suppose, for example, that Businessman wants to sell his business to ABC Corporation and, to establish a value for the business, Businessman gives ABC Corporation a copy of the financial reports his accountant prepared for him several months ago when he was preparing tax returns for the business. Based upon the accountant's numbers, ABC Corporation agrees on a price for the business but several months after it has purchased the business it discovers that the accountant's numbers are seriously flawed, to its detriment. Businessman has taken the cash from the sale and moved to the Bahamas. Can ABC Corporation sue Accountant on the contract he had with Businessman and pursuant to which he prepared the erroneous financial reports? Most courts would say, "No." Because even though ABC Corporation relied on the reports, they were not prepared on its behalf or for purposes of the sale of the business. The intended beneficiary of those reports was Businessman to whom the Accountant had a direct obligation under that accounting contract.

Government Contracts

What about contracts in which the government and a private entity are parties? Can third parties sue the government to enforce benefits they stand to receive under the contract? The answer is: it depends. The analysis is the same as we have seen in contracts between private parties but the evidence of intent is specific to the nature of government contracts. Again, you are looking for the intent of the parties to the contract (private entity and federal agency) and whether the government had a direct obligation to the third party under its terms. But to address these issues the court must consider the underlying statute or regulation that authorized the contract and the terms of the contract. With regard to the enabling statute, the court must decide what the legislative purpose or intent of the statute was and what class of citizens was it intended to benefit.

▶ A federal dam project, for instance, intended to provide local farmers with irrigation, may also benefit recreational facilities in the area. The recreational facilities have no standing to sue the government on the irrigation contracts resulting from the dam project if the government eliminates the dam. Unless the recreational companies were within the class Congress intended to benefit by the enabling legislation for the dam project, the federal government has no *direct* obligation to provide any benefits to these facilities.

The second line of inquiry for identifying the intended beneficiaries of the government project is to analyze the terms of the contract itself and to inquire what remedy is provided for its breach and to whom the remedy flows.

▶ For instance, if a government agency provides low rent housing for citizens within a certain economic bracket by reimbursing participating landlords, does a tenant in the low rent housing have a cause of action against a landlord who breaches the terms of its contract with the government agency? If the contract provided a remedy for tenants, then clearly tenants were intended beneficiaries of the contract and the answer would be "yes." If the contract indicates the parties' intent to benefit the tenants the likely answer is "yes" as well.

Construction Bonds

Another nuanced context for analysis is contracts for construction bonds.

▶ Imagine that a general contractor undertakes to construct a church. As a part of his commitment, he secures a labor and materials bond. If the general contractor fails to pay his sub-contractors and material men and they, in response, stop working on the church, can the church sue for the proceeds on the bond? The answer is: no, in spite of the fact that the church did benefit from the bond. Without the bond the sub-contractors and material men would undoubtedly file a lien against the church's property, thereby encumbering the church's title. Thus, the church received a benefit from the bond. However, that benefit was only incidental to the direct and, therefore, intended purpose of the bond: to assure payment to the sub-contractors and material men.

Consumer Contracts

Finally, the nexus between privity, on the one hand, and the realities of an advanced industrial and consumer society, on the other has led to other, more complex issues. As you know, in our consumer society, the ultimate consumer or user of a product rarely has any contract with the producer of the product. If the product is "defective" (tort law terminology) or "nonconforming" (contract law terminology), the consumer usually has no contractual relationship, and therefore no privity, with the producer. This situation differs markedly from the society in which the doctrine of privity was developed. Privity is a common law doctrine that implicates both tort taw and contract law. However, as we changed from a rural society to an advanced industrial/consumer society, tort law found it easier to do away with privity than did contract law. The reason for the difference in the approaches may lie in the difference in purpose between the two fields of law. The purpose of tort law is to give a remedy for harm to a foreseeable class of parties injured by the negligence of another. Whoever caused the harm should be liable for the remedy as long as they could foresee their conduct could cause harm to that class of people. However, the purpose of contract law is to enforce the bargain of specific parties to a specific contract. That purpose seems inherently to demand privity: this Buyer and this Seller entered into a transaction with each other. They have made a private law between themselves to which they are bound ... to each other. Those outside the reciprocal promises of that private law are not bound. Can Consumer sue Producer for a product she bought from Retailer? (Vertical privity.) Can Consumer sue Retailer for a product she received from Purchaser? (Horizontal privity.) There are few "bright line" answers to those questions in contract law. The issue of *vertical* privity remains a state-by-state case law issue. Most states grant vertical privity to the consumer who buys nonconforming goods from a retail store. That means there is no Privity bar to a consumer's lawsuit against the producer. The common law bar of privity has generally been abrogated by state common law and state statutes. The issue of *horizontal* privity has been addressed by the Uniform Commercial Code Article 2 by a series of three options in Section 2-318. The UCC drafters afforded these three alternatives for states to "bend" privity to accommodate modern mass market transactions, recognizing that modifying common law principles is a gradual, ongoing process which, over a period of time, may go beyond the modifications suggested by Section 2-318. It should be recognized that tort law presents another alternative to third party beneficiaries seeking remedies for injuries inflicted upon them by nonconforming goods. These concepts are covered in an advanced contract class on the UCC.

Part II: Rights and Duties of Third Parties

Other Enforceable Interests of Third Parties: Assignments of Rights and Delegation of Duties

This Part II deals with these two kinds of transfers to third parties. The key distinction between Part II and the Part I analysis of third parties is that Third Party Beneficiary (Part I) rights arise, if at all, within the terms of the *original* contract. While in Part II, the rights and duties arise, if at all, in transactions *subsequent* to the original contract. Contract law includes the ability to assign rights and delegate duties that arise from a contract or from a breach of a contract. Generally either party to a contract may assign his rights or delegate his duties under the contract.

First, we should give a note on the terminology. When a party to a contract assigns her rights, she is granting to a third party all or part of the benefit she expects to receive from the other party. By contrast, when a party delegates her duties, she is making a third party responsible for conferring the promised contractual benefit to the other party in the contract. For example, say Sara promises computer support services to Tom in exchange for $100. If Sara decides that the $100 payment from Tom should go directly to David, then Sarah may assign her right to receive the $100 to David. If Sara later arranges to have Beth be responsible for providing the promised computer support, then Sara may be able to delegate her duties to Beth, providing the delegation does not prejudice the rights of the party who receives the performance

After any initial contract between the original parties (A and B for example), one of the parties may want to transfer (assign) her rights under the contract to someone else. Or, one of the parties may want to transfer (delegate) his duties under the contract to someone else. An assignment or delegation may be made in an oral contract. In other words, generally the scope of statutes of frauds does not include assignment or delegation. The party making the assignment or delegation must manifest an intention to transfer the right at the time of the transfer. The strength of the modern goal of keeping commerce and contracts moving in the market can be seen by the fact that even when parties state that the contract prohibits assignment of the contract, an assignment may be effective. Courts respect and enforce assignments of contract rights unless the party resisting an assignment can show that the assignment would materially change the duty of the obligor, or materially increase the burden or risk imposed on him by his contract, or materially impair his chance of obtaining return performance, or materially reduce its value to him. Of course if the assignment is forbidden by statute or violates public policy, a court would hold it unenforceable. Courts interpret a contract that states that an assignment of "the contract" is prohibited as effectively barring only the delegation of performance rather than assignment of the contract right to payment or to damages for breach of the contract. In such cases, courts will enforce the breach of the contract term by damages but will allow the assignment.

This approach allows for the power to assign rights unless the other party's interests are affected negatively by an assignment. This does not mean that the contract term has no effect. The inclusion of such a provision provides evidence for a court on the question of whether the assignment materially changes the obligor's duty. Similarly, if the parties include in their contract a provision that provides assent to future assignments of rights, courts will give effect to this provision.

Assignments of Rights

An assignment of a right is the effective transfer of a party's right to receive a benefit to a third party. It is like the transfer of an item of property, such as a car or land, except that in the context of a contract assignment, the property transferred is a contract right. The defense of lack of consideration is not effective with regard to an assignment since the assignment is not a promise but is a completed transfer of a right. Thus, this is a transfer of a property right to enforce a contract. At traditional common law, future rights were not assignable. The modern approach is to allow assignment of a future right to payment that is to arise out of an existing employment or business relationship. This is effective even though it is not in existence at the time of the assignment.

Assignment of a right to payment under a contract does not increase the obligor's risk. Like a Third Party Beneficiary contract, the assignment moves a right to performance from the original holder to another person. The clearest case is the transfer of a right to payment. To make an effective assignment, an assignor of a contractual right must completely divest herself of the right when she conveys it to an assignee. Unlike the third party beneficiary setting, in which the original party retains standing to sue on the original contract if the promisor does not deliver performance, an assignor of a right under the original contract also transfers her standing to sue for performance. Rights under the original contract are assignable unless the performance is conditioned on performance by a particular person or the assignment will materially change the terms of the contract and increase the promisor's (obligor's) risk.

The clearest case is the transfer of a right to payment. Suppose that A enters a contract with B to paint B's house for $5,000. The contract does not mention C. Thus, C is not a third party beneficiary of that contract. However, after that contract is signed, A may assign his right to the $5,000. This assignment of a right to payment does not increase the obligor's risk. It merely changes the party who receives payment.

Not all assignments are enforceable. If the assignment would materially change the obligation of the other party, a court will not enforce the purported assignment. On the same contract to paint a house, suppose B assigns his right to the house painting by A to C. C's house is larger and in a remote location. A's obligation is now materially altered and A is not bound by the assignment. Likewise, an assignment will not be enforced if it changed the burden or risk or materially impaired the other party's chance of obtaining the return performance.

The Assignee stands in the shoes of the Assignor and has all of the rights Assignor under the contract. Moreover, the obligor or promisor under the original contract with Assignor retains all the defenses he may have under that contract against Assignee. (For example, the defenses of mistake; lack of consideration; violation of public policy; impracticability are viable defenses against the assignee). You will learn more about those defenses in today's commercial markets in a course in secured transactions covering Article 9 of the UCC.

Delegation of Duties

A delegation of a duty is similar in concept to the assignment of a right. The rules enunciated above regarding Assignment of Duties also relate to delegation of duties. There is an important distinction. An assignment divests the assignor of his rights. By contrast, a delegation of duties does not rid the delegator of obligations under the original contract unless there is a new contract that expressly releases the delegator.

A court will refuse to enforce a delegation if it finds the delegation is contrary to public policy. Additionally, some contracts require performance by a particular person. If that is the case, an attempt to delegate the duty to another person will be ineffective if the obligee (the person who is to receive performance under the contract) has a substantial interest in having the original party perform the obligation.

Novations

Sometimes, it is desirable that a party assign all his rights and delegate all his duties under a contract to third party, while simultaneously releasing the original party from the obligations. The new contract is called a "novation." It requires the consent of the party with a right to performance of the duty under the original contract. Generally, the novation will include all three parties. You can envision three parties holding hands and one party removing himself from the triangle by joining the hands of the other two together. The party who left the circle is no longer a party to the contract at all. The contract cannot be enforced against him, nor does he have any rights under the contract.

The following chart summarizes the points set forth above relating to third party contract rights.

Third Party Beneficiary	Assignee of Rights	Delegatee of Duties
1. Arise by intent of parties at the time of contract.	1. Arise subsequent to the first contract and must be intended.	1. Arise subsequent to the first contract and must be intended.
2. Promisee retains rights under contract to enforce promisor's performance.	2. Assignment divests assignee of the interest and transfers it to assignee.	2.Delegation makes delegatee responsible for the duty, but does not divest delegator of the duty, unless specifically agreed to by the other party.
3. Beneficiary stand in promisee's shoes BUT	3. Assignee stands in assignor's shoes BUT	3. Delegatee stands in delegator's shoes BUT
4. Benefit is revocable (by modification or discharge of contract by the parties) unless beneficiary reasonably relies to his material detriment.	4. Assignment is revocable if gratuitous; irrevocable by consideration or reliance.	4. Delegation is revocable if gratuitous; irrevocable by consideration or reliance.
5. Privity analysis is required. Intended third party beneficiary has standing.	5. Rights are assignable unless: they materially disadvantage they other party	5. Duties are delegable unless: they materially disadvantage they other party

Checkpoints

- The doctrine of privity usually bars third parties from suing to enforce a contract.

- But intended third party beneficiaries do have standing to enforce a contract.

- This exception to the Privity Rule recognizes that in modern commercial practice, contracts may be made for the purpose of benefiting a third party.

- To a limited extent third parties may use this exception to privity to sue producers of non-conforming goods (an exception to vertical privity) and the retail seller of non-conforming goods (horizontal privity).

- Parties to a contract may also assign their rights under the contract to third parties, which divests the original party of the right.

- Parties to a contract may delegate their duties under the contract to third parties, but this does not divest the original party of the duty, unless specifically agreed to by the other party.

Conclusion

This book has organized the principles of contract law encountered in the first year contracts course around five sequential questions. These sequential questions provide a map for analyzing a contracts case. First, did the parties enter an agreement that the law would consider to be a contract? Second, are any of the terms of the contract enforceable? Third, was there a nonperformance (or a defective performance of a promise) that amounts to a breach? Fourth, what remedies are available to compensate the non-breaching party? And fifth, may a third party interest be enforced? Although this sequence is not followed strictly by courts, it provides a useful approach to understanding the principles at play in contracts cases. Thus, one way of mastering contract law is to master the principles of these five sequential questions.

This book has noted how common law rules often change in society, and now changes in business practice, put pressure on the legal rules to change, too. Legal rules change to accommodate shifts and developments in the economy otherwise the law would become irrelevant to the marketplace of contracts or—worse—an impediment to commerce. As examples of the changes in the common law brought about by changes in the marketplace (you saw such changes in the chapters covering Formation, and Performance), consider the following common law rules affected by the pressure of commercial activity: The Perfect Tender Rule, the Illusory Contract, the Statute of Frauds, and The Parol Evidence Rule. In those chapters you saw how longstanding rules changed to meet the demands of changes in the marketplace.

It is the genius and enduring strength of the Common Law that it will tolerate a change to accommodate market demands only to the extent that the modified rule remains consistent with the underlying purpose and principles of the older doctrine. For example, the "Perfect Tender" yields to substantial performance in Sequential Question #3 (was there a nonperformance amounting to a *breach*) and to a diminution of value remedy only where there is extreme waste created by the *remedy* of completion required by Perfect Tender, and only to the extent that it is reasonable to conclude that the resulting remedy for the non-breaching party will give him the benefit of his bargain without imposition of a "perfect tender." The "Illusory Contract" Rule gave way to

modern commerce under later versions of the common law, ultimately memorialized in the Uniform Commercial Code's Article 2, Section 2-306 (covering requirements contracts, output contracts and exclusions dealing contracts)
but only with the addition of "implied in law" ("constructive") terms like "good
faith" and "best efforts" which eliminated the illusory nature of these kinds of
modern contracts by binding both parties to objective standards. Judge-created
as well as statutory modifications (see, e.g. UCC § 2-201; 2-202) have been
made in both the Statute of Frauds and the Parol Evidence Rule to narrow (but
not eliminate) their application where other factors indicate they are over-
broad. Understanding that evolution is part of the law helps you understand
not only where the law has been, but also where it is likely to go (and why).

Mastering Contracts
Master Checklist

Chapter 1 · Preliminary Matters

☐ How Should You Think about a Contracts Problem?
  - The Five Sequential Questions of Contract Analysis
  - Promises: The Seriousness of Promising
  - Interests Protected
  - Implied-in-law Contracts and Implied-in-Fact Contracts
☐ What are the Sources of Contract Law in the U.S.?
  - Common Law
  - Statutory and Regulatory Law
  - Reading the UCC and Statutes Generally
☐ What are the Basic Transnational Sources of Contract Law?
  - The Movement Toward Greater Uniformity
  - International Law
  - Tensions among Different Sources of Law

Chapter 2 · Basic Concepts and Guiding Principles

☐ What is a Contract?
☐ What is an Agreement?
☐ What is Freedom of Contract?
☐ Which Contracts are Illegal?

Chapter 3 · Interpretation

☐ Why Interpretation? The Purpose of Interpretation
☐ What are the Rules for Interpretation?
  - Interpretive Rules for Statutes
  - Public Policy Considerations
  - Contract Interpretive Rules
  - Canons of Construction
  - Extrinsic Evidence of Contract Construction
  - UCC Rules for Constructing Contracts
  - Parol Evidence Rule

Chapter 4 · Formation: Mechanics of Mutual Assent

- ☐ How Do Parties Assent to a Contract?
  - Capacity
  - Formation
- ☐ To What Forms of Contract May They Assent?
  - Unilateral Contracts
  - Bilateral Contracts

Chapter 5 · Consideration

- ☐ What is Consideration?
- ☐ What are the Two Tests for Consideration?
  - The Benefit/Detriment Test
  - The Bargain Test
- ☐ What Is Not Consideration?
  - Lack of Consideration
  - Moral Consideration
  - Gifts
  - Illusory Promises
  - Why Requirements, Output and Exclusive Dealing Contracts Are Not Illusory
  - Sham Contracts
  - Past Consideration and Pre-existing Duties
- ☐ If There Is No Consideration, What Happens to the Contract?
  - Invalidity
  - Rescission

Chapter 6 · Defenses and Obstacles to Performance Liability

- ☐ Under What Circumstances May a Party Not Be Required to Perform under a Contract?
  - The Starting Point—Strict Liability
  - The Prerequisite of Consent
  - Fraud and Misrepresentation
  - Duress and Other Forms of Unfair Advantage
  - Mistake
  - Impossibility and Impracticability
  - UCC Special Rules for Excusing Performance
  - Modification
  - Risk Allocation: Conditions and Contingencies
- ☐ What Happens to the Contract if Performance Is Not Required?
  - Rescission
  - Reformation

Chapter 7 · Modification

- ☐ What Changes Give Rise to Attempts to Modify Contractual Obligations?
- ☐ When Will Modified Contracts Be Enforced?
- ☐ What Circumstances Foreclose Modifications?
- ☐ What Distinguishes Modification from Obstacles to Performance?
- ☐ Parties sometimes resolve an obligation by a performance that alters the original agreement under the doctrine of Accord and Satisfaction.
- ☐ Courts respect the discharge of the original contract when parties enter "accord" (the new contract) and follow through with the "satisfaction" (performance of the new contract).
- ☐ To be effective, the accord must arise from a good faith dispute on the original obligation or be based on new consideration.
- ☐ The original contract obligation is discharged upon performance (satisfaction) of the new accord.
- ☐ The doctrine of Accord and Satisfaction differs from modification in that it suspends obligation of the first contract rather than discharging it.

Chapter 8 · Exceptions to Bargain Theory: Contracts without Consideration

- ☐ Under What Circumstances Will Contracts without Consideration Be Enforced?
  - Equitable Estoppel
  - The Seal
  - Charitable Subscriptions
  - Restitution and Modification Events
  - Promissory Estoppel/Reliance
    - *Restatement 90 (First) of Contracts*
    - *Restatement 90 (Second) of Contracts*
- ☐ The Conundrum of Letters of Intent

Chapter 9 · Special Issues of Enforceability

- ☐ Under What Circumstances Will a Valid Contract, or Any Part of It, Not Be Enforced?
  - Statutes of Limitations: The Doctrine of Laches
  - Statutes of Limitations: The UCC
  - Statutes of Fraud
  - The Parol Evidence Rule

Chapter 10 · Performance and Breach

- ☐ Why Do Parties Contemplate a Breach?
  - Contract Enforcement Considerations

- The Temptation to Breach
- "Efficient" Breach
☐ What distinguishes a Nonperformance as Breach from a Nonperformance premised on a Condition?
  - Relationship of Condition and Performance
  - Conditions
  - Terminology: Condition Precedent; Condition Subsequent
  - Types of Conditions
  - Waiver
  - Independence of Obligations vs. Dependence of Obligations
  - Kinds of Breach: Material; Immaterial and the Perfect Tender Rule
  - Standards of Performance as Conditions and the Requirement of Good Faith
  - Forfeiture
  - Conditions are Distinguishable from Timing Requirements
  - Identifying Conditions
  - Anticipatory Repudiation
  - Assurances of Performance
  - Warranties as Conditions

Chapter 11 · Remedies

☐ What is the Context in Which the Rules for Contract Remedies Have Been Developed?
  - Specific Performance
  - Historical Background
  - Constitutional Dimensions
☐ What Are the Categories of Contract Remedies in Addition to Specific Performance?
  - Expectation Interest Damages
    - Purpose
    - The Foreseeability Limitation
    - The Degree of Proof Limitation
    - The Compensation Limitation
    - The Disproportionality Limitation
    - The Measure of Damages Limitation
    - The Avoidable Consequences Limitation
    - The Lost Volume Seller Exception
    - The Emotional Harm Limitation
  - Reliance Interest Damages
  - Restitution Interest Damages

- Liquidated Damages
- Nominal Damages
- Attorney Fees and Court Costs

☐ Can a Party Recover in More Than One Category of Remedies or Would That Always Constitute an Impermissible "Double Recovery"?

☐ How Does the UCC Treat the Categories of Remedies?

Chapter 12 · Third Parties' Interests

☐ Under What Circumstances Will a Third Party Receive an Enforceable Benefit under a Contract Formed by Two Other Parties?
- The Problem of Privity
- The Doctrinal Rationale for Protecting Third Party Interests
- Rules Applicable to Specific Kinds of Third Party Contracts
  - Government Contracts
  - Construction Contracts
  - Consumer Contracts

☐ What Are the Enforceable Interests of Third Parties When a Party to the Contract Either Assigns the Third Party Rights under the Contract or Delegates Certain Duties to the Third Parties?
- Assignment of Rights
- Delegation of Duties

Index